MW01629934

Texas Fish & Game®

presents

Where, When and How to
Wadefish
TEXAS

By Bink Grimes

**Texas Fish & Game
Publishing Co., L.L.C.**

1745 Greens Road
Houston, Texas 77032
1-800-750-4678
www.fishgame.com

Although the author and publisher have extensively researched all brand names and sources to ensure the accuracy and completeness of information in this book, we assume no responsibility for errors, inaccuracies, omissions or any other inconsistency herein. Any slights against people, products, manufacturers or organizations are unintentional.

Published by
Texas Fish & Game Publishing Co., L.L.C.

1745 Greens Road
Houston Texas 77032
Phone: 281-227-3001 Fax: 281-227-3002
Website: www.fishgame.com

First Edition

All photos by Bink Grimes unless otherwise credited.

Layout, design by Wendy Kipfmiller

Production by Doug Berry

Edited by Don Zaidle.

ISBN: 0-929980-17-4

To the two most beautiful girls in the world, Shelly and Mallory.
Thanks for loving Daddy.

To Dad and Mom, thanks for giving me every opportunity
to succeed. To my sister, Danyelle, thanks for risking your
life in the batting cage.

Contents

Introduction

When my father, Danny, and I made our first trip to Trinity Bay with Randy Stacy on a cold December night in 1981, little did we know the impact that winter redfish trip would have.

Twenty-three years later, I remain as passionate about each saline experience as that first night at the Spillway at the ripe age of 10. It is this passion that prompted me to write this book, my first, filled with anecdotes and know-how learned from thousands of fishing trips with hundreds of Texas professionals, friends, and just plain ol' good fishermen.

I grew up east of Houston in the town of Mont Belvieu, sandwiched between petrochemical plants, rice prairies, and Trinity Bay. My home was just a short 10-minute jaunt from the Gou Hole Road boat ramp and the Trinity River bridge ramp off Interstate 10, affording easy access for late afternoon excursions, especially in the fall.

I graduated from Barbers Hill High School, attended Sam Houston State and East Texas Baptist universities on baseball scholarships, and graduated from ETBU with a bachelor's degree in kinesiology and English. I was an All American first baseman for the Tigers and played a year of professional baseball before receiving a master's degree from Stephen F. Austin State University in 1997.

Besides duping speckled trout on topwaters, I love to fool wary ducks and geese in the winter, and have been a waterfowl guide since age 19. My love for waterfowl prompted my wife, Shelly, to name our first and only child "Mallory" after a mallard duck. I swear, I had nothing to do with it.

These days, I am a full-time freelance writer and photographer living in Bay City, and regularly contribute to more than a dozen national and state publications. I have written the Weekly Coastal Fishing Report for the Texas Parks and Wildlife Department since 1998, and created the Weekly Migratory Bird Hunting Report in 2000, both distributed by the Associated Press to every Texas newspaper.

For reasons known only to them, my peers in the Texas Outdoor Writers Association have awarded me more than 30 Excellence in Craft awards since 1999, including 12 first place finishes. I also share a hat rack with members of the Outdoor Writers Association of America. In my spare time, I teach English and coach baseball for the Bay City Blackcats. I hold a Coast Guard captain's license, and run charters out of Matagorda in the fall and summer.

Unless there is one I do not know about, I have fished every bay system in Texas. Once, I fished Sabine Lake (the northernmost estuary on the coast) and South Padre Island (the southernmost estuary in Texas) within 24 hours.

I am prone to impulsive behavior, such as jumping in my truck at 2:30 a.m. to be wading by 6:00 a.m. on Stewt's Island on Sabine Lake, or towing my Pathfinder two hours south to Rockport after a friendly "great fishing report" call from a guide buddy. The words in this book reflect many red-eyed, way-too-early alarms.

I simply write what I know, learned by doing—getting my feet wet, so to speak. It does not happen on the phone, hacking away on the keyboard without ever leaving the concrete jungle. You cannot fool outdoorsmen; they can sniff out a fake before the ink dries. If you do not hunt or fish on a regular basis, you cannot write it, only report it. Outdoor writing is unique in this aspect. Most baseball, football, and basketball writers never played the sports on which they report, especially at a higher level like college. Most never had the ability and, if they had, it is hard to obtain a journalism degree, be an athlete, and become a working member of the school newspaper, which many college journalism departments require. Yet, look at Texas' three leading metropolitan newspapers and ask their baseball writers if they have ever hit the long ball. There are exceptions, you know, but not very often.

Now, ask your favorite outdoor writer if he has ever caught a trophy trout, called in a hot spring gobbler, shot a banded greenhead, watched a Boone & Crockett buck waltz into a sendero, fished on Lake Fork, or made a morning wade. Chances are, he has, and has taken you there in the pages of *Texas Fish & Game* or your local newspaper. That's the difference I hope you will find in Wadefish Texas.

In this book, I divulge GPS coordinates of some of my favorite locales, including the spot where Capt. Chuck Uzzle and I caught and released nine fish over 28 inches one morning in June 1999. You also find information on where, when, and how to fish these spots, and patterns for each bay system in Texas for every season.

The idea is to help you become a better student of fishing. To that end, I included tips such as why you should keep a fishing journal; how to process weather, wind, and water information to eliminate unproductive water before you ever make the first wade of the day, and so on.

I thoroughly enjoyed writing the sections on fishing the surf—one of my favorite things. There are warnings about riptides and the perils of wading around passes, where strong tidal movement could prove deadly; heed them.

Some anglers never leave the boat for fear of what lies beneath the surface. These pages include the know-how to avoid encounters with barbed marine life and cartilaginous fish with large dorsal fins and sharp teeth. Knowledge spawns confidence, and as with anything in life, confidence is everything. The confident angler catches more fish.

This tome will not answer every question (some have no answer), nor is it the final word on wadefishing in Texas (there may not be such a thing). What this work hopes to achieve is to give the novice the know-how to take that first plunge, or give an experienced angler another angle on the game.

When all is said and done, all anglers are alike. We all love a good sunrise or sunset, the chance to share a day with our dad, mom, child, or friend, and count it a blessing to live in Texas and fish her salty waterways.

Catching fish is just a bonus.

Chapter One

Gearing Up

You want to bail over the gunnels and plunge into one of Texas'
pristine estuaries, but you do not know where to start. Most first-timers
don the oldest, nastiest pair of tennis shoes in the garage, tie a stringer
to the belt loop of a pair of cutoff jeans, pile wads of plastics and jigheads in a front pocket, and stick a plug or two on their hat. And, that
works. Nevertheless, manufacturers have refined equipment to outfit
the Texas wader. Some of it is useful, some useless, some gaudy to catch
the eyes of rookies, but there is quality tackle out there. Here is how to
get started.

RODS

My favorite rod is a 6-foot, 6-inch medium light graphite, though
most Texans work a 7-footer. When wading, you want a rod that is an
extension of your arm, not laborious to work, and doesn't cramp your

forearms.

If your budget is limited, you have to make a choice. How often do you throw plugs and how often do you toss soft plastic? There are specialty rods with stiffer actions to fit the plugger, and others with a lit-

Besides seeing below the surface, polarized shades blocks ultraviolet rays and lets your eyes relax. There is nothing worse than forgetting your sunglasses and squinting the entire day, not to mention the headache associated with it.

tle more play in the tip for working soft plastic "tails."

There are plenty of inexpensive but capable rods out there. Before making your purchase, ask yourself: "How often do I fish?" and "What can my wallet handle?" All Star, American Rodsmiths, Castaway,

Falcon, Kistler, Laguna, and Shimano make quality, moderately priced rods. By "moderate" I mean in the $60-$100 range.

The differences between an $80 rod and a $200 rod are the graphite blank and guides. A 40,000-modulus graphite blank costs double what a 20,000-modulus blank does, but the more expensive blank weighs considerably less. It is also more apt to break when banged around in a pickup truck bed or run through a ceiling fan.

I like the titanium rods. Many mistakenly believe titanium rods are made entirely of the exotic metal. Only the guides are titanium, which are lighter and do not corrode with saltwater exposure. They do cost much more than regular guides—around $8 apiece. Do the math: eight guides at $8 each and you are looking at $64 before they even go on the blank.

Tim Locker at American Rodsmiths built my first titanium to my specifications four years ago, and it remains the best all-around stick I own. The Laguna Texas Wader is the best feeling stick I have ever had in my hand. The All Star Titanium 783PC is another favorite that allows me to toss topwaters or tails all day and never feel the fatigue. Most pricey rods carry lifetime warranties.

REELS

When choosing a reel, you must decide between bait-casting and spinning. Most Texans choose the bait-caster, but in Alabama and Florida, you are hard-pressed to find a tackle shop that sells anything other than spinning tackle.

In my experience, you cannot go wrong with Shimano. They, by far, have the best selection of reels in every price range, and their warranty work is second to none. If you have a problem with a reel, send it to the factory in Irvine, California, and comes back in working condition in two weeks. The most they have ever charged is $15, even when they replaced six bearings and a worm gear. Most tackle shops charge $15 per bearing.

I use the entire line of Shimano reels, from the Calcutta to Curado and Chronarch. The Curado is the best reel on the market for the money, in my opinion. It is no coincidence that I see more Curados on rods than any other reel. Priced at $119.99 for the 200B and $129.99 for the 100B, it is the best value for the dollar. I think I have about eight of them, give or take.

I also use the Chronarch SF and Mg. These cast out of sight and require very little maintenance other than a shot of oil to the bearings and grease to the worm gear. They are the best in the industry, in my opinion, especially with the warranty they carry.

Since we are discussing maintenance, the best thing to do for your reel at the end of a day wading is to spray it down with products like Reel Magic or Corrosion X, then wipe it off with a towel. Hosing off a reel with freshwater actually forces salt and grime into the inner works. If you must wash off with water, give the reel a trickle of water and wipe off the rest. Since I quit hosing my reels and began using Reel Magic exclusively, I have had fewer problems with corrosion and stiffening of working parts. My Chronarch Mg hasn't been torn down in over a year, and it is still as smooth as the day it came out of the box, despite hard use. (I fish more than 100 days a year.)

MONOFILAMENT

Monofilament line in the 12- to 15-pound-test range is the standard in Texas. Mono deteriorates over time, especially in arid conditions and direct sunlight. A fresh spool casts farther, resists memory and tangling, and holds up better to oyster shell nicks.

I have witnessed lines broken by a two-pound trout, and the angler and wondered why. When asked, "How old is your line?" most respond, "I changed it last summer."

I lost a quality trout on Hodges Reef with Capt. Jack Innmon due to worn-out line. That was during my younger, dumber years. There is really no excuse. Line is cheap and takes minimal time to spool.

A reel does not function and cast at optimum unless the spool is full of line. When I outcast somebody by 30 yards, a glance at their reel spool usually discloses why—it is only half full. As stated, line is cheap. You can save even more buying bulk spools of 1,500 yards or more. Just keep it inside in a cool, dry place.

BRAIDED LINES

Capt. Melvin Talasek introduced me to a braided line called "Power Pro" five years ago. It scared me at first. I had heard all the horror stories of braided line cutting guides and burying in the spool. It was not until Talasek and I traveled to Florida to fish with my friend Mark Nichols of D.O.A. Lures that I became a believer.

Nichols "took me to school," so to speak, on tight-lipped snook at the St. Lucie Inlet. He threw his rootbeer TerrorEyz, let it drift with the outgoing tide, and stuck giant snook when he felt them close their mouths. Problem was, he was feeling the subtle bite and crossing their eyes while I was still waiting and wondering if I would ever get a bite. He was using Power Pro and I was using monofilament. I am no genius, but I know when I get out-fished—and I do not like it. Nevertheless, I conned Nichols over barbecue ribs to give up a spool of Power Pro for the next day. He obliged, and I have used it every day since.

I fish topwaters 80 percent of the time. The no-stretch braided line allows me to walk-the-dog with just a twitch of the rod and gives me the ability to set the hook when a fish hits right at the end of the cast. With monofilament, you have to reel down to get the bow and stretch out of the line. With a braid, just set the hook.

One note of caution: loosen your drag a bit. Because braided line has limited stretch, a fish can jerk the rod out of your hand if the drag is tight.

I have noticed a better hookup ratio during the winter months when trout are lethargic and subtly gumming the bait. The sensitivity of braided line helps you feel the strike.

Texans are catching on to braids, though the number of Lone Star anglers who use it does not compare to Floridians. Those I have talked to who have tried it swear they will never go back to monofilament.

Braided line is more expensive than monofilament, but does not wear as quickly, and, you do not use as much when spooling. The key is to fill the first half of the spool with mono, then tie the braid to the mono and fill the spool. This cuts the cost in half and reduces waste. Another way to save line is to wind used line onto the base of another reel. This will put the used portion of the line on the bottom of the spool and fresher line on the top of the new reel.

WADING BOOTS

Most waders use zip-up wading boots by Hodgman or Shimano, while others prefer "reef boots" with added protection from sharp shell and stingrays. Though no boots are 100 percent "stingray proof," they do protect the ankle and calf region where most injuries occur. Hodgman Reef Boots and ForEverLast Ray Guards are the major players.

ForEverLast Ray-Guard Wading Boots, a Texas company based in Hallettsville.

A stingray encounter is a numbers game for me. My baseball background prompts me to play the percentages. If I wade 70 percent of the time compared to a guy who wades 20 percent of the time, odds for a ray encounter favor me over the other guy. Every trip I wade and do not get hit, my percentage increases on the next trip. So, I wear protective boots. I have been hit twice in the last three years, and protective boots deflected both.

Sure, old tennis shoes work, but they also collect shell and other debris that make wading uncomfortable.

WADING BELT

Though a wading belt is not mandatory, it does help carry tackle and provides back support during death-march, four-hour wades. Most belts are 3 inches wide, but Team NuMark and Texas Tackle

Large wading belts, like the Wade-Aid belt shown here, add back support for hours of wading. Though the Wade-Aid is not a United States Coast Guard approved life preserver, it does have buoyancy and will float you if you wade too deep.

Factory make 5-inch models that really shine in the back support area. Wade-Aid's belt offers comfort to the back and flotation in deep water. Shimano makes a quality belt as well.

Most wading belt packages come with a stringer, set of pliers, and tackle box with holder ($25-$50). Though I have yet to find a set of pliers that hold up to the rigors of saltwater, it is tough to live without them, especially when extracting trebles from rubber-lipped redfish. I can do without the tackle box; when wading the surf and breakers are crashing, you are sure to deposit your favorite plugs in the sea. Current and waves eventually pound and shake the box loose. I was a mile down the beach one afternoon before I realized the Gulf had eaten $50 worth of my topwaters. Now, I wear shirts with pockets for jigs and plastics, and hook my plugs to the float at the end of my stringer. I have not lost one since.

First light at the Community Bar near Port O'Connor.

A bag supported by a floating ring ("do-net") is an option in lieu of a stringer. You just plop fish through the donut and it swims in the bag. You do not have to worry about a fish squirming from your grasp while trying to thread it onto a stringer. Some models have tackle boxes attached with a rod holder, but most do not come with a set of pliers.

CLOTHING

The basic dress for wading is a long-sleeved shirt, long pants (to protect against jellyfish), hat, and polarized glasses. The long sleeves and hat protect from excessive sun exposure. Day after day of wading in short sleeves sets the forearms ablaze and promotes skin cancer.

I like to wear shorts when the jellyfish are not thick, but during the summer months, I carry a pair of long pants in my boat.

Polarized shades are a must, not only for sun protection, but also for visibility below the surface. Without polarized shades, I feel like I am fishing naked, not to mention the severe headache I get from squinting all day. Costa Del Mar, Maui Jim, Ocean Waves, Oakley, and Bausch & Lomb produce quality glasses. Prices range from $50-$300.

Chapter Two

Lures & Baits

What to feed the fish

I am tired of hearing all the debate about artificial vs. live bait. Can't we all just fish, have fun, and toss the egos overboard? Sure, I prefer tossing artificials, and do 95 percent of the time. However, I fondly remember great popping cork sessions when trout creamed a feisty shrimp as soon as it landed on the reef, and the thump of a jetty redfish as it nailed a live Carolina-rigged pogey or finger mullet.

Fishing is fishing. Some like to sit on a bucket and soak dead shrimp, some plug all day for that one big bite. Fishing gives everyone a different pleasure.

Hanging out with Capt. Chuck Uzzle of Orange and spending weeks on family vacations together have given me a new perspective of fishing.

"I just like to fish," he said. "I have fun catching trout on live shad in the river, or poling around in the marsh and sight-casting to tailing redfish. I enjoy it all."

Enjoyment. That is what we are after, isn't it? You do not have to catch fish to enjoy the experience, though I know it helps at times. I shot some of my best photography on days when I caught very little. During those "slow" days, I noticed beauty in the bay I never took the time to look for. A great blue heron with a mullet in its beak, an autumn sunset, and a white shrimp bounding to the surface are what make an estuary a special place. Yogi Berra once said: "You can see a lot just by looking."

So, I charge you: Leave the mode and method of fishing to the participant. Enjoy your time on the water and leave the artificial egos at the dock.

TOPWATER PLUGS

To say I enjoy firing a topwater bait as far as my reel will allow is like saying a dog enjoys a bone. I never get enough of the water-thrashing, plug-sucking sound a trout makes when it decides to kill my fake plastic mullet.

Though topwaters do not always garner the most attacks, they do produce better quality fish. Often, when I am working (tough job, I know), I fish a topwater all day trying for one solid "picture fish." As mentioned elsewhere, it is a numbers game. The more you throw topwater, the more opportunity to connect with a speck of a lifetime.

Popular surface plugs include MirrOlure She Dog, Top Dog, Top Dog Jr., He Dog, and Top Pup; Pradco Super Spook, Super Spook Jr., Jumpin' Minnow, and Spit'n Image; Producer Ghost and Mega-Ghost; and Rapala Skitter Walk and Skitter Walk Jr.

Trout and redfish will eat all of them, though at times the smaller versions are better when tiny baitfishes such as glass minnows are present. Redfish have an easier time with plugs like a Top Pup, Spit'n

Popular surface plugs (topwaters) include: from left to right, Spit-N-Image, Super Spook Jr., She Dog, Ghost, Top Dog, Jumpin' Minnow and Super Spook.

Image, and Skitter Walk Jr. due to their down-pointing mouths.

SUSPENDING PLUGS

If you want to throw a big plug for big fish, but the fish do not want to come up and bang a surface plug, go below with a suspending, slow-sinking plug. It is one of the "in-betweeners" that dance in the middle of the water column when fish are not feeding on top or bottom. These baits are popular year-round, especially during the winter and spring when the water temperature does not know if it wants to warm or cool. Hence, the fish remain in limbo as well.

Suspending big fish baits include Paul Brown's original Corky, Fat Boy, and Corky Devil; MirrOlure 51M, 52M, and Catch 2000; Tidal Surge Crazy Croaker; and Pradco Swim'n Image. Just ask a few Troutmasters Tournament participants about their bait of choice during the first tournament of spring (if they will tell).

SOFT PLASTICS

Use of soft plastic baits outpaces all other artificials. Day in and day out, they produce more strikes than any other artificial offering.

Jerkbaits get their side-to-side, up-and-down action from the rod tip. Most mimic a sand eel or worm. The Bass Assassin was the bait that started the jerkbait revolution in Texas in the early 1990s. Someone decided to thread it on a jighead instead of the standard weedless, weightless hook. It must have worked. The funny thing is, most Texans have never worked the bait weightless, which solves the problem of floating grass.

Other popular jerk baits include Norton Sand Eels, Texas Trout Killers, Hogie Eel Diablos, D.O.A. CAL baits, Mister Twister Slimy Slugs, Tidal Surge, and Kelley Wigglers.

Swim baits wiggle or "paddle" with the slightest current.

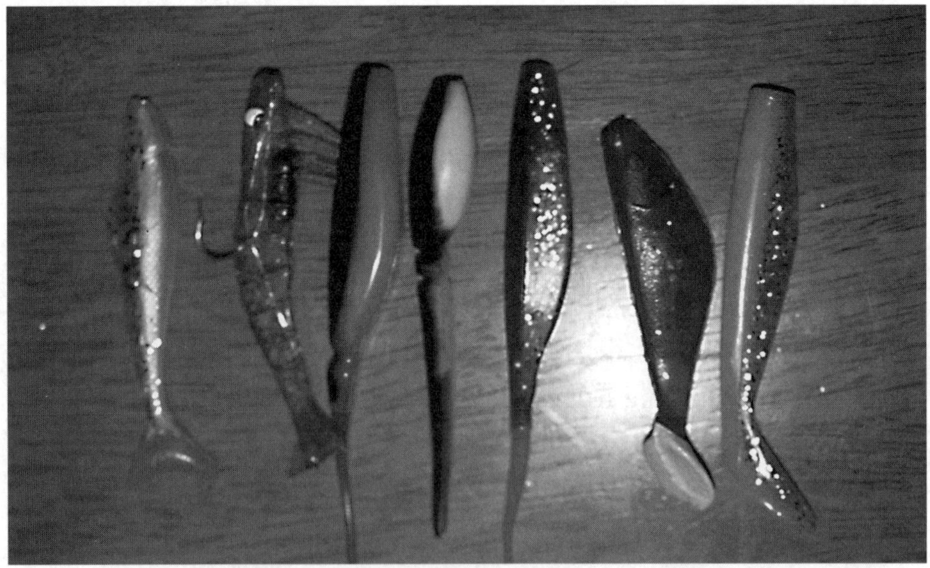

Popular soft plastic baits include: from left to right, Stanley swimming minnow, D.O.A Shrimp, Texas Trout Killer, Norton Sand Eel Jr., Bass Assassin, Hogie's shad and Norton Bull Minnow.

Though most anglers pop the rod when working swim baits, a simple turn of the reel will produce a lifelike "swimming" action. Ease of use makes them popular with novices.

Popular swim baits include Bass Assassin Sea Shad, Norton Bull Minnow, Texas Tackle Factory Red Killer, and Hogie Major Minnow.

Jigheads to rig with these baits are available in 3/8-, 1/4-, 1/8- and 1/16-ounce. Obviously, if you are fishing a strong current and want the bait to get to the bottom, use the heavy head. If you want the bait to fall slowly and suspend, use the 1/8- or 1/16-ounce head. Carry a few of each in your pocket for every wading condition.

COLORS

The best color bait is the color you prefer. A few years ago, I was a big believer that color mattered in topwaters, but my position has changed. I believe if the fish are there and they want a topwater, color is not a big issue—most of the time. There are times when chartreuse outperforms chrome, orange outperforms bone, and black outperforms everything. Got that clear in your mind? Yeah, about as clear as Galveston Bay in a stiff southwest wind.

For soft plastics, the rule of thumb is dark colors in stained water and light colors in clear water. In dirty water, dark colors cast a shadow that makes it easier for fish to locate. Then again, I have caught plenty of fish in Port O'Connor's clear waters on black/chartreuse, plum/chartreuse, and red shad. Likewise, when wind churns East Matagorda Bay into chocolate milk, I caught fish on glow/chartreuse and limetreuse. Go figure. Only the fish really know.

LIVE BAIT

"Ain't nothin' like the real thing baby." Though I don't know the rest of the song, the lyric is a truism for waders dragging a bait bucket behind. Live bait swims, smells, and sounds naturally, so, it naturally catches more fish than anything else does.

Live shrimp under a popping cork is the most popular presentation. Pre-rigged corks with weights and rattling beads make rigging as simple as tying it on, or you can make your own with a weighted cork, leader, and hook. Most are rigged to present the bait 18 to 24 inches beneath the surface. Kahle and circle hooks in sizes 1/0 to 5/0 get the job done. Circle hooks penetrate in the side of the jaw instead of deep in the stomach—critical if you get into a school of undersized trout and catch-and-release becomes mandatory.

When fish are on bottom, free-lining shrimp is a proven method. All it takes is a hook, the smallest split shot weight you can effectively cast without backlashing, and a shrimp. Allow the shrimp to do the work as it sinks to the bottom. Be aware that other species besides trout, redfish, and flounder enjoy shrimp, too; hardhead catfish, croaker, and piggy perch forged their bait-thief reputations on shrimp.

Carolina-rigged mullet or shad is deadly as well. Slide a bullet weight on the line and tie on a swivel. Tie leader material below the swivel and attach a Kahle or circle hook. Match weight to current.

From May through September, free-lined 4- to 6-inch croaker are deadly on trout. Allow it to swim freely and croak in harmony. Most insert the hook just above the anal fin, while others hook through the mouth. The mouth method seems to keep them livelier longer. When hooking through the anal fin, you drag water behind the gills when reeling in to cast again. This will drown the croaker, and a dead croaker is not as effective as a croaking one.

Chapter Three

Tide, Technique & Terrain:
The moon over Matagorda and other mysteries

One thing is certain in fishing: fish swim. They move from guts, to sand flats, to mud, to shell, to back lakes, to the pass, to channels, to bars, to spoil islands, to grass, to the first gut, to the second gut, and to the short rigs, not necessarily in that order.

Water temperature, hours of daylight, tide levels, moon phases, the presence of bait, and many other undetermined factors figure in when and where to wade-fish. Fish like constants: too cold, and they retreat to warmer, deeper water; too hot, and they retreat to cooler, deeper water. More often than not, fish frequent the same areas as they did a year ago, give or take a few weeks.

The simplest advice for deciding where and when to fish is simply "simplify." Here is a game plan to get you started.

LOG BOOKS

The pros keep a logbook, diary, or journal. "Diaries are girls' stuff," I used to say as I wiped the sweat and layers of dirt from my face after countless afternoons of playing baseball. Mr. Craig, my senior English teacher at Barbers Hill High School, consistently urged us to keep a diary of our daily lives and occurrences. I thought diaries were for those (mostly girls) who came home from school, ate a snack, and curled up with their favorite teenage love story until time for supper.

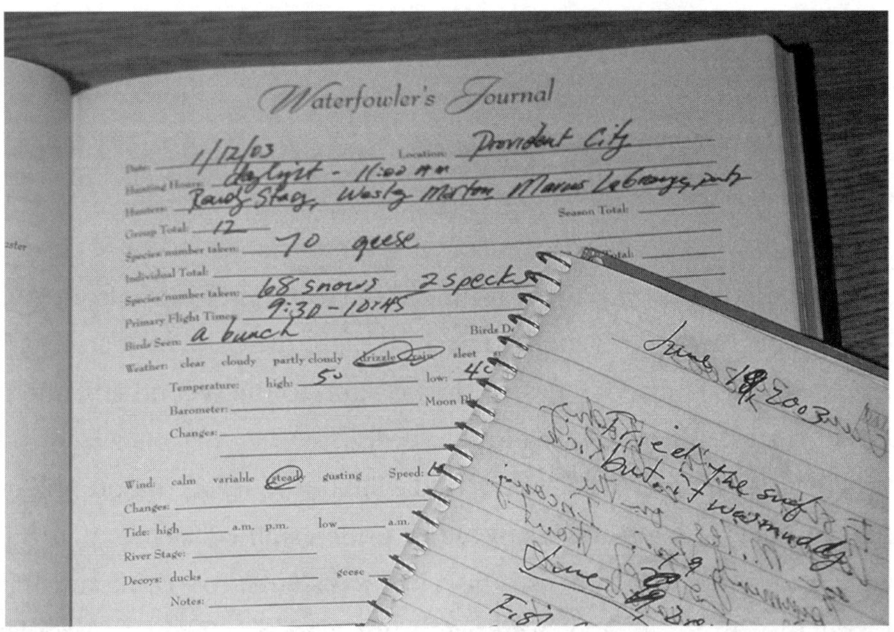

Keeping a log book or journal will help you remember fishing patterns from previous years.

A few years ago, I began a journal of all my outdoor experiences—good and bad—logging the date, temperature, wind speed, sky conditions, water temperature, tidal flow, location, and lunar phase. Depending if it was a fishing or hunting trip, I included the baits used, the fish caught, or the birds harvested.

What is the advantage of keeping an outdoor journal or log? Wildlife movements, feeding times, and locations follow a pattern annually. Chances are, if you caught fish in a particular spot a year ago, they will often be in the same vicinity a year later.

Serious anglers know the value and success that comes from keeping up with fish movements and patterns. Be it a journal, log, or diary, writing down your detailed experiences and exploits is the best recipe for return success on the water.

Capt. Gary Gray works the Port O'Connor/Seadrift area and has logs dating back to 1986. Though he says he still keeps a log, it is not as detailed as in his earlier years in the guide business: "Logs are important, especially for the everyday angler. When you do it day in and day out, like most guides, you begin to memorize it. Then, something goes wrong and you lose your fish and search for answers. That is when you can look back at your log. When everything is going good, it doesn't matter. But when it goes bad, you have the log."

Outdoor journals are not foolproof; times change. My log from years of recording told me the shrimp migration and bird activity in East Matagorda Bay began in late September, right at the conclusion of teal season. For years, the shrimp began their exodus to the Gulf of Mexico right on schedule. However, one year, during a period of drought, the shrimp and bird action did not crank up in autumn. I made note of it in my log.

"Note little coves or reefs to fish when the fishing pressure is heavy, like on weekends. These have paid off for me, especially with all the people on the water these days," said Gray.

When fish slime covers the deck, nobody cares. Yet, when your livewell is full of the same kicking crustaceans you had when you left the dock, or your soft plastic jerk bait is void of a tooth mark, a fishing journal gives you another option or plan.

Every good fisherman has a checklist in his head of where he wants to fish before he leaves the dock. Most have a good memory, but it never hurts to write it down.

If you are out of the loop and do not know the current pattern, refer to newspapers or Internet sites with fishing reports. Yeah, I know, you can't trust everything you read. However, do not search for precise locales to fish. Read through the lines and look for patterns, then fish the appropriate terrain (e.g., sand, shell, grass, mud) for the conditions.

One good one is www.txfishing.com. Click on "Coastal Report." I know it is reliable—I have written it since 1998. It is the same Weekly Coastal Fishing Report distributed by the Texas Parks and Wildlife Department and the Associated Press, and you can refer back several years to reports to see if the pattern is holding true.

THE MOON

My mom says she knows it is a full moon without looking to heaven because people act differently. The magnet of the moon affects wildlife more strongly.

"I book all my trips around the moon," said Capt. Melvin Talasek. "Your best fishing is going to be five days before and five days after a full moon or new moon. I can check my big fish records all the way back to the 1970s and the pattern holds true."

"Ninety percent of my biggest fish have been around the full moon," said Capt. Mickey Eastman of Baytown.

Eastman said he caught the two legitimate 10-pounders of his life while wading a full moon. In 1989, while fishing the full moon on Anahuac National Wildlife shoreline in East Galveston Bay, Eastman's 10-fish stringer weighed a gargantuan 97 pounds.

"You are going to get a good push and a good pull from the

tides during a bright moon," Eastman said. "The mullet and bait-fishes migrate and gang up. Because the bait is on the move, the trout are also active following them. You will find the fish on the breaks and tide lines."

My dad and I were standing side by side on the Kenedy shoreline halfway between the mouth of the Landcut and Port Mansfield, armed with chartreuse, red-headed Top

Wading at night with topwaters can be rewarding. Notice the full moon over my buddy Walt Wendtland's right shoulder.

Dog Jr's. We worked the shoreline tight early that morning before daylight, hoping to lure a sow in shin-deep water. A redfish was all we could muster.

By 8:00 a.m., we, along with the mullet, moved to deeper water. Bait littered scattered patches of grass in waist- to chest-deep water. Throughout the morning, spotted predators blew up on our plugs, but no hook-ups. Consecutive casts seldom escaped a trout popping them out of the water. The specks were not in feeding mode, just agitated at the pseudo-mullet noisemaker.

Dad was frustrated.

"Am I doing something wrong?" he asked.

"No. Remember, we are on the full moon," I replied. "Just wait until around 11:00 a.m. These fish will quit playing with the bait when they start feeding."

As if Cookie banged the triangle on a cattle drive, the feed commenced at the aforementioned hour. There were no pops or patsy nudges like before, but full-blown attack. When the fish decided they wanted the plastic dog-walker, you did not have to set the hook; just make sure your drag is loose so your tackle would not be snatched from your palms. We remained in the same 50-yard radius until the action slowed around mid-afternoon.

Typically, the best bite occurs around the full or new moon just before daylight, then from late morning to early afternoon, give or take a half an hour.

Spring Wading Terrain

Under cloudy, damp March skies, Capt. Lynn Smith, Art Wright, and I made a mile wade along an Ayres Bay shoreline. This particular locale had humps, guts, undulations, and grass—the amenities a trout desires. A warming trend raised water temperatures into the low 60s.

We caught plenty of trout that day on topwaters and limetreuse Bass Assassins, Trout Killers, and Eel Diablos. However, had the water temperature been a few degrees lower, the flat probably would have been barren

Spring is full of uncertainties. The weather does not know if it wants to hold onto winter or loosen its grip for spring. Hence, the fish have the same attitude. Get a week of sunlight and warmth, and the fish head to the flats. Then, a late-season cold front drops water temperatures back into the 50s and the fish retreat to winter haunts.

Spring fishing terrains are mud, shell, grass, and sand. Fish use the mud when mercury readings chill. Mud is warmer and acts as an insulator. Often, scattered shell mixes with the mud. The shell holds baitfishes, which are also trying to stay warm.

As the sun shines, trout move to the sand and grass. Sunlight warms the sand quicker than mud, and attracts mullet and other finfishes to the warmth. Where the baitfishes go, so go the game fishes.

For flounder, the cuts and drains leading to the bay, and the openings leading to the marsh, are prime spots. Flounder use these highways to enter and exit and wait to ambush prey.

SUMMER WADING TERRAIN

Mike Trevathan, Mark Collins, Eddie Sullivan, and I arrived at the Hump just as the sun etched through the horizon. The 32-mile boat ride from Matagorda Harbor is a long one, but well worth the extra fuel and predawn navigation to this far western locale of West Matagorda Bay. (Some consider it part of Port O'Connor. It is only a five-minute boat ride from the Fishing Center and Clark's.)

The Hump is a flat in the middle of the bay, with depths ranging from 1 to 5 feet. Water ranging from 6 to 14 feet surrounds it, and it is within two miles of the Port O'Connor jetty and two miles from Pass Cavallo. It is a trout magnet, to say the least, especially from May to September.

As tides rise and fall, shrimp, mullet and other baitfishes fall on and off the bar. Baitfishes use the grass and undulations on the bay floor as cover from predators. Predators use this structure as ambush points.

(The spots on a trout are perfect camouflage against sea grasses.)

On this particular day, an incoming tide pushed a line of mullet on the flat. We knew there were fish, evident by the sweet smell of fresh slicks popping all over. We caught over 100 fish that day (caught, not kept), mostly on She Dogs and Top Pups.

Back at the harbor, Capt. Bill Pustejovsky was filleting a catch of the same magnitude, yet he had only burned a few gallons of gas on mid-bay reefs in East Matagorda Bay.

That is the dilemma summertime wading presents: fish use the sand, grass, shell, and mud.

Pustejovsky had fished the reefs because a crop of brown shrimp was moving through the bay in route to the Gulf (June/July). Since reefs are some of the only structure in the open bay, the shrimp used it for refuge. However, the trout were on their tails and hanging out at the "Halfshell Restaurant" for a buffet of healthy crustaceans. Trouble is, these mid-bay reefs are only fishable when light winds persist. Strong winds turn the middle of mud-bottomed, reef-laden bays like East Matagorda and San Antonio to chocolate milk.

Fish use the mud in the summer when tides are lowest and temperatures are highest. The mud acts as an insulator in the winter and performs the same function in the summer. When southwest winds persist in July and tides drop to more than a foot below normal, trout will not haunt the shallow shorelines; they are too hot. Find a muddy bottom and work from there. The temperature change from the flats to the mud will be only a few degrees, but one degree can make all the difference.

AUTUMN WADING TERRAIN

October is by far my favorite time of year. The sunsets are brilliant, cooler days and nights send a bolt of energy through my veins, migrant waterfowl arrive daily, and the fishing is fabulous.

White shrimp flood the bays from the nearby marsh and prompt large schools of trout and redfish to gang up and follow like bullies.

Equinox tides flood shorelines and rejuvenate the shallows with fresh recruits of baitfishes. Mud, shell, sand, and grass all hold fish. Shrimp bounding to the surface indicate a speck, spot, or dot is near.

Again, open bay reefs are prime wading venues due to balls of shrimp seeking cover. If you think there are lots of brown shrimp in the summer, wait until you see the clumps of fall "whites." You know they are there by the hovering gulls.

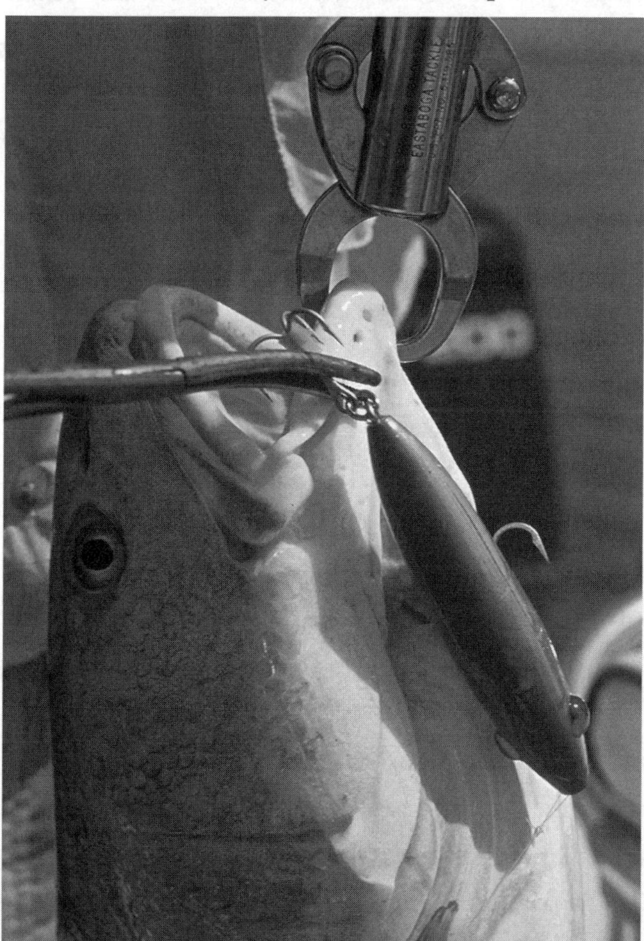

Back lakes as well are solid for trout and reds. Those shrimp that have not found their way to the bay remain in the back lakes. Often, herds of reds—sometimes 50 to 100 in a school—roam the shallows and gorge. Loosen your drag; most are brutes.

Like in springtime, autumn flounder are on the move to spawn in

Large redfish often require surgery to extract a topwater.

the Gulf. Cuts and

passes leading to the ocean, including the Ship Channel and Intracoastal, are fine wading spots. Jigs tipped with shrimp or Carolina-rigged mud minnows dupe migrating flatfish.

WINTER WADING TERRAIN

More oft than not, winter wading is mostly over mud. Mud bottoms are the warmest part of the water column during a frigid winter, and it is no coincidence top pros get muddy when Old Man Winter appears. Sabine Lake, Trinity Bay, East Galveston Bay, West Galveston Bay, Christmas Bay, and East Matagorda Bay have lots of mud.

Wading the mud is not for the meek or faint of heart. It requires a level of physical fitness—unless you enjoy pain, muscle cramps, and a sweat-laden forehead.

Capt. Jesse Arsola can't wait for January in East Matagorda Bay: "Right about the time hunting season is winding down, you can catch some beautiful trout over mud. It is one of my favorite times of the year. There is not a lot of traffic due to the cold, and most people will not wade in the muck."

Arsola is not a small man, but he said wading muddy bottoms requires a different style: "Go slow, very slow. Try to keep the pressure on your toes and pick up your feet with every step. These trout will be in very shallow water, so sound is a big factor. I get in mud to my knees and water to my waist, so I am in about two feet of water."

Arsola likes to fish a mixture of mud and oyster shell, and said 11 a.m. to 3 p.m. is the best time to fish in winter: "The water heats up and the fish head to the mud flats to warm up. I like working a Corky real slow over the mud and shell, sometimes dragging it over every piece. I also like to use braided line so I do not lose so many baits to the sharp shell."

Capt. Chris Martin of Seadrift fishes the mud exclusively during the winter and early spring. He said finding structure in the mud is the key to his success: "I work the muddy edges of reefs that have a drop-off where a strong current is moving. When I find a trough, combine that with the warmth of the mud and active bait, I can almost guarantee the fish will be there."

Martin said winter trout are often lethargic and looking for a larger, protein-rich meal. Trout are not as apt to chase a bait like they do in the summer: "Give them a slower presentation. They will eat a Corky Devil, especially if you pop it and let it fall slowly."

Martin drags avocado and pumpkinseed Norton plastics over the shell and mud, creating a mud cloud that simulates a shrimp or eel bursting out of the mud: "Sometimes trout are suspended in the middle of the water column. By stirring up the bottom with the bait, we entice those trout to take a look."

West Galveston Bay is only a cast away from Capt. James Plaag's Tiki Island home. A short boat ride away is his muddy, winter trophy trout haunt. Plaag and his constituent at Silver King Adventures, Dana Bailey, have each won the Troutmasters Pro Angler of the Year award along with numerous individual tournament wins.

Plaag said catching a big fish in frigid water is a bit of an anomaly. He prefers temps at least in the 50s. The key is the presence of mullet and a little bit of mud and shell: "We all know that water over mud warms faster, and whatever bait is present in the bay will be over the mud for that reason. The prime water temp for catching big trout is 50-62 degrees. I am always looking for mullet in the winter, and so are the trout."

Do not expect fast and furious action. On a normal day, Plaag gets about five bites and his parties average 10-11 fish a day. Nonetheless, his customers know fishing the mud is about quality over quantity: "We had one day when a few buddies and I caught 52 trout with a 5-3/4-pound average. We got on them that day, but it does not happen like that in the winter very often. Overall, we catch quality fish wading in Galveston, Sabine, and Calcasieu."

TIDES

When I plan to fish, the first thing I check the day before is the weather forecast, which determines where I fish. The next thing I look at is the tide forecast, which determines when I fish.

Knowing the tides before you hit the water helps eliminate unproductive water.

Incoming tides push fish closer to shorelines, depending on the height of the tide. The outgoing tide pulls fish away from the shoreline. Typically, trout and redfish stage in guts, channels, and drop-offs until the next incoming tide pushes more water and bait onto the flats.

When fishing around cuts, drains, and back lakes, work the outside on a falling tide and the inside of the back lakes on a rising tide.

The best tides occur around the moon and new moons. Four-tide days are best on the upper coast, while two-tide days produce along the middle and lower coast.

One thing is certain: as long as the water is moving, you have a chance.

Chapter Four

Upper Coast Strategies
& Hotspots:

Sabine Lake to Sargent

I took the largest trout of my life, along with my heaviest one-day stringer of speckled gorillas, while wading Sydney Island on Sabine Lake in June 1999. Growing up within 10 minutes of the boat ramp on Gou Hole Road, which winds through the marsh and eventually to Trinity Bay, and now residing 20 minutes from the nearest ramp to Matagorda Bay, I have fished the last dozen years of my life on the upper Texas coast.

The upper coast is a fish-producing machine and receives more pressure than any other region in the state due to its proximity to Houston. The calling card is extensive marsh and wetlands. Not by coincidence, these estuaries are prime fishing venues where anglers hook a plethora of specks, reds, and flatfish.

All upper coast waters have one thing in common: the marsh is the backbone. One thing is for sure on the upper coast: after a day of wading, the inside of your boat needs a rinse at the car wash.

Wading along a marshy shoreline can be excellent, especially when fishing near a cut or bayou on a falling tide when bait empties from the back reaches of the marsh.

Surrounding marshes are nurseries where a plethora of shrimp, shad, and tiny game fishes grow. Unlike bay systems in southern Texas, each estuary on the upper coast has a surrounding marsh.

According to biologist Bill Balboa of the Texas Parks and Wildlife Department (TPWD), marsh areas are always near rivers and tributaries where fresh- and saltwater meet: "The organic matter from the river and marsh are pumped into the bays. Marshes are critical on the upper coast of Texas to the productivity of finfishes and shellfishes. It provides a shelter due to its shallow waters and reduced salinity. Algae, little shrimp, and smaller fish can feed on the organisms. The marsh is very important to the bottom of the food chain."

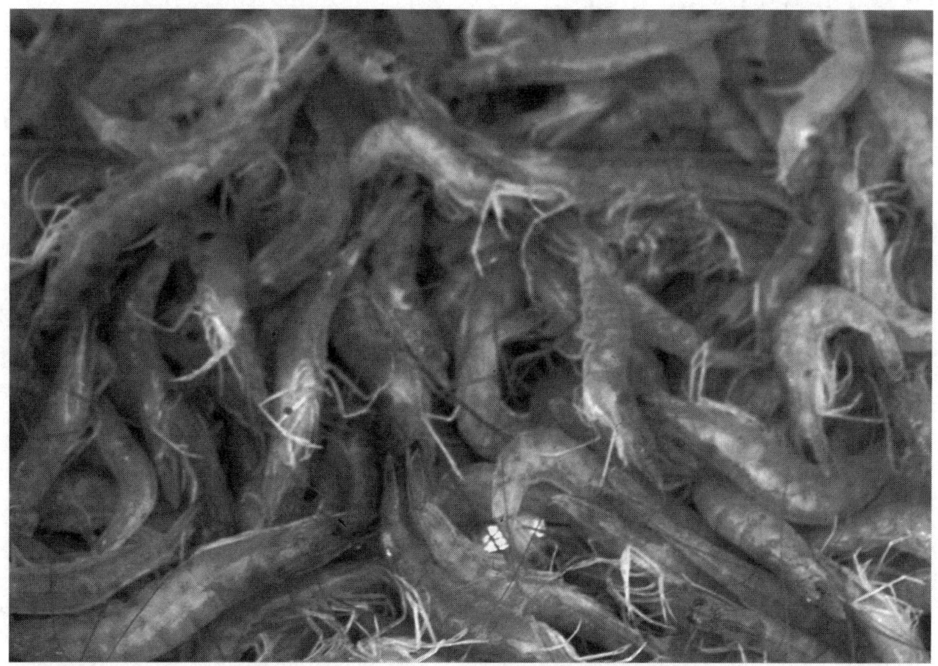

On most occasions, live shrimp is your best bet for bending a rod.

Balboa said brown shrimp use the marsh in early spring, and white shrimp use it in late summer and early fall. Brown shrimp prefer a saltier environment while "whiteys" like a fresher environment. Hence, there is a direct correlation between the marsh and Texas' prime autumn bays. East Matagorda, East Galveston, and West Galveston bays and Sabine Lake are established estuaries where shrimp begin their exodus from the marsh to the Gulf.

"There are four times more young fish and crabs in the marsh than in the bay," said Andy Sipocz, habitat assessment biologist for TPWD in Dickinson. "On average, there are 800 shrimp per square meter in the marsh."

Balbao said the marsh is important to the health and vitality of adjacent bays. The marsh consumes organic matter from rivers and hosts decomposing vegetation throughout the year. Higher than normal tides in spring and tropical storms surges flush the organic matter into the open bays. "The organic matter fertilizes the bay and gives food to

Young Mitchell Mize of Friendswood caught this solid East Matagorda Bay flounder on a Bass Assassins while wadefishing with Capt. Bill Pustejovsky.

Capt. Chuck Uzzle catch this seven-pound trout on fly while on the East Flats in Corpus Christi Bay. Notice the abundance of spots on this trout that was caught over grass.

organisms on the bottom of the food chain," Balbao said.

The lower coast does not have the rivers and marsh of the upper coast. Pristine waters like Laguna Madre rely on decomposing sea grasses and photosynthesis to pump nutrients back into the estuaries.

Sipocz said the bacteria and fungi that grow from decomposing plants in the marsh keep bay waters clean. He pointed to air pollutants, nitrogen-based fertilizers, and pesticides as the major sources of pollution in the Galveston Bay Complex: "What goes up must come down. The pollution in the air eventually falls into our bays. These organisms in the marsh can break down some nasty chemicals such as benzene

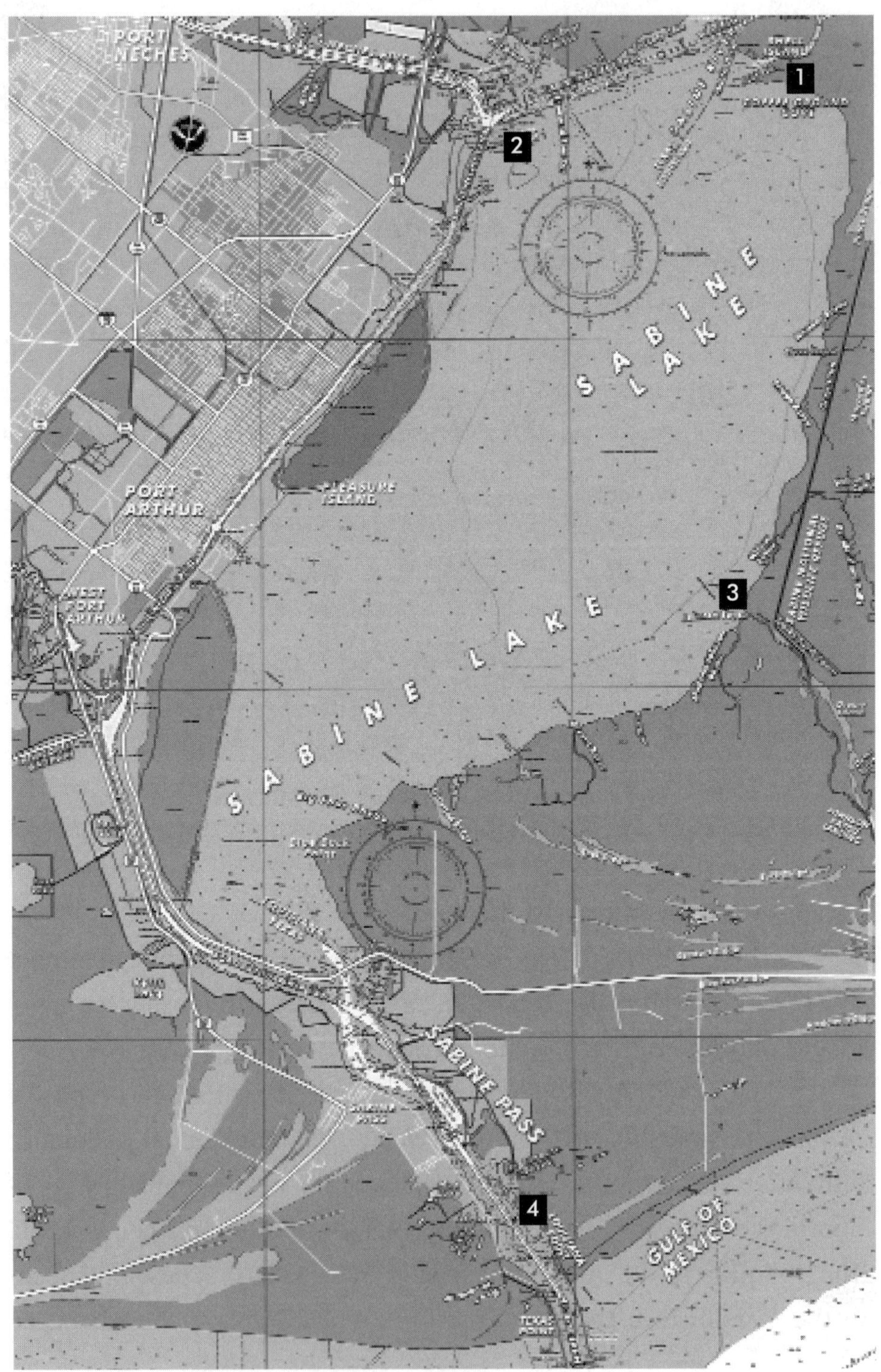
PORT NECHES
PORT ARTHUR
WEST PORT ARTHUR
PLEASURE ISLAND
SABINE LAKE
SABINE LAKE
SABINE PASS
GULF OF MEXICO
1
2
3
4

and ammonium nitrate and keep our water clean. The marsh and wetlands are the basis of the food chain and water quality."

Sabine Lake (see map on page 34)

Sabine Lake occupies a special place in my heart. It is where I met my new best friend, Capt. Chuck Uzzle, and we shared quite possibly the best morning of wading either of us will ever experience.

On the morning in question, he, the late Sammy Noland, and I caught and released nine trout over 28 inches. We caught 27 total, the smallest measuring 24 inches. I lost one I know was pushing 33 inches. I can say that with a straight face because I had danced with a half-dozen 28-inchers that morning, and the "big one that got away" was definitely in another class.

Uzzle was a conservationist before conservation was cool. He insisted we let the "big girls" go and I respected him for it. I consider him one of the pioneers that helped shift the attitude of Texans to release big trout.

Sabine Lake is a border lake with the western half in Texas and the eastern half in Louisiana. Marsh surrounds the entire lake, with the Louisiana shoreline providing most of the wading terrain. Mud and silt is the predominant bay floor and the reason the water looks like a large glass of weak tea or coffee.

1 Coffee Ground Cove (GPS N29 58.561, W93 46.372) begins at the mouth of Black Bayou and catches runoff from East Pass. Its proximity to marsh drains and cuts makes it a hotspot on a falling tide, especially in the fall when shrimp and shad are abundant.

When tides swell, work tight to the shoreline for redfish and trout. As tides fall, work close to the cut for flounder, trout, and reds. As the bait exits the marsh, the game fish follow close behind. A north or northeast wind is best.

2 Stewt's Island (GPS N29 57.780, W93 51.161), Sydney Island, and Rabbit Island are spoils islands on the north end of the lake bordering the Sabine-Neches Canal (Intracoastal). The south side of the islands has solid footing for wading, while the north side is a bit of a quagmire with mud past your knees in some spots.

With the canal so close, trout and reds wait for an incoming tide to swim onto the flats. When the tide recedes, they fall back to the deeper water, Work Barrel Channel, that separates Stewt's and Sydney islands. The best winds are northerly or light southerly.

3 The Willow Bayou and Johnson Bayou shorelines (GPS N29 51.032, W93 47.281) are on the south end of the lake on the Louisiana shoreline. Deep cuts filter into the marsh. The shoreline is best on a falling tide, as the bayou drains trout, reds, and flounder from the marsh. Footing is solid for the most part, but there are boggy spots. The best winds are south, east, and southeast.

Blue Buck Point on the Louisiana shoreline has many humps and scattered shell. Its proximity to Big Four Bayou allows baitfishes

Capt. Bobby Gardner of Matagorda unhooks the trebles from a West Matagorda Bay trout. Note his hat holding his extra topwaters.

to flow in and out of the marsh with fluctuating tides. The best fishing is normally on an incoming tide as trout, redfish, and flounder hit the shoreline from the nearby deeper water. The best winds are south, east, and southeast.

4 Lighthouse Reef (GPS N29 43.363, W93 51.180) is located in a shallow cove right off the Sabine Pass Channel. Fish use the channel as a highway to and from the Gulf and are attracted to the reef on an incoming tide. This is big fish territory, but be aware of fluctuating water levels, especially when huge oil tankers roll past. The best winds are east and northeast.

She Dogs, Super Spooks, and SkitterWalks get the job done on top. Pumpkinseed, plum, and red shad Bass Assassins, Trout Killers, Sand Eels, and shrimp tails top the soft plastic choices. Live finger mullet and Carolina-rigged shad are solid natural baits.

Pluggers should let the fish play out before trying to land it; or, risk a handful of treble hooks.

TRINITY BAY (SEE MAP ON PAGE 40)

I spent many mornings of my high school and college years fishing and duck hunting in Trinity Bay. The Spillway is only 15 minutes from my parents' driveway in Mont Belvieu.

The bay is consistent as long as floodwaters do not swell the Trinity River. If this occurs, most of the fish retreat to East Galveston Bay, and Trinity becomes a freshwater mud hole.

The North Ridge beginning in the **1** Anahuac Pocket (GPS N29 42.752, W94 42.411) on the east shoreline is solid wading along a line of spoil banks. The Old Trinity River channel runs parallel to the shoreline. The area is particularly good in the fall when the first crop of white shrimp leaves the marsh. The boat ramp at Oak Island puts you on the spot. The best winds are north, northeast, south, and southeast.

2 Little Pipeline Reef (GPS N29 36.760, W94 43.333), **3** Little Hodges Reef (GPS N29 36.040, W94 43.652), and **4** Hodges Reef (GPS N29 35.302, W94 44.404) line up in that order on the east shoreline and provide oyster shell that holds baitfish. I have caught quality trout on topwaters and plastics here and have lost a few big ones, too. Don't overlook the backdoor of the reefs in the Old Trinity River Channel as shrimp bury in the mud and trout and reds hang close to root them out. The water stays clean here with easterly winds.

Keep heading south and you will run into Vingt-et-un Island (pronounced "van-tune" in Texanese) and surrounding reefs. **5** Roundtable Reef (GPS N29 33.702, W94 46.821) sits on the tip of the island and is particularly strong when the upper portion of Trinity Bay is fresh. There are other unnamed bits of shell in the area worth wading if baitfishes are present. Again, the area is protected from easterly winds.

On the north shoreline, from **6** Jack's Pocket (GPS N29 46.000, W94 45.003) to the **7** HL&P Spillway (GPS N29 45.131, W94 48.851) is quality wading. Jack's Pass, Long Island Bayou, Cove Bayou, Cross Bayou, and Reds Bayou all dump baitfishes along the shoreline on a falling tide. However, the shore is very shallow and requires good tides to flood the flats. In the wintertime, especially with persistent north winds, the shoreline is dry. It is best under light northerly winds in spring and autumn.

The North Flats on the west shoreline from Point Barrow to Umbrella Point is good at high tide. **8** Elliot's Reef (GPS N29 42.228, W94 51.187), **9** Trinity Reef (GPS N29 41.762, W94 51.480), and **10** Fisher Shoals (GPS N29 40.301, W94 51.190) are a mile-long set of reefs running south. **11** Beazley Reef (GPS N29 39.232, W94 52.651) and **12** Dow Reef (GPS N29 38.851, W94 54.202) are exceptionally strong as they drop off to seven feet of water on their southern tip. The area is protected from westerly winds.

Live shrimp under a popping cork, finger mullet, shad, and croaker are solid live bait offerings. Red shad, black, plum, pumpkinseed, fire tiger, and glow are proven soft plastic colors. Any topwater will work.

EAST GALVESTON BAY (SEE MAP ON PAGE 44)

East Galveston Bay floor is predominantly muddy but wadeable due to its entire shoreline bordering the marsh. Tidal flow from Rollover Pass and Bolivar Roads give it a constant flushing on its extreme east and west ends. Fish stack in this bay when Trinity Bay floods with freshwater.

Reefs litter the North Flats from Smith Point to Robinson Bayou. **1** Richard's Reef (GPS N29 31.401, W94 44.280), **2** Drum Village Reef (GPS N29 31.710, W94 41.633), **3** Stephenson Reef (GPS N29 32.040, W94 41.101), and **4** Buckshot Reef (GPS N29 32.241, W94 40.400)

BURNETT BAY
WOOSTER
SCOTT BAY
HOUSTON SHIP CHANNEL
ALEXANDER ISLAND
SAN JACINTO
BAYTOWN
TABBS BAY
SPILLMANS ISLAND
MORGANS POINT
LA PORTE
HOUSTON POINT
Big Hog Bayou
Smith Bayou
LAKE ANAHUAC
TRINITY RIVER
ANAHUAC
RED BLUFF
Clear Point Oil Field
SEABROOK
CLEAR LAKE
12

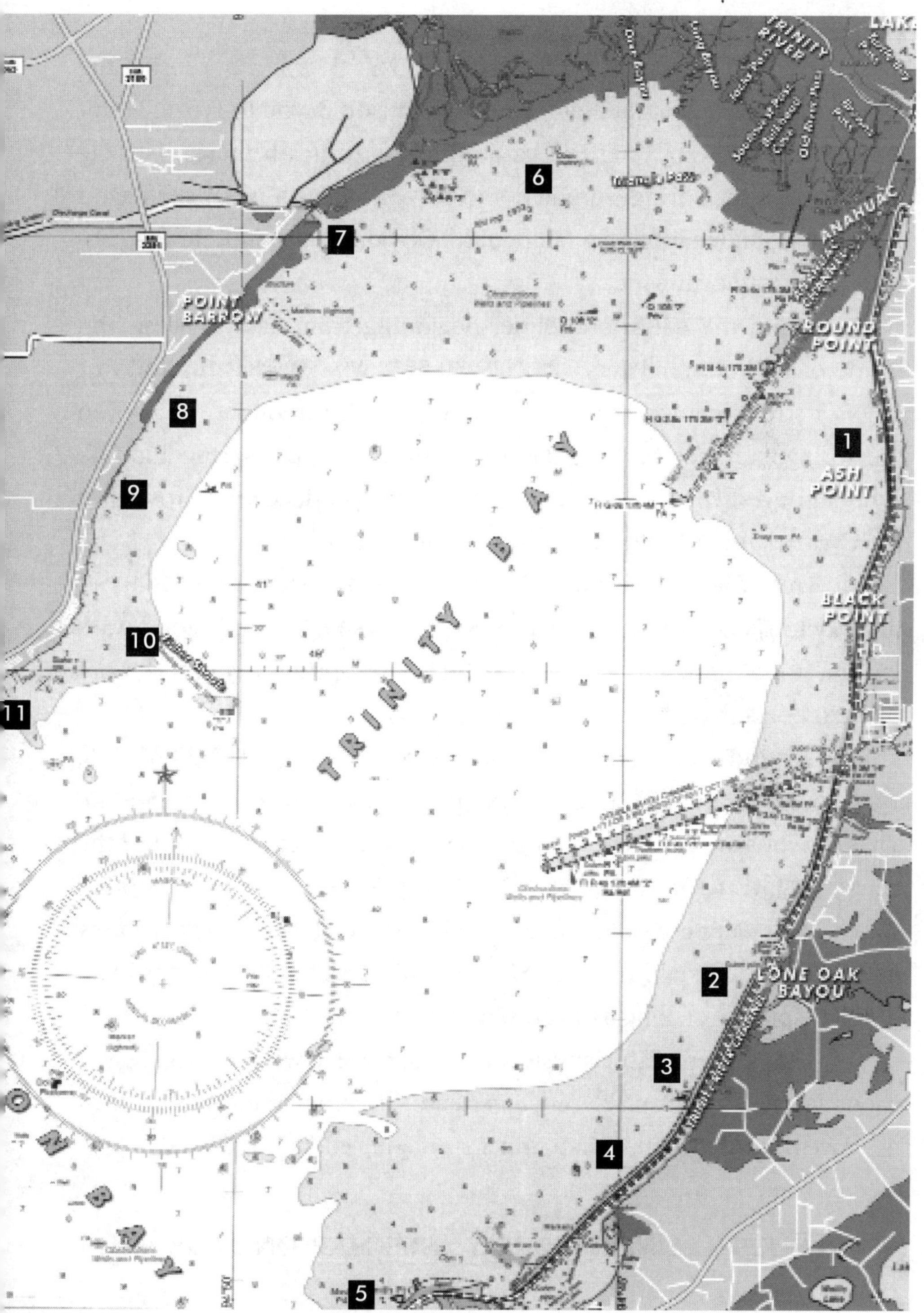
TRINITY RIVER
ANAHUAC
ROUND POINT
POINT BARROW
ASH POINT
BLACK POINT
TRINITY BAY
LONE OAK BAYOU
1
2
3
4
5
6
7
8
9
10
11

provide structure to wade.

5 Wildlife Flats (GPS N29 33.317, W94 31.938), bordering the Anahuac National Wildlife Refuge from Robinson Bayou to Frozen Point (name derived from a herd of cattle freezing to death there), is a big trout spot in the spring, summer, and fall. The mouth of Oyster Bayou is a great flounder spot on a falling tide. Obviously, the shoreline is protected from a north wind.

Along the south shoreline, beginning from east to west, the inside of **6** Rollover Pass (GPS N29 30.583, W94 30.084), in Rollover Bay is a strong choice anytime. Trout and redfish frequent the area in the spring, summer, and fall. Flounder are best in the spring and fall. Tandem-rigged Lil' Fishies and D.O.A. Shrimp produce when tossed in the channel and allowed to swim with the current.

From **7** Little Pasture Cove (GPS N29 31.316, W94 32.164), all the way to **8** Long Point (GPS N29 31.844, W94 34.390), is good wading due to its proximity to Rollover Pass. One spring, I counted more than 20 boats there when the fish were thick.

Around Long Point lie **9** Big Pasture Bayou (GPS N29 30.226, W94 35.699), and **10** Yates Bayou (GPS N29 29.622, W94 35.877). These bayous are best when shrimp, shad, and mullet empty out of the marsh. **11** Fat Rat Pass (GPS N29 28.551, W94 38.832) is a popular spot as well. Pepper Grove Cove and Elm Grove Flats receive tidal flow from the Intracoastal by way of Sievers Cove, and the Pig Pen has been a stellar spot for as long as I can remember.

For pluggers, East Galveston is a great place to walk the dog. Jiggers choose glow, red shad, plum, red, limetreuse, black, and pumpkinseed plastics. Live-baiters go with shrimp under a popping cork or free-lined.

WEST GALVESTON BAY (SEE MAP ON PAGE 48)

Jamey Knight of Bridge City helps his brother, Capt. Chuck Uzzle, weigh a 28-inch Calcasieu Lake trout before releases it back to its southwest Louisiana waters.

West Bay often goes overlooked and under-fished, except among those who live close to Galveston or just know how good it can be. It does not receive the traffic Trinity or East Galveston bays endure, probably because it is off the beaten path. If you plan to fish West Galveston Bay, chances are you will be there the entire trip. Whereas, Trinity and East Galveston offer easy access to each other and Bolivar Roads in the same day.

The locals like to keep it quiet when the fishing is good, and I

SMITH POINT
LAKE SUPRIS
STEPHENSON
POINT
1
2
3
4
EAST BAY
HANNA REEF
BOLIVAR PENINSULA
SOLIVAR
PORT BOLIVAR
TEXAS CITY DIKE
PELICAN
ISLAND
GALVESTON

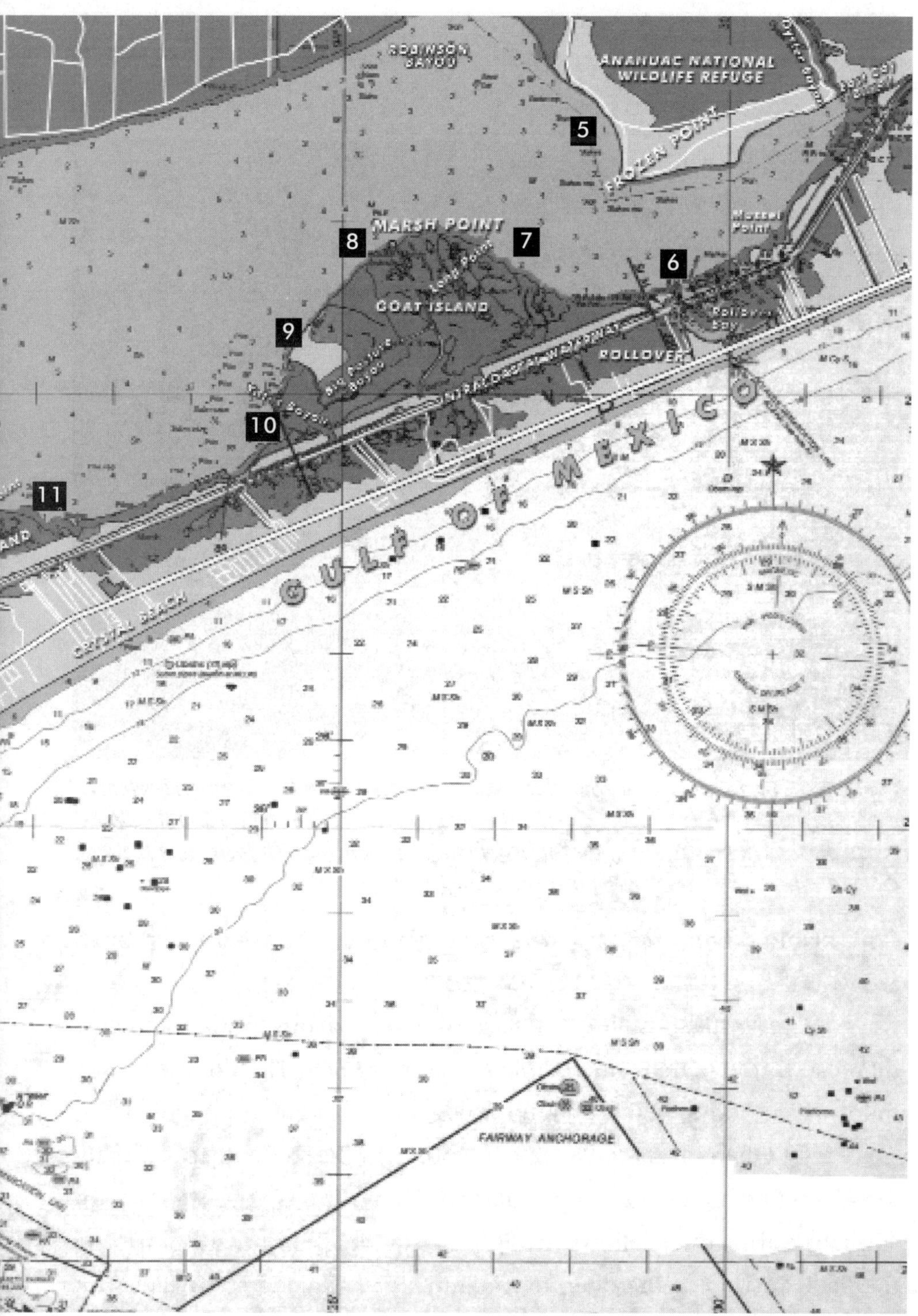
ROBINSON BAYOU
ANAHUAC NATIONAL WILDLIFE REFUGE
FROZEN POINT
5
MARSH POINT
8
7
Long Point
6
Mottel Point
GOAT ISLAND
Rollover Bay
9
Big Pasture Bayou
ROLLOVER
INTRACOASTAL WATERWAY
10
GULF OF MEXICO
11
CRYSTAL BEACH
FAIRWAY ANCHORAGE

Capt. Chuck Uzzle releases a 28-inch trout after duping it on fly. Catch-and-release, especially on trophy trout, has become the norm and not the exception on the Texas coast. Most waders are opting for replica mounts of their big fish instead of the traditional skin mount. The result is a healthier fishery for all.

can't blame them. The narrow bay can get quite crowded when birds are working and trout are crushing plugs.

The south shoreline is a maze of coves, bayous, points, and guts that lead to the marsh—incredible structure to fish. The floor is mostly mud, which bodes well for winter pluggers wanting that one, big bite.

1 Offatts Flats (GPS N29 16.666, W94 52.267), adjacent to 20-feet-deep Offatts Bayou is a popular winter wading spot. As afternoon sunlight warms the shallows, trout leave the deep bayou and warm on the flats. Casting to the deep bayou and slowly jigging soft plastics on the bottom also catches fish. Long Reef, parallel to the deep channel running to Offatts Bayou, provides shell and structure that holds bait year round.

2 Confederate Reef (GPS N29 15.810, W94 55.302) wraps around the west shoreline of North Deer Island and South Deer Island. Each island has superb wading with easy-walking flats and scattered shell throughout. Since the reef and islands are in the middle of the bay, wind must be light to fish clear water.

The shoreline from Virginia Point (where the causeway begins) to Campbell Bayou is strong when tides fall out of Swan Lake. Very few locales enjoy protection from late summer's southwest winds, but one does.

Starvation, Hoeckers, Dana, Carancahua, Jumbile, Bird Island, and Snake Island coves all provide shelter from southerly and easterly breezes. The Pirates Beach Marina channel runs through Hoeckers Cove, while West Bay Marina offers close access to **3** Snake Island Cove and Reef (GPS N29 09.753, W95 02.351).

On the north shoreline, from **4** Carancahua Point (GPS N29 12.845, W95 01.826) to **5** Alligator Point (GPS N29 10.277, W95 07.250), is solid wading along the spoil islands bordering the Intracoastal. North winds are best for fishing, and a moving tide shuffles fish from the deep channel to the flats.

6 Bird Island Flats (GPS N29 06.230, W95 08.611) and **7** Mud Cut Flats (GPS N29 06.233, W95 09.502) are on the far west shoreline of the bay. Bastrop Bay empties onto the shoreline through Mud Cut. Christmas Bay empties by way of Cold Pass, and strong tidal flow from San Luis Pass brings this shoreline to life. This is one of those spots protected from a southwest wind.

Christmas Bay has good wading on the grass-laden north shore, and plenty of shell near the mouth of Drum Bay. The south shoreline

CARANCAHUA LAKE
GREENS LAKE
INTRACOASTAL WATERWAY
CARANCAHUA REEF
WEST~BAY
CARANCAHUA COVE
DANA COVE
DALEHITE COVE
STARVATION COVE
MELAGER COVE
LAKE COMO
PIRATES COVE
JAMAICA BEACH
GALVESTON
PALM BEACH
SPANISH GRANT
PIRATES BEACH
BERMUDA BEACH

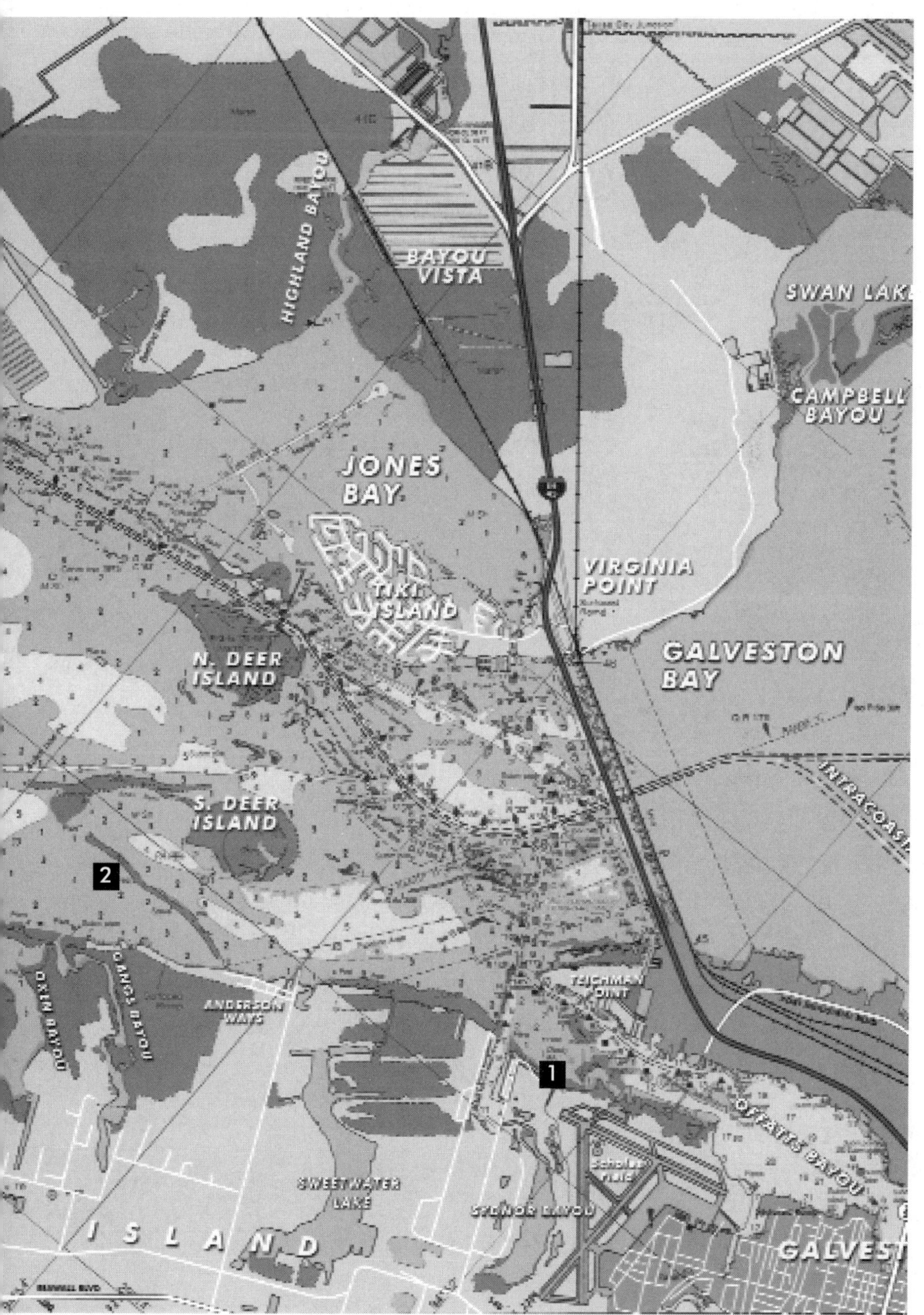
HIGHLAND BAYOU
BAYOU VISTA
SWAN LAKE
CAMPBELL BAYOU
JONES BAY
TIKI ISLAND
VIRGINIA POINT
N. DEER ISLAND
GALVESTON BAY
S. DEER ISLAND
GRITS
INTRACOAS
2
OXEN BAYOU
BASINS BAYOU
ANDERSON WAYS
TEICHMAN POINT
1
OFFATTS BAYOU
SWEETWATER LAKE
Scholes Field
SIGNOR BAYOU
ISLAND
GALVEST

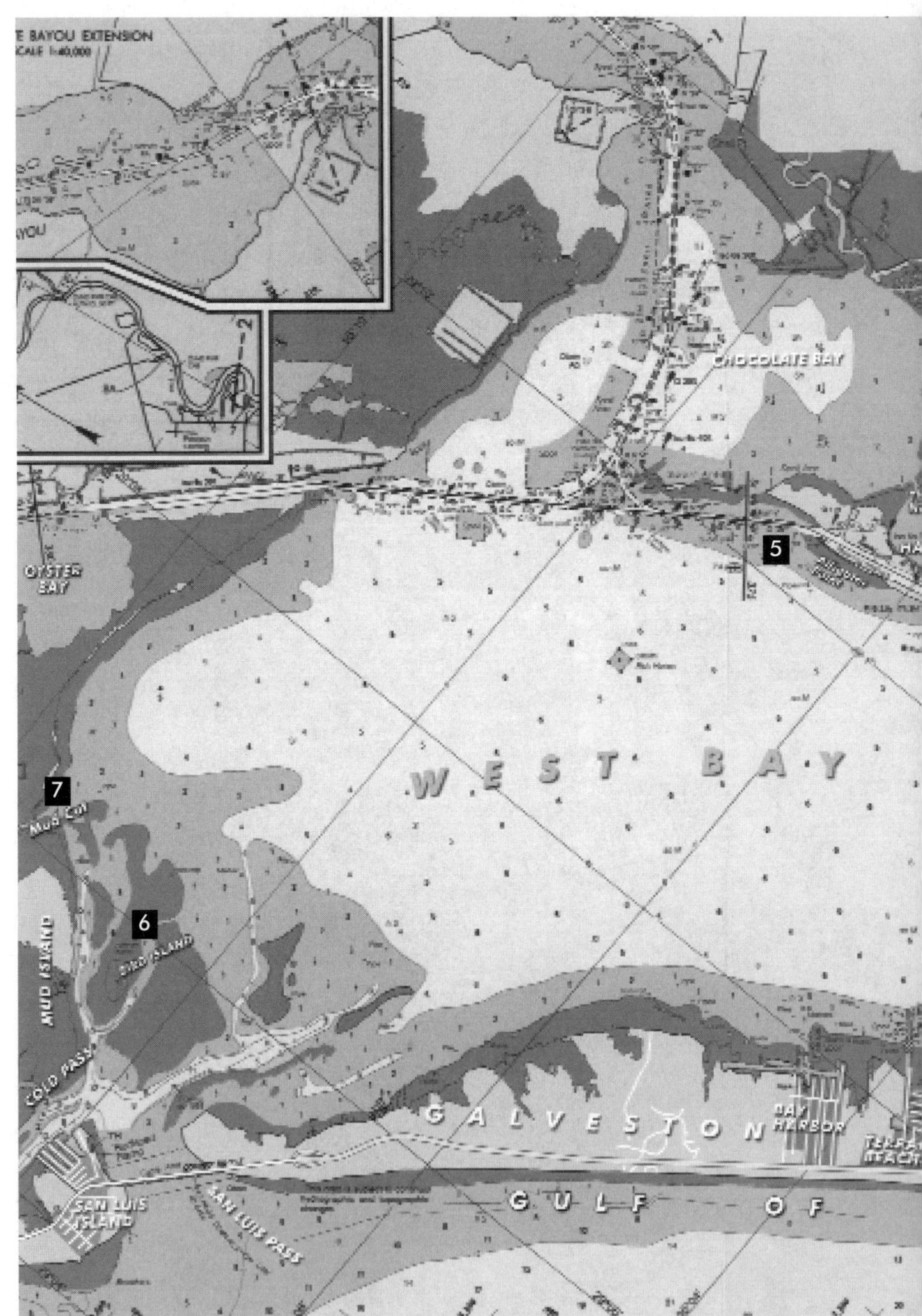
E BAYOU EXTENSION
SCALE 1=40,000
BAYOU
OYSTER
BAY
CHOCOLATE BAY
5
W E S T   B A Y
7
Mud Cove
6
MUD ISLAND
BIRD ISLAND
COLD PASS
SAN LUIS ISLAND
SAN LUIS PASS
G A L V E S T O N
BAY HARBOR
TERRA BEACH
G U L F   O F

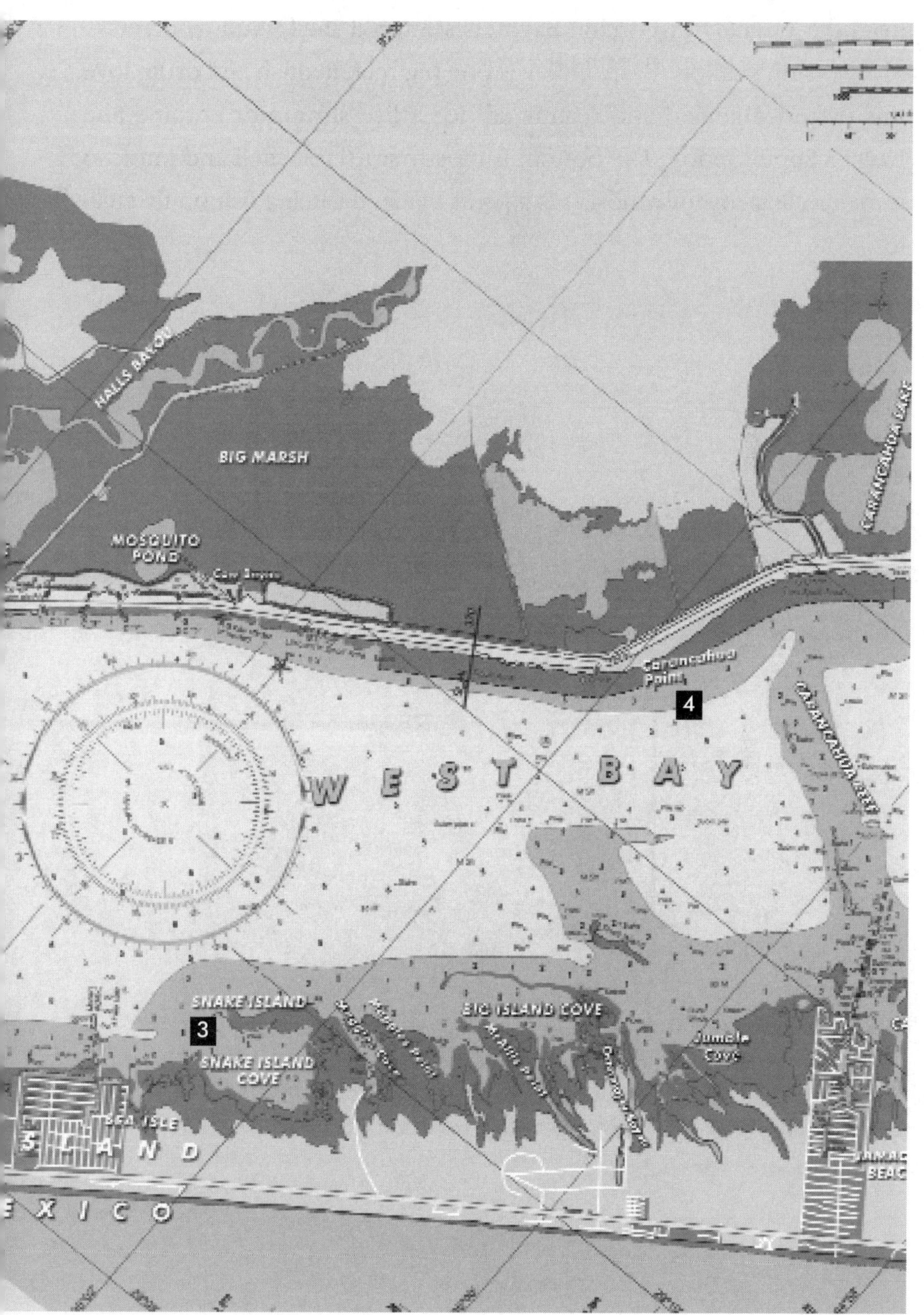
HALLS BAYOU
BIG MARSH
MOSQUITO POND
CARANCAHUA LAKE
Carancahua Point
CARANCAHUA REEF
4
W E S T   B A Y
SNAKE ISLAND
3
SNAKE ISLAND COVE
BIG ISLAND COVE
Jungle Cove
SEA ISLE
I S L A N D
E X I C O
BEAC

from the Targets to Churchill Bayou is scattered shell, mud, and grass.

Tiny, shallow, Bastrop Bay is one big reef. Redfish and drum love this oyster minefield and readily fall for a live shrimp or chrome She Dog or Super Spook. The bottom is mostly scattered shell and mud, so remains clear in stiff winds. It is a great place to catch a fish on fly tackle.

Chapter Five

Middle Coast Hotspots:
Wading the Golden Crescent

Opinions vary as to where the middle coast begins and ends. Sargent south to the JFK Causeway in Corpus Christi is my interpretation. The middle coast starts with mud and shell in East Matagorda Bay, then transforms to turtle grass shorelines from West Matagorda Bay south to Corpus Christi Bay.

Most of my days on the middle coast are from Matagorda to Port O'Connor. I head south to Rockport and annually spend a week in the spring and summer fishing and vacationing with the family. More anglers are jumping on U.S. 59 and heading south to get away from upper coast crowds. I have had some of my best days in the bay on the middle coast. Here are a few of the spots I fish.

EAST MATAGORDA BAY (SEE MAP ON PAGE 54)

I probably fish East Matagorda more than any bay in Texas. One

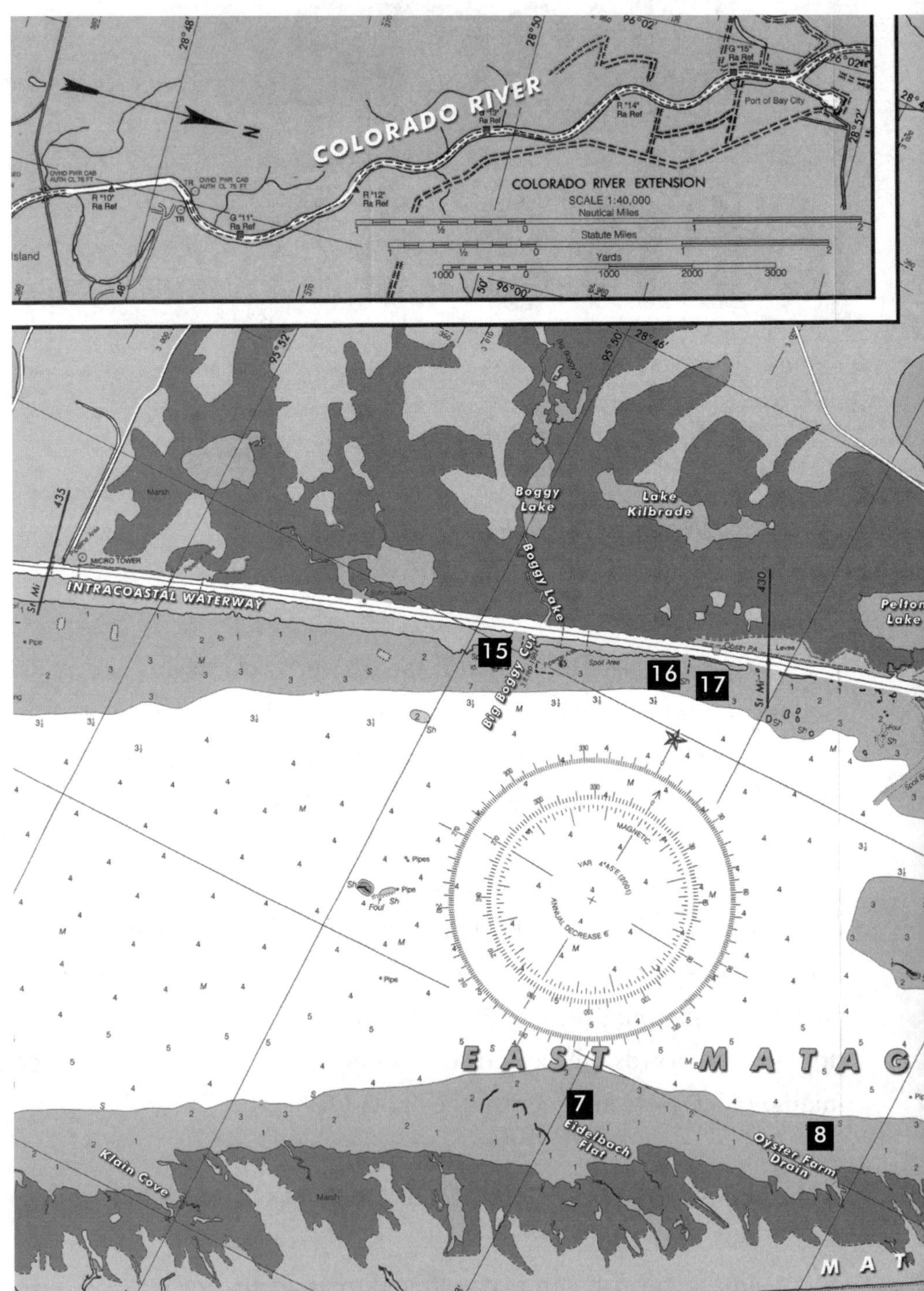
COLORADO RIVER
G "15"
Ra Ref
96 02
96 02
Port of Bay City
28 52
R "14"
Ra Ref
R "13"
Ra Ref
COLORADO RIVER EXTENSION
SCALE 1:40,000
Nautical Miles
Statute Miles
Yards
1000   0   1000   2000   3000
R "12"
Ra Ref
OVHD PWR CAB
AUTH CL 75 FT
OVHD PWR CAB
AUTH CL 75 FT
R "10"
Ra Ref
G "11"
Ra Ref
Island
96 00
28 48
N
Boggy
Lake
Lake
Kilbrade
Pelton
Lake
INTRACOASTAL WATERWAY
MICRO TOWER
Big Boggy Cut
15
16   17
EAST   MATAG
Klain Cove
Eidelbach
Flat
Oyster Farm
Drain
Marsh
7
8
MAT

EAST MATAGORDA BAY
Lake Austin
CARANCAHUA BEND
Caney Creek Cutoff
Caney Creek
Dead Caney Lake
Surfaced Ramp
FM 457
INTRACOASTAL WATERWAY
CANAL DR
PONTOON BRIDGE
HOR CL OPEN 140 FT
OVHD POWER CABLE
AUTH CL 94 FT
SMALL BOAT PASS
HOR CL 13 FT
VERT CL 4 FT
Cable and Pipeline Area
GULF OF MEXICO
Lake Austin
Chinquapin Bayou
Live Oak Bayou
CHINQUAPIN
CHINQUAPIN LANDING
Marsh
CANOE BAYOU
LIVE OAK BAYOU
Spoil Area
Foul area
LIVE OAK BAY
Boggy Bayou
INTRACOASTAL WATERWAY
St. Mi.
BAY
9
10
Catchall
Foul Area
Spoil Area
Submerged pile
Foul Area
PENINSULA
GULF OF MEXICO

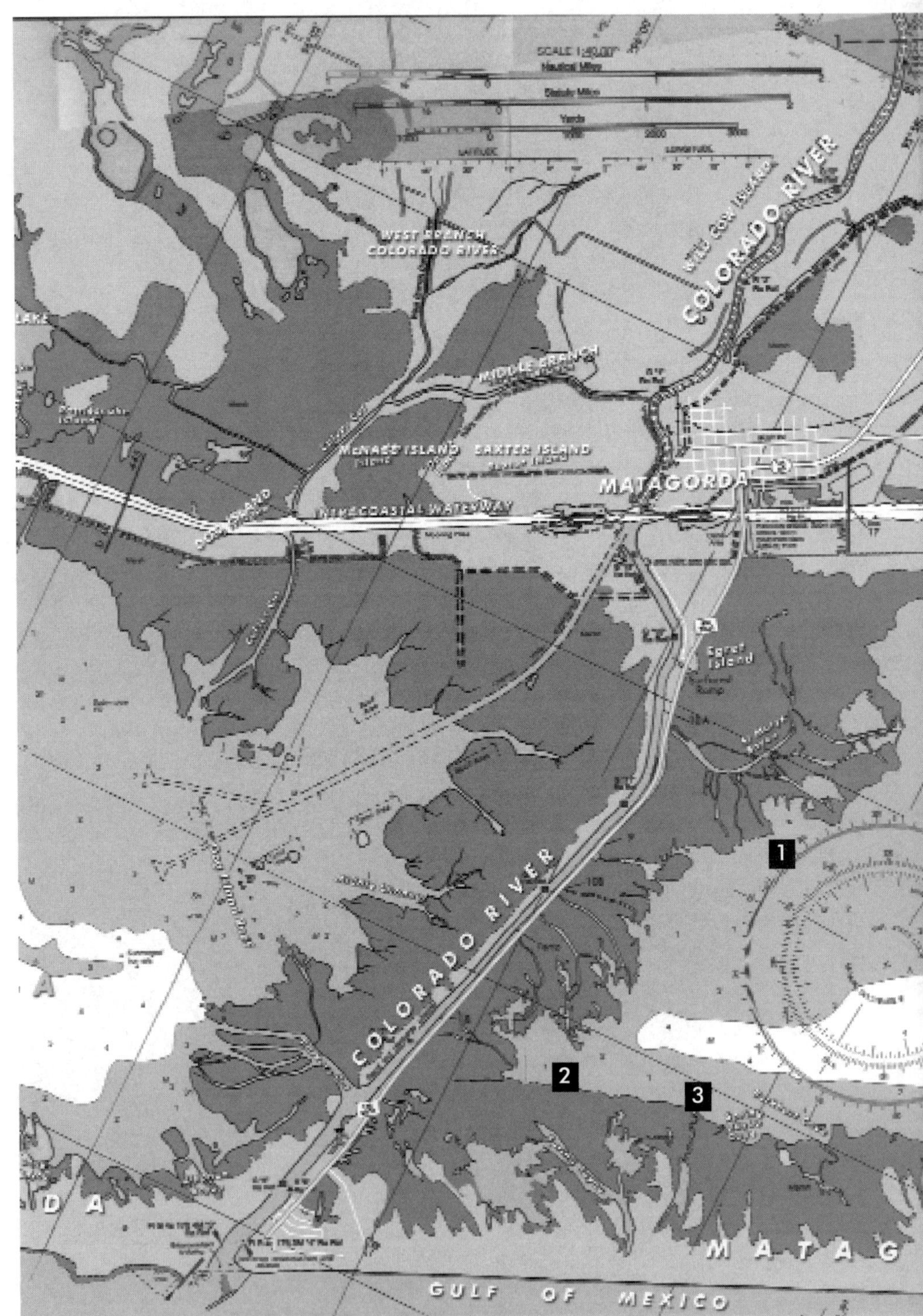
SCALE 1:40,000
Nautical Miles
Statute Miles
Yards
WEST BRANCH
COLORADO RIVER
COLORADO RIVER
MIDDLE BRANCH
McNABB ISLAND
BAXTER ISLAND
MATAGORDA
INTRACOASTAL WATERWAY
Egret
Island
COLORADO RIVER
1
2
3
MATAG
GULF OF MEXICO

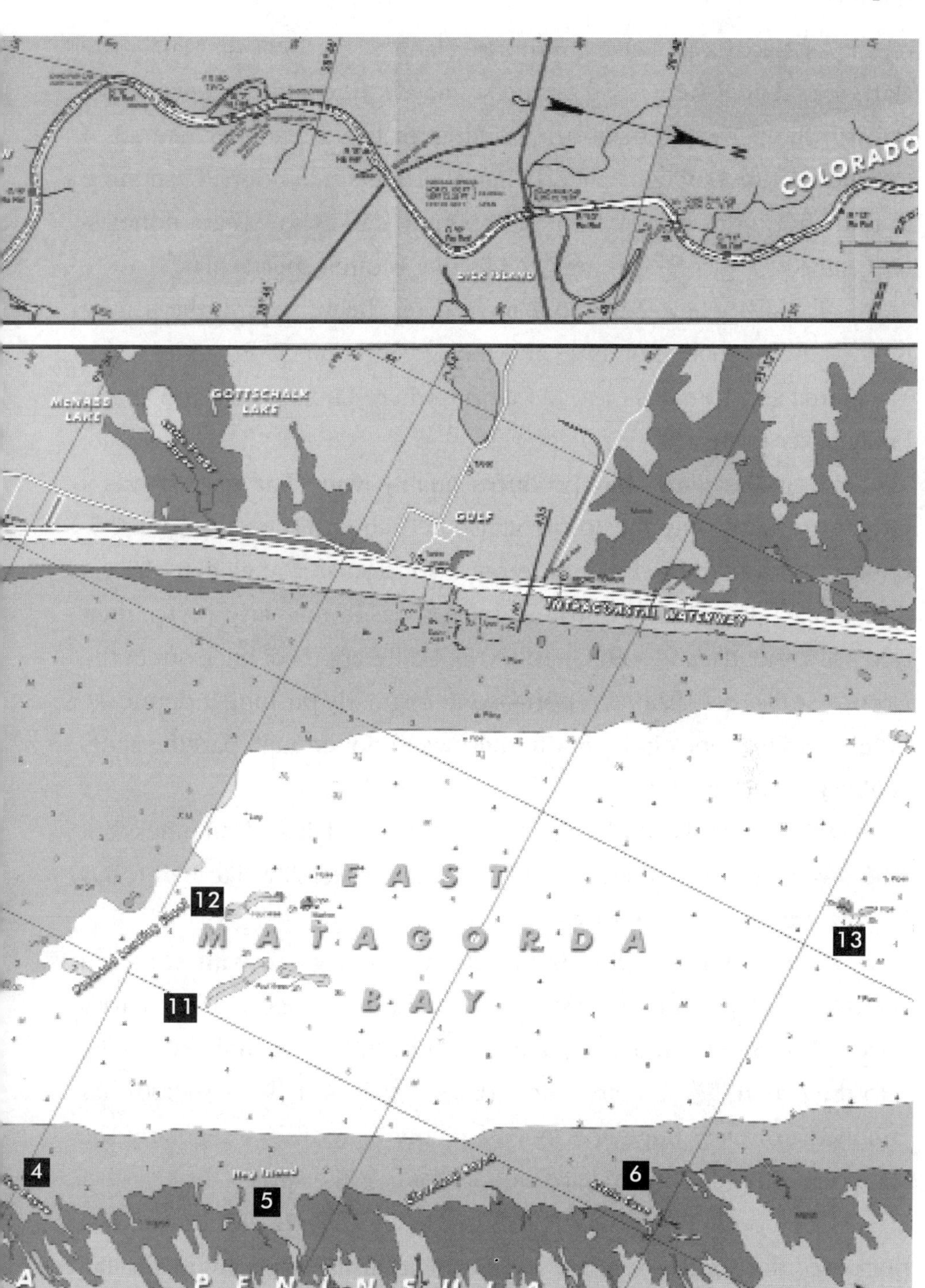
COLORADO
DUCK ISLAND
McNABB LAKE
GOTTSCHALK LAKE
GULF
INTRACOASTAL WATERWAY
E A S T
M A T A G O R D A
B A Y
12
13
11
4
5
6
Hog Island
A   P E N I N S U L A

reason is that I can leave my house, launch my boat at Matagorda Harbor, and be fishing in 30 minutes. I have it down to a science, especially in the fall when birds are working. In late September and all of October, before Daylight Savings Time shortens sunlit hours, I fish three to four afternoons a week from 4:30 p.m. to dark. Crowds are nonexistent, sunsets are gorgeous, and the fishing is often spectacular.

I really believe I live in a sportsman's heaven. Sure, the fishing is not always good; but is it anywhere? My home is 20 miles from Matagorda and 30 miles from El Campo, where I hunt ducks and geese. I may never move.

East Matagorda Bay produces quality trout. For years it was a hidden treasure only the locals whispered about. Then reports of 5-pound trout under the birds prompted Houston-area anglers to drive a little longer. They found out how good it was in the early 1990s, then told a few friends, and so on, and so on. Daily reports of big trout in the *Houston Chronicle* fishing report—some regularly pushing 9 pounds—didn't help matters, either. Soon, there were not enough parking spots at Matagorda Harbor.

Today, the bay still gets crowded in the fall and summer, but when word gets out of another bay producing steadily, like Baffin Bay or Port Mansfield, traffic slows.

The south shoreline is mostly mud and grass, with scattered shell. Beginning from the west shoreline and heading east is St. Mary's Bayou. The spot is mud and scattered shell, and the mouth leads deep into the marsh. **1** St. Mary's Reef (GPS N28 39.431, W95 56.800) has coughed up many huge specks and plenty of redfish. I regularly see state record holder Jim Wallace camped out on the spot.

2 Condo Cove (GPS N28 37.631, W95 57.442) in the far west pocket of the south shoreline holds quality fish, especially in the fall and spring when tides are high. **3** Three Mile Reef (GPS N28 37.878,

Capt. Bruce Shuler of Port Mansfield hefts a large Laguna Madre trout. Shuler owns and operates the Get-A-Way Lodge in Port Mansfield.

W95 56.223) sits in front of Three Mile Cut, which opens to the Gulf when a tropical storm or hurricane hits the peninsula (most recently, Hurricane Claudette). Three Mile is best on a falling tide when it is closed to the Gulf, but good on an incoming and outgoing tide when the cut is open to the ocean.

4 Boiler Bayou (GPS N28 38.760, W95 53.720) is located in a large cove with mud, grass, and scattered shell. When I need to get away and make a quick wade to blow off some steam, I drive in from the beach and cross over the dunes, then drive across the peninsula to the south shoreline. An August morning wade put me on the board in the Matagorda Troutmasters a few years ago.

5 Hog Island (GPS N28 39.191, W95 52.784) and **6** Kain Cove (GPS N28 40.367, W95 50.387) are probably the most popular spots fished. Floating grass can be bad at times, so be prepared to go

Often trout will hang tight to the shoreline when tides are above normal.

weedless. Redfish hold tight to the shoreline. A deep gut runs parallel off the point of Kain Cove, and is reportedly where a 9-pounder was taken during the 2001 Matagorda Troutmasters. My buddy, Glenn Ging, whipped me pretty good one day on a roach-colored Hogie under a Mansfield Mauler.

7 Eidelbach Flats (GPS N28 41.206, W95 48.999) extend from the point of Kain Cove to the **8** Oyster Farm (GPS N28 41.512, W95 48.077). Tight to the shoreline, you have to wade mud, but the farther from shore you walk, the harder the sand is packed. Turtle grass grows sporadically from year to year, depending on salinity levels. The area is best when tides are high. Because of the grass beds, I duck hunt the flat in the winter for redheads, buffleheads, pintails, and bluebills.

The Oyster Farm is another consistent producer, easily identifi-able by the four reefs protruding past the surface. Work all the shell, but do not forget the shoreline and bayous behind the reefs. Flounder, reds, and trout hang in the mud and scattered shell to ambush shrimp and mullet exiting the marsh. In November of 1996, Captains Melvin Talasek and Bill Pustejovsky, along with Talasek's three-man charter, caught 50 trout, half of which went over 7 pounds.

I like to begin on the shoreline and work toward the reefs with a She Dog or Top Dog. When mullet are flipping, I have never waded without catching a trout or redfish on topwater. Work a Bass Assassin, Trout Killer, or Sand Eel and expect to catch flounder. To my surprise, a sheepshead hanging close to the reef once wrapped its ivories around my Spit'n Image.

9 Catchall Basin (GPS N28 41.860, W95 46.564) is another large cove on the south shoreline. It has humps, guts, mud, and grass, and is best when tides are high. Flounder giggers frequent the cove, especially in the fall and spring. Topwaters are good when there is no floating grass. Soft plastics under a Mansfield Mauler, and a Corky are good choices, too.

The far east end of the bay is **10** Brown Cedar Flats (GPS N28 43.653, W95 42.759), named for its proximity to old Brown Cedar Cut, which has silted in over the years. It opened for about a month in the wake of Hurricane Claudette.

Tight to the shoreline is grass and mud, but farther from the shoreline it becomes strictly mud. It is a good summer spot when tides are high because trout like to lay in the cool mud, though the water clarity does become muddy with stiff winds. It is good in the fall when shrimp bury in the mud. Trout and redfish know they are there, and hang in the area until they pop out.

One July day, I had not caught a fish all morning. I went to Brown Cedar Flats and saw mullet everywhere, but water visibility was less than an inch. Exhausted of options, I stayed and fished, and around

Blain Talasek fights a Port Aransas speck on a rare calm day in the Coastal Bend.

noon got one bite—a 28-inch trout. Brown Cedar is a big fish hangout due to its proximity to the Intracoastal. Don't be afraid to fish it if the water is off-colored but bait is present.

East Matagorda's mid-bay and north shoreline reefs hold quality fish year-round. The problem is, winds must be light or water clarity will become chocolate milk. Whenever conditions are right, I reef-hop throughout the bay. Eventually, I usually find fish.

11 Long Reef (GPS N28 40.121, W95 53.361) is my favorite mid-bay reef. Hence, it is a long reef that takes about two hours to fish from tip to tip. When the fish are there, I have stayed on it for more than five hours. It is great in the summer when brown shrimp are in the bay, and likewise in the fall when the whites are exiting the marsh. Rarely have I ever caught small trout on the reef, and several summers I have caught and released a dozen over 27 inches. My favorite bait is the chartreuse/bone/chartreuse or chrome She Dog. Capt. Bill Pustejovsky swears by his Bass Assassins, too.

For years, anglers never knew Long Reef was there, and most

still do not; they run right over it unless they see a wader with a bent rod.

12 Three Beacon Reef (GPS N28 40.605, W95 53.519), **13** Drull's Lump (GPS N28 42.328, W95 49.760), and **14** Halfmoon Reef (GPS N28 43.331, W95 46.410) are all solid shell for trout on topwaters, soft plastics, and live shrimp. The good days are too many to remember.

On a north wind, **15** Boggy Cut (GPS N28 44.026, W95 49.736), **16** Windmill Cut (GPS N28 44.556, W95 48.086), and the **17** Chinquapin Reefs (GPS N28 44.482, W95 47.226) are good on an incoming tide. Summer and fall is best as shrimp enter the bay from the Intracoastal.

WEST MATAGORDA BAY (SEE MAP ON PAGE 68)

West Matagorda Bay is forgiving, and often holds cleaner water than East Matagorda due to its jutting points and grassy shorelines that harbor waders from winds. Depth reaches 14 feet. West Matagorda is particularly popular in the spring, when glass minnows move onto the grass and attract trout and redfish. The heat of the summer is good, too, as trout and reds move onto the flats on an incoming tide, and fall to the deep when the water recedes.

The bay is rather large, extending from the Colorado River to Pass Cavallo in Port O'Connor. The east end of the bay holds mostly mud and shell due to sediment discharged during flooding from the Colorado River. The closer you get to Port O'Connor, the more sand and grass and the clearer the water.

Beginning on the north shoreline is **1** Shell Island (GPS N28 37.701, W96 03.829), a huge reef in the northeast corner of the bay that extends from the bank to more than a mile into the bay. Very few wade it, but the ones who do catch big fish. It is a popular spot for boat

Capt. Lynn Smith works Ayres and Mesquite Bay for spring trout like this one.

anglers using live shrimp.

The only drawback to fishing the north shoreline is south winds usually dominate. Since the bottom is comprised of mud, the water quickly becomes dirty. Spring and fall tides combined with light winds are a recipe for fillets at Shell Island.

2 Southeast Pocket (GPS N28 36.328, W95 59.796) is a muddy wade, but well worth it on an incoming tide. If mullet are present and brown pelicans are diving, get out of the boat and make a wade. I cannot begin tell you how many large trout and redfish frequent the area. Again, if the water is muddy but the bait is present, you can catch fish here. Go with a bait that makes a lot of noise like a She Dog or Super Spook.

3 Hooper Bayou (GPS N28 35.851, W96 00.947), **4** Forked Bayou (GPS N28 35.486, W96 01.724), **5** Gold Bayou (GPS N28 35.289, W96 02.363), **6** Big Bayou (GPS N28 34.663, W96 03.759), and **7** Green Island (GPS N28 34.083, W96 05.207) are good spots for red-

Feeding pelicans are a good indicator that fish are in the area.

fish anytime of the year.

8 Fencepost Reef (GPS N28 32.967, W96 07.601) is a topwater spot on a strong incoming tide and nearby **9** Pipeline Reef (GPS N28 32.967, W96 09.921) can be fished in the same manner or with plastics or live shrimp under a popping cork.

10 Cotton's Bayou (GPS N28 31.205, W96 11.988), **11** Middle Grounds (GPS N28 30.743, W96 12.670), and **12** Green's Bayou (GPS N28 30.341, W96 14.107) are the most popular locales in West Matagorda Bay. All three have acres of grass and sand humps with undulations that hold fish, especially in the spring and summer. If the fish are not there, wait them out, according to Capt. Bobby Gardner: "The area is too good to leave if the fish are not there right away. Know your tides and the fish will eventually show."

One April afternoon, my buddy, Eddie Sullivan, and I dodged

hordes of redfish crashing glass minnows at Green's. One actually swam through Sullivan's legs. The glass minnows were so thick that day I found some in my pants when I undressed that night.

13 Tom and Jerry's (GPS N28 28.227, W96 17.380) near the old military landing strip and fishing camps on the peninsula, has fish-holding guts and grass.

14 Jetty Reef (GPS N28 26.718, W96 19.335) is great on an incoming tide. The shell runs parallel with the shore, and often holds mullet and pogey. It receives strong tidal flow, since it is within eyeshot of the Port O'Connor jetty. I caught a ride on Capt. Bill Pustejovsky's boat and fished it with him on the final day of the 2000 Port O'Connor Troutmasters. Had we been there the day before, we would have been in the money—an often-heard story at the weigh-in. Like Capt. Terry Shaughnessy of Hackberry, Louisiana says: "You should've been here yesterday!"

15 The South Jetty Pocket (GPS N28 25.580, W96 21.140) can be productive on an incoming or the beginning of the outgoing tide. A bar runs east and west, even with the point of the jetty, and holds fish. From the bar back to the shore is grass holes and guts, some chin-deep. Capt. Melvin Talasek and I fished it for three weeks by our lonesome in June 2000. Though it is a 30-mile boat ride from Matagorda, the payoff was too good to worry about the long ride. It receives great tidal flow from the jetty.

The Cedars (GPS N28 24.569, W96 22.268) and Decros Point (GPS N28 23.914, W96 22.988) have grass and guts along the entire shoreline and usually stays clean, even in the stiffest southerly wind. Fish move in and out since the locales are smack dab between the jetty and Pass Cavallo.

The Hump (GPS N28 25.295, W96 22.498) is my favorite spot to fish in West Matagorda Bay. It is only a five-minute boat ride from Clark's in Port O'Connor, but almost an hour in my Pathfinder from Matagorda Harbor. If I want to be on the spot at daylight, I must leave a little before 5 a.m. and navigate 30 minutes in darkness. I have had too many great trips there to name; ask to see my logbook, and I can tell you exactly how many.

Talasek calls it the "Community Bar" because of the number of people who use it on the weekends. Word to the wise: wear a bright shirt. There are many boats in Port O'Connor, and even more operators who do not know the basics of boating—like watching where they are going. Be visible so you do not have to dodge a fiberglass bullet.

Know your tides for the day. If the bar is dirty, it often cleans on an outgoing tide. If the Gulf is dirty, the bar will be dirty on an incoming tide as water filters through Pass Cavallo and the jetty. The bar ranges in depth from 1 foot to neck-deep and is surrounded by 9-14 feet

Springtime double-hook-up on the grass flats of Ayres Bay.

WEST
MATAGORDA
BAY
MATAGORDA
GULF OF MEXICO
PE
9
8
SCALE 1:40,000
LOGARITHMIC SPEED SCALE

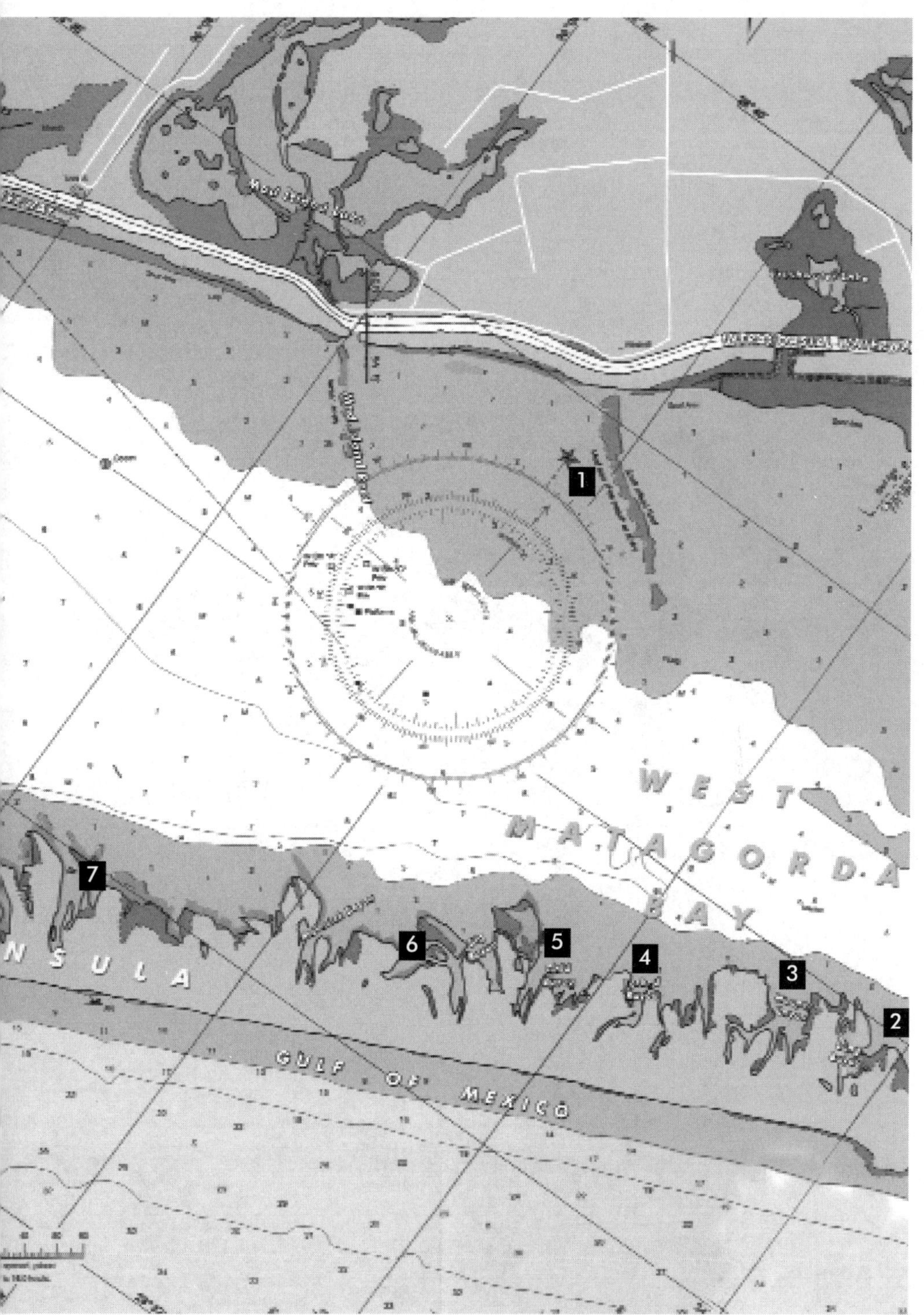
WEST
MATAGORDA
BAY
GULF OF MEXICO
1
2
3
4
5
6
7

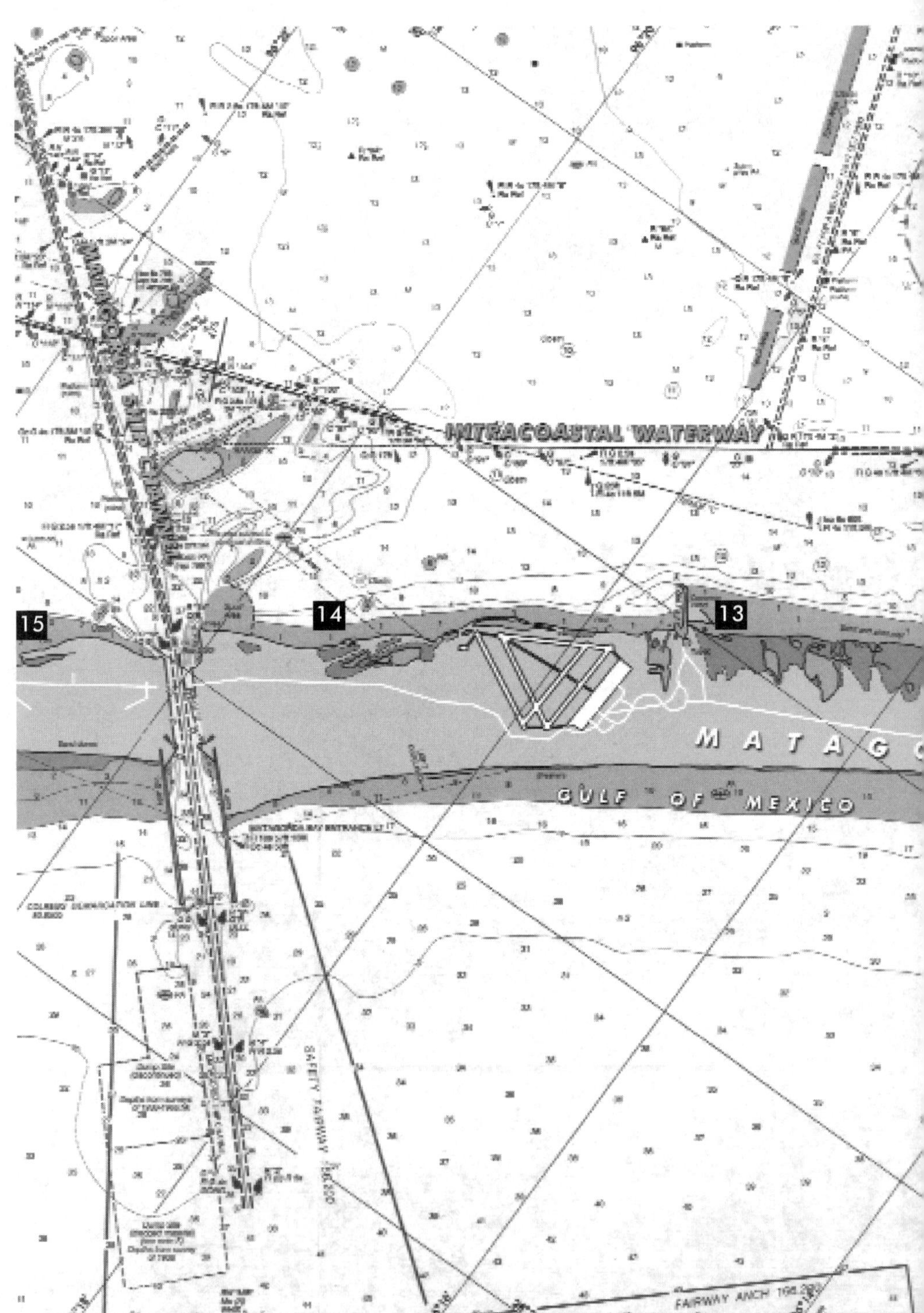
15
14
13
INTRACOASTAL WATERWAY
MATAGO
GULF OF MEXICO
FAIRWAY ANCH

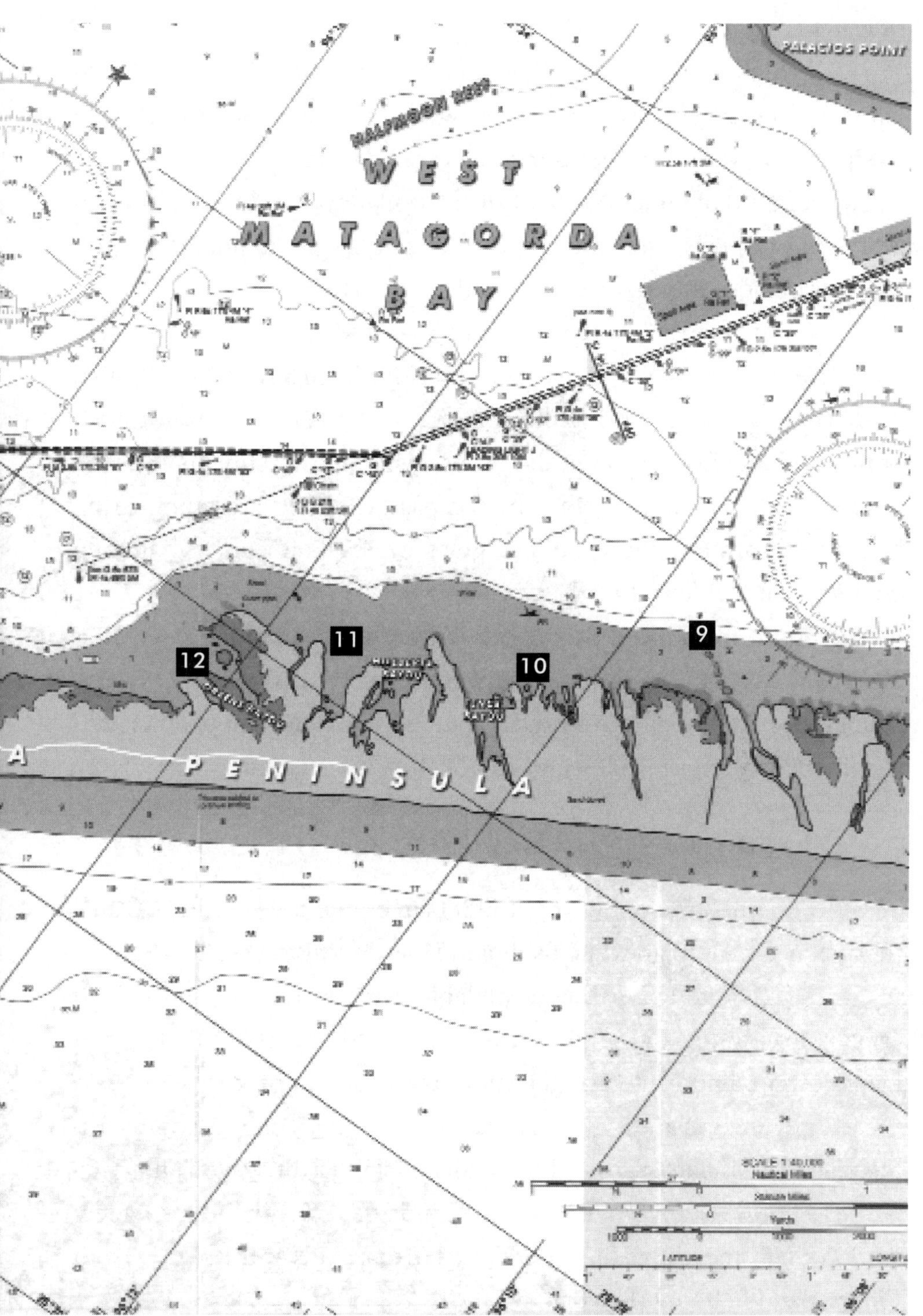

PALACIOS POINT
WEST
MATAGORDA
BAY
PENINSULA
12
11
10
9
A

of water.

At high tide, the fish will be on top of the bar. When it begins to fall, work the edges of the bar. I have waited for two hours for the tide to shift, then was rewarded as the fish came knocking.

A friend of mine, Rodney Corporron, jumped a 4-foot tarpon on a Norton Sand Eel. There are plenty sharks, too, but, do not let the dolphins scare you; they get close enough to pet at times.

Coast Guard Flats (GPS N28 24.364, W96 24.128), City Slickers (GPS N28 26.215, W96 23.849), and the J-Hook (GPS N28 23.419, W96 24.202) are awesome during the summer, and receive a constant flush of tide and fish from Pass Cavallo. Capt. Lynn Smith frequents the area often: "I will be hanging close to the pass. The fish are going to be somewhere around there on the grass or shell. If you fish it long enough, you will find them."

Smith introduced me to the Powderhorn Shoreline (GPS N28 30.790, W96 28.937) a few summers ago as we waded with topwaters. Numerous bars and guts extend far from the shore and run parallel with it. When Powderhorn Lake empties, the area is even better.

ESPIRITU SANTO BAY (SEE MAP ON PAGE 74)

I do not know about you, but if I am bound to leave this life anytime soon, I want to go while fishing in Holy Spirit Bay (Espiritu Santo).

Man, there are so many wadable acres in this bay, most with crystal clear water and turtle grass—where do you start? First, get a map. Second, find bait. Last, get out of the boat and probe.

1 Grass Island (GPS N28 22.919, W96 26.595) is a good starting place. Grass flats surround the entire island. **2** Farwell Island (GPS N28 21.899, W96 26.988), just south of Grass Island, is good for waders working chrome topwaters, pepper/chartreuse Bass Assassins, Trout Killers, Sand Eels, and live bait.

3 Lighthouse Cove (GPS N28 20.789, W96 26.362) and **4** Big Pocket (GPS N28 21.675, W96 26.181), both in the southeast corner of the bay, are protected from easterly winds and are especially grand with high tides. Redfish love to root in the grass, and flounderers regularly score there.

Often overlooked, but right around the corner from main boat ramps, is the **5** Blackberry Island shore (GPS N28 25.801, W96 25.539) in Barroom Bay, and nearby **6** Bill Day's Reef (GPS N28 24.989, W96 26.170). Autumn equinox tides and light winds push fish to the reefs and grass, where mullet are trying to hide. Corky, She Dog, Super Spook, and SkitterWalk baits all get dunked. The **7** Dewberry Island (GPS N28 23.415, W96 30.136) shore is solid footing as well.

Know where you are going before

Pat Davis of Conroe with a 28-inch trout at the Oyster Farm in East Matagorda Bay.

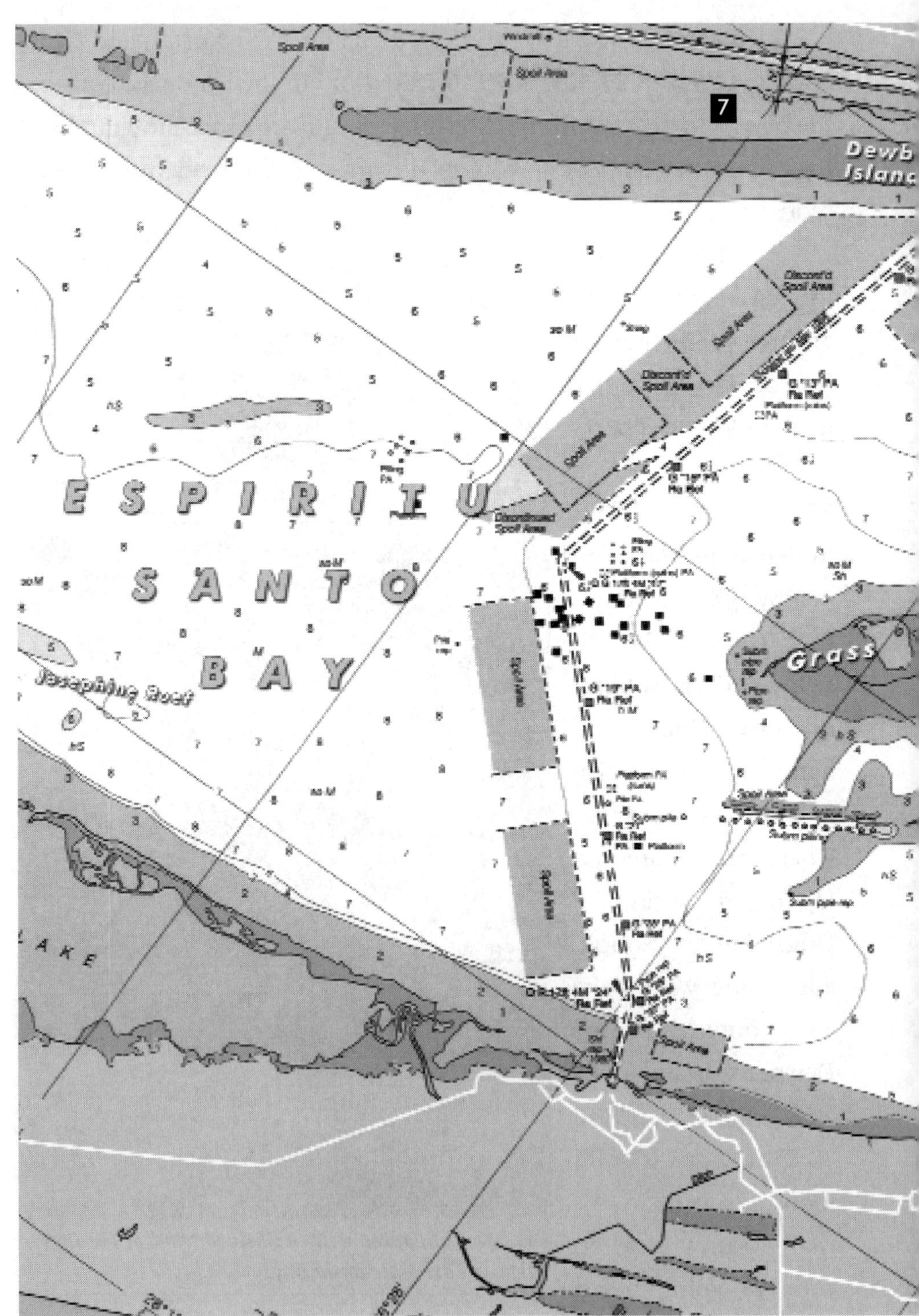
Spoil Area
Spoil Area
Dewb
Island
Discont'd
Spoil Area
Spoil Area
Discont'd
Spoil Area
Discont'd
Spoil Area
E S P I R I T U
S A N T O
B A Y
Josephine Boat
Grass
LAKE
Spoil Area

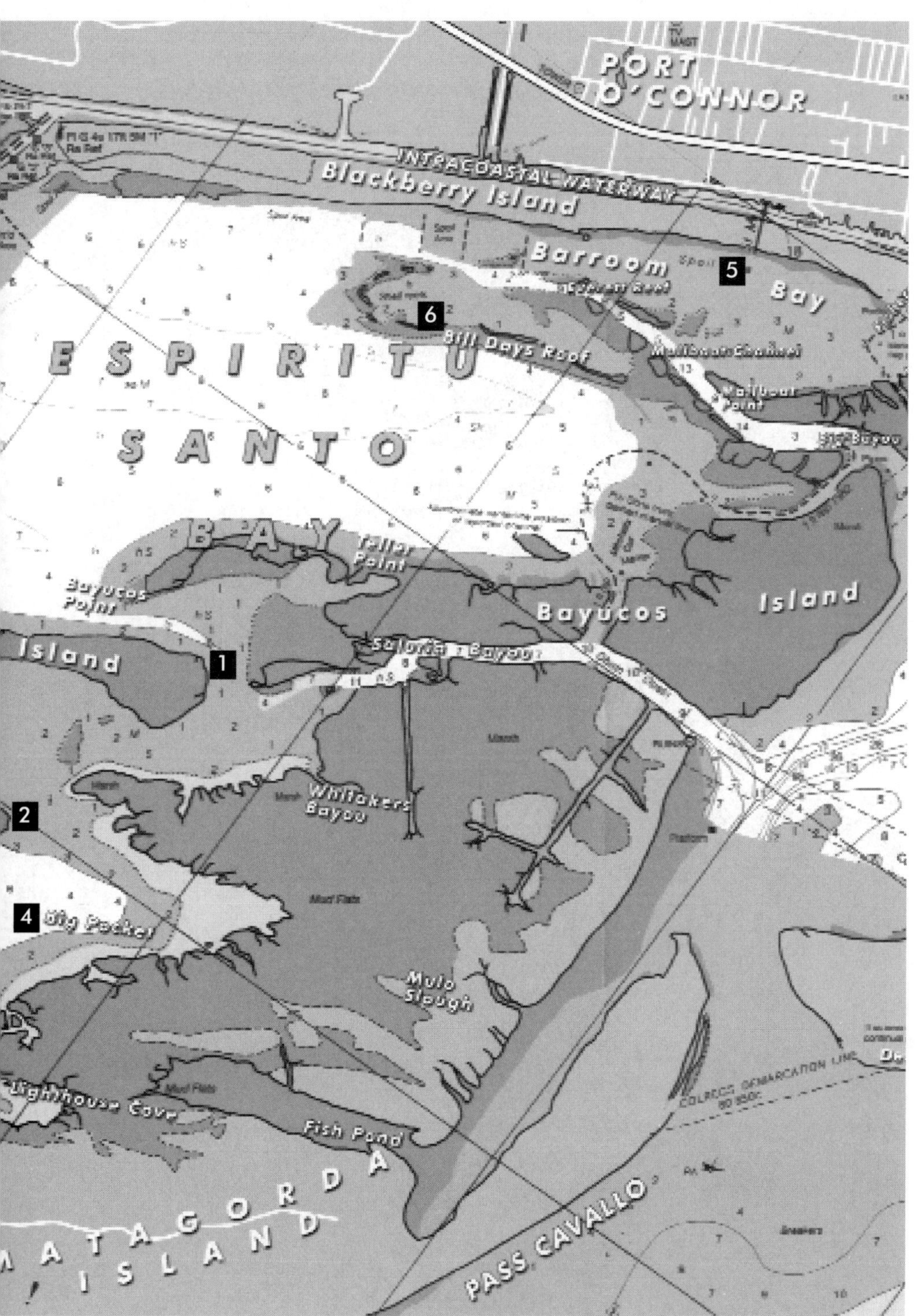
PORT O'CONNOR
INTRACOASTAL WATERWAY
Blackberry Island
Barroom
Bay
5
6
Bill Days Reef
E S P I R I T U
S A N T O
B A Y
Teller Point
Bayucos Point
Island
Bayucos Island
Saluria Bayou
1
Whitakers Bayou
2
4 Big Pocket
Mulo Slough
Lighthouse Cove
Fish Pond
MATAGORDA ISLAND
PASS CAVALLO

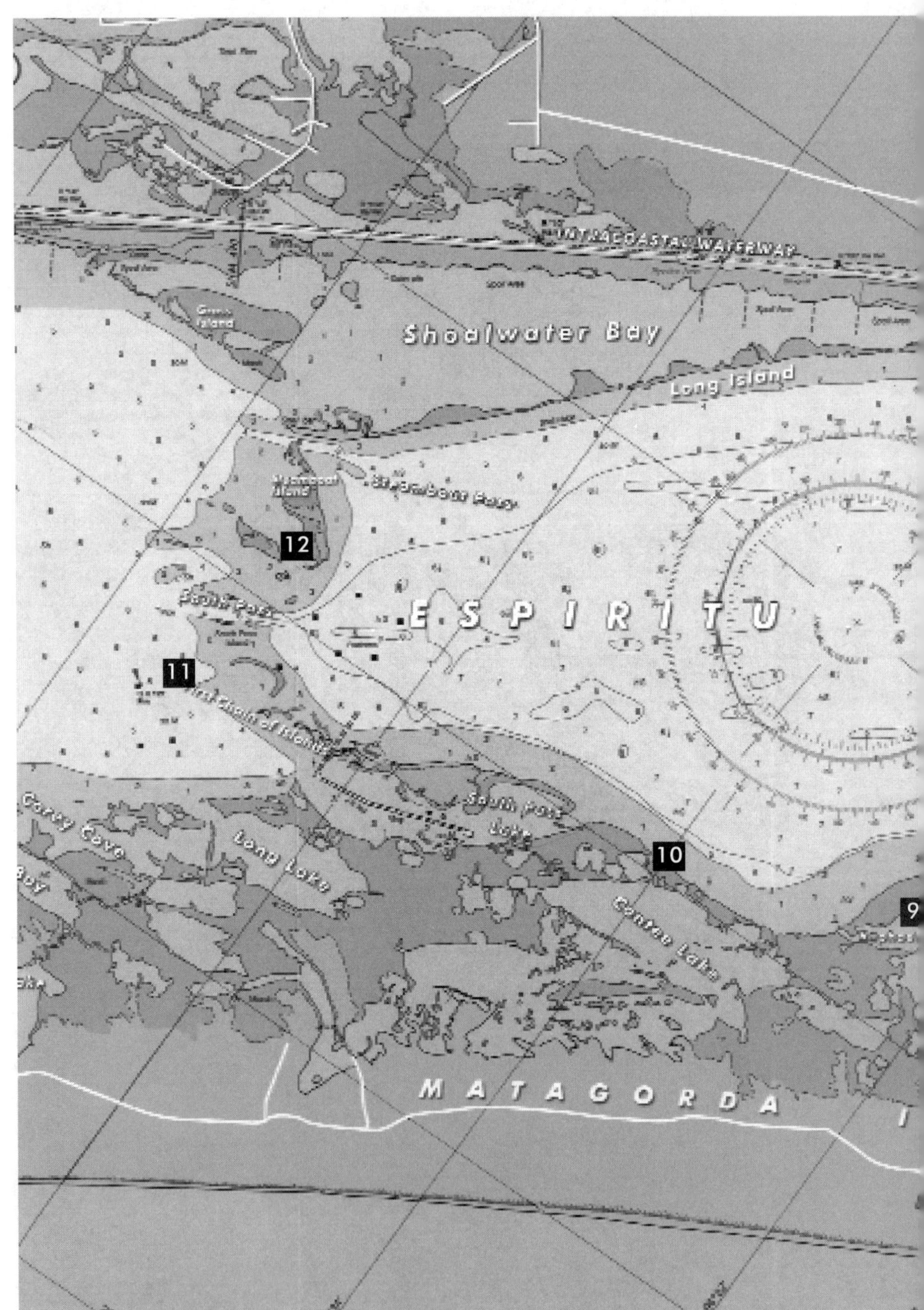
INTRACOASTAL WATERWAY
Shoalwater Bay
Long Island
Steamboat Island
12
Panther Point
11
Chain of Islands
Contee Cove
Long Lake
South Pass Lake
10
Contee Lake
9
MATAGORDA
ESPIRITU

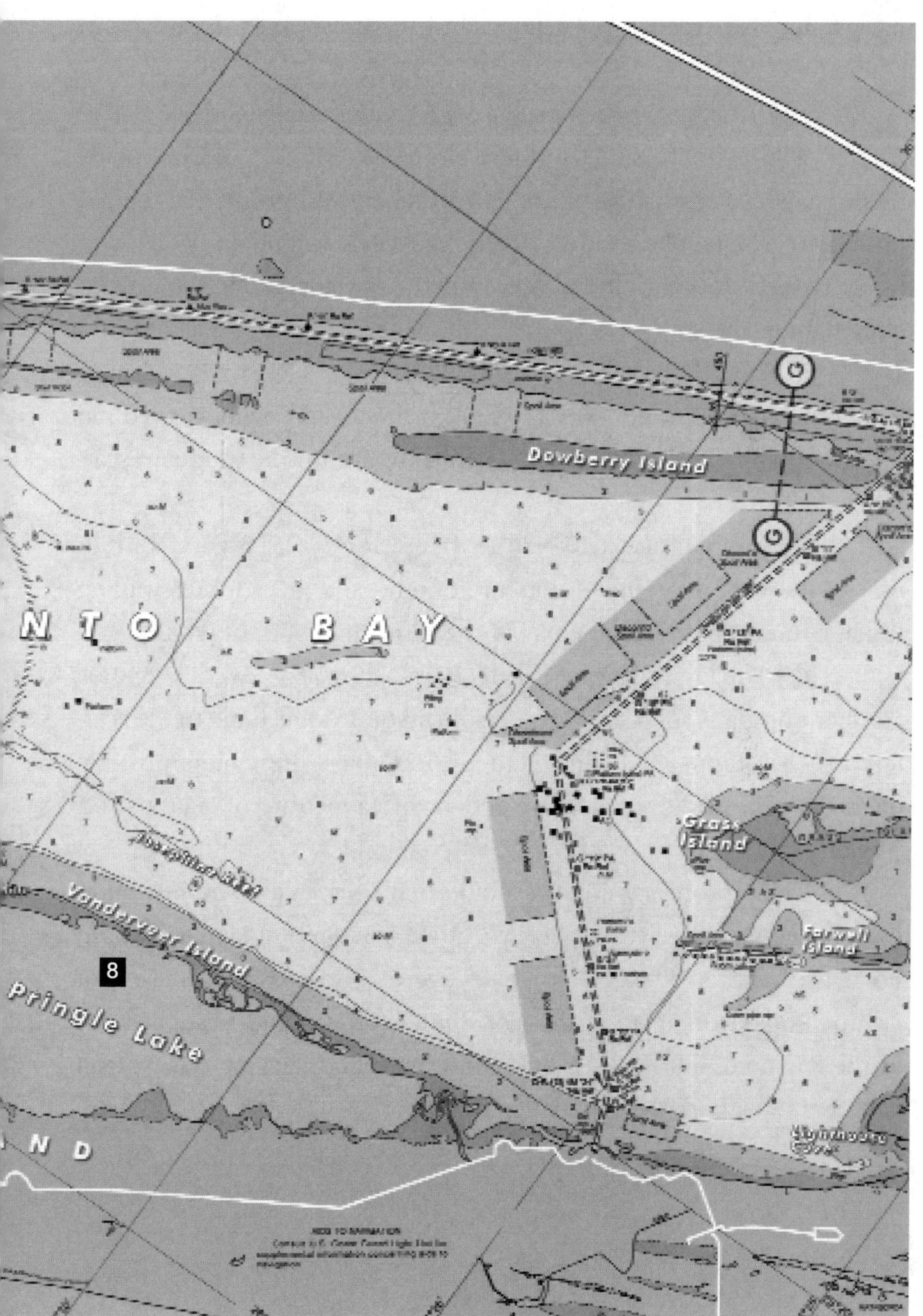
Dowberry Island
NTO BAY
Grass Island
Farwell Island
Vandervert Island
Pringle Lake
8
N D

navigating. Many reefs, obstructions, and shallow water can put you in a bind.

Back on the south shoreline, **8** Vanderveer Island (GPS N29 19.570, W96 30.677) is the northern shore for Pringle Lake and holds plenty reds and trout. The above GPS numbers will put you in the cut leading to Pringle. The south shoreline of Pringle is mud and grass, and holds redfish throughout the year. When tides are swollen, big trout hang tight to the shore.

9 Rahal Bayou (GPS N28 18.420, W96 32.796) is good on a falling tide as Pringle empties. Capt. T.J. Christenson, who showed me the spot, likes to fish it in spring when trout are on the mud and scattered shell.

10 Contee Lake (GPS N28 18.154, W96 33.125) is good for redfish on the west shoreline. A mixture of mud and grass makes wading tough at times, but often the payoff is a three-man limit of reds.

11 The First Chain of Islands (GPS N28 17.855, W96 37.330) is another popular spot. Capt. Jesse Arsola first introduced me to the scattered shell. He put on a clinic with a Corky, and I drew quite possibly the biggest blowup of my life. We ended with a mixture of big reds and 3-pound trout.

Christenson proved you could catch trout in a 25-mph wind at **12** Steamboat Island (GPS N28 18.385, W96 37.059) in March. I would not have believed it had I not been there. Christenson, Jeff Neu of Laguna Rods, Doug Pike of the *Houston Chronicle*, and I caught trout in the harsh conditions by tossing into a gut and clicking our Norton Sand Eel Jr's across the shell-laden bottom.

SAN ANTONIO BAY (SEE MAP ON PAGE 80)

San Antonio Bay can be divided into two parts: north of the Intracoastal and south of the Intracoastal. The north bay is mainly mud and reefs, with little cover from the wind. The south shoreline below the Intracoastal is littered with points, guts, grass flats, and plenty of leeward coves.

1 Twin Lakes (GPS N28 14.664, W96 39.340) and **2** Cedar Lake (GPS N28 13.813, W96 39.950) offer protection from southeast winds. **3** Panther Point (GPS N28 12.943, W96 42.206) and **4** Panther Reef (GPS N28 13.166, W96 42.289) hold trout and reds regularly. Christenson and Capt. Chris Martin like to wade to their necks off the point and toss jalapeno Sand Eel Jr's.

5 Rattlesnake Island (GPS N28 11.728, W96 49.785), **6** Second Chain of Islands (GPS N28 11.650, W96 48.883), **7** Point of Ayres (GPS N28 11.276, W96 47.786), and **8** Chicken Foot Reef (GPS N28 12.871, W96 47.463) are on the west end of the bay. Some consider these spots part of tiny Ayres Bay. Capt. Lynn Smith likes to hang out on this end of the bay in the spring: "Whenever I can get to San Antonio Bay, I go. But, when the wind blows, it muddies the bay and it is tough to fish. You can hop from reef to reef when the wind is light and eventually you will run into a mess of fish."

North of the Intracoastal, San Antonio Bay is a minefield of oyster reefs and soft mud.

9 Bird Island Reef (GPS N28 16.610, W96 44.113), **10** Dagger Point Reef (GPS N28 17.269, W96 47.332), **11** Refuge Reef (GPS N28 18.103, W96 46.480), **12** Half Moon Reef (GPS N28 20.227, W96 46.420), **13** Turtle Reef (GPS N28 19.345, W96 45.136), and **14** Big Reef (GPS N28 19.798, W96 43.654) are just a few of the many reefs cluttering the bay. There are many more, unnamed, which hold fish.

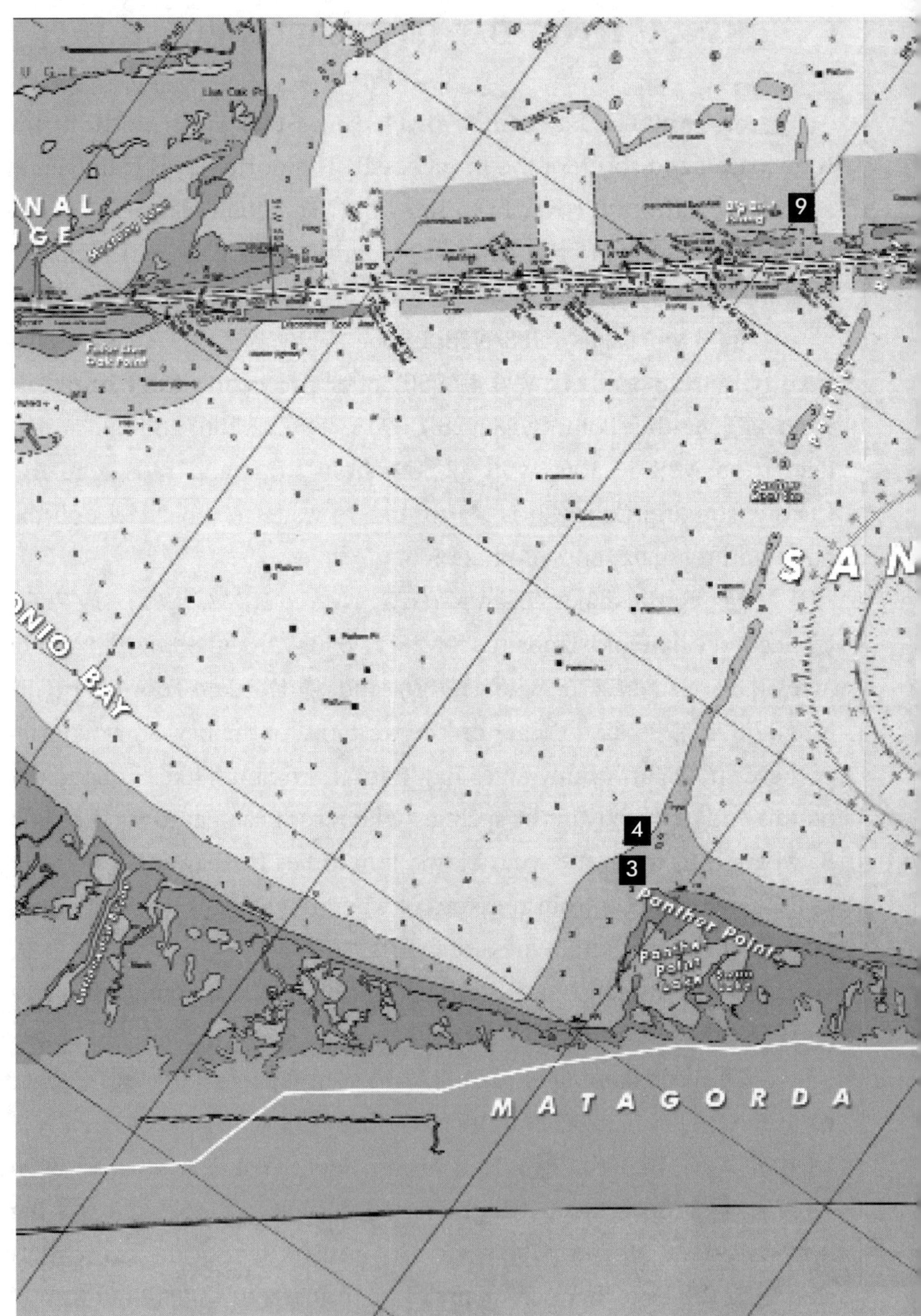
NAL
GE
NAL
Shoalwater Bay
Live Oak Pt
9
ONIO BAY
SAN
4
3
Panther Point
Panther
Point
MATAGORDA

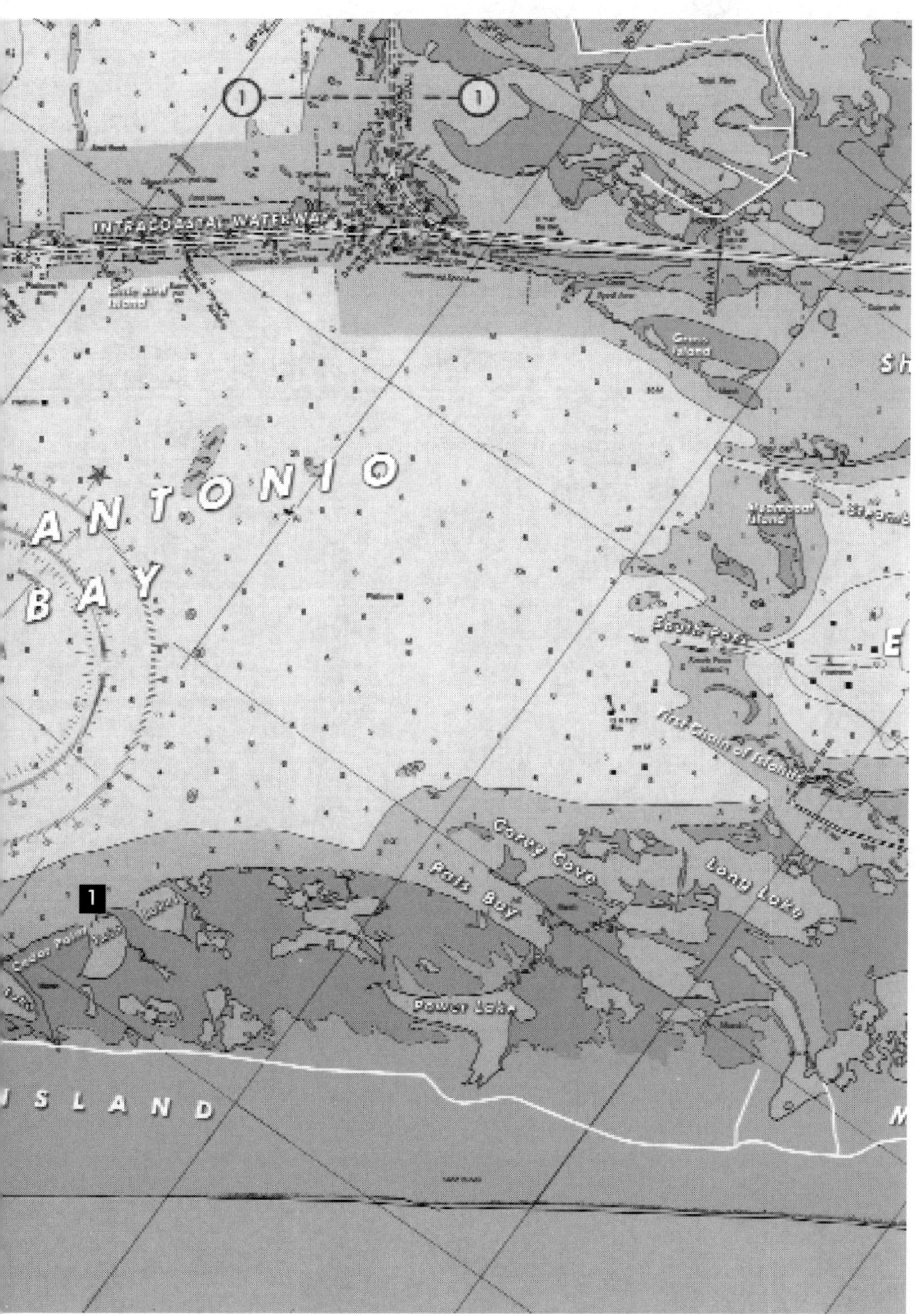
INTRACOASTAL WATERWAY
ANTONIO
BAY
ISLAND
Cony Cove
Pats Bay
Power Lake
Long Lake

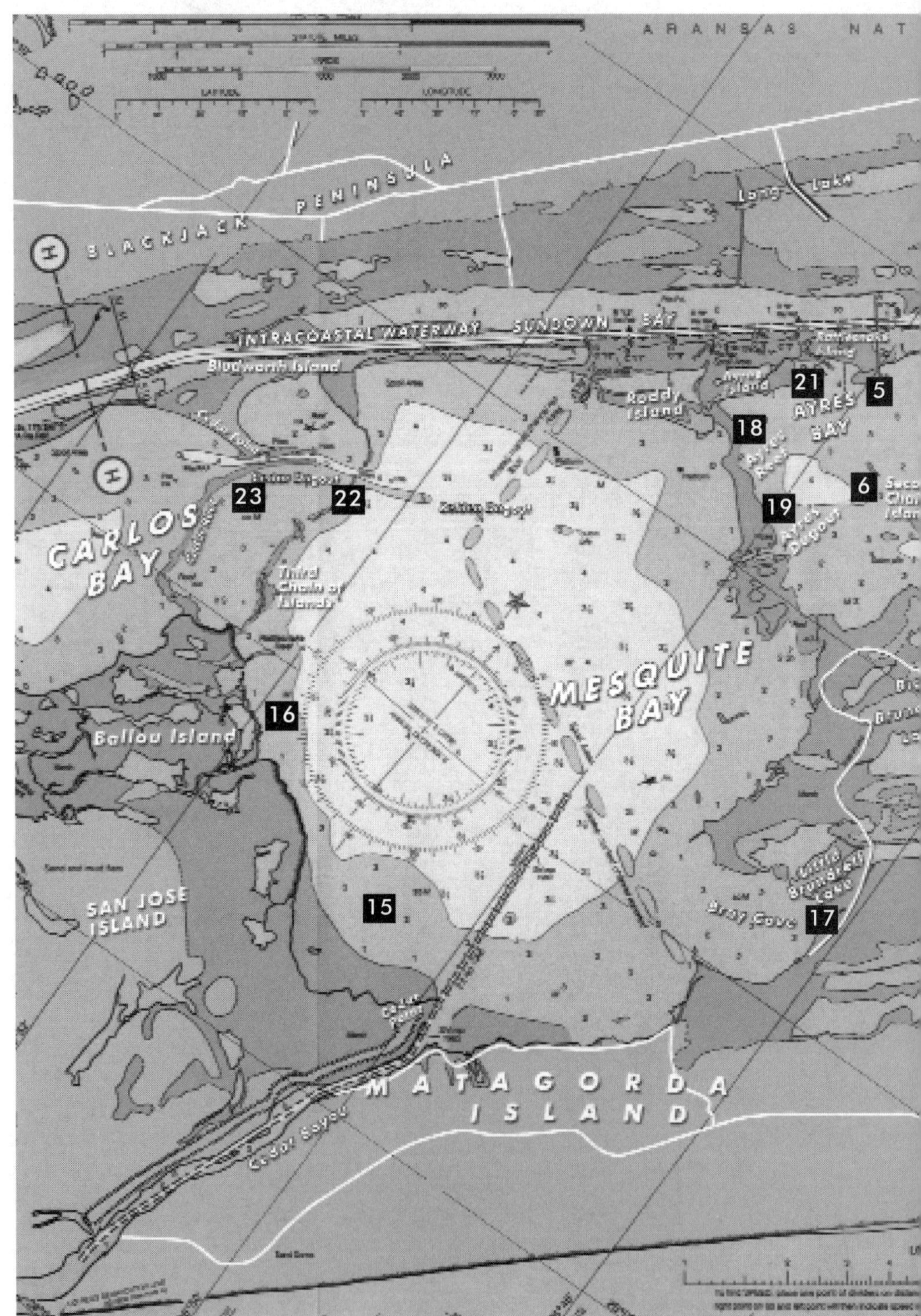
ARANSAS NAT
BLACKJACK
PENINSULA
Long Lake
INTRACOASTAL WATERWAY
SUNDOWN BAY
Bludworth Island
Roddy Island
21
5
18
AYRES BAY
23
22
19
6
CARLOS BAY
Third Chain of Islands
16
MESQUITE BAY
Ballou Island
SAN JOSE ISLAND
15
Bray Cove
17
MATAGORDA ISLAND

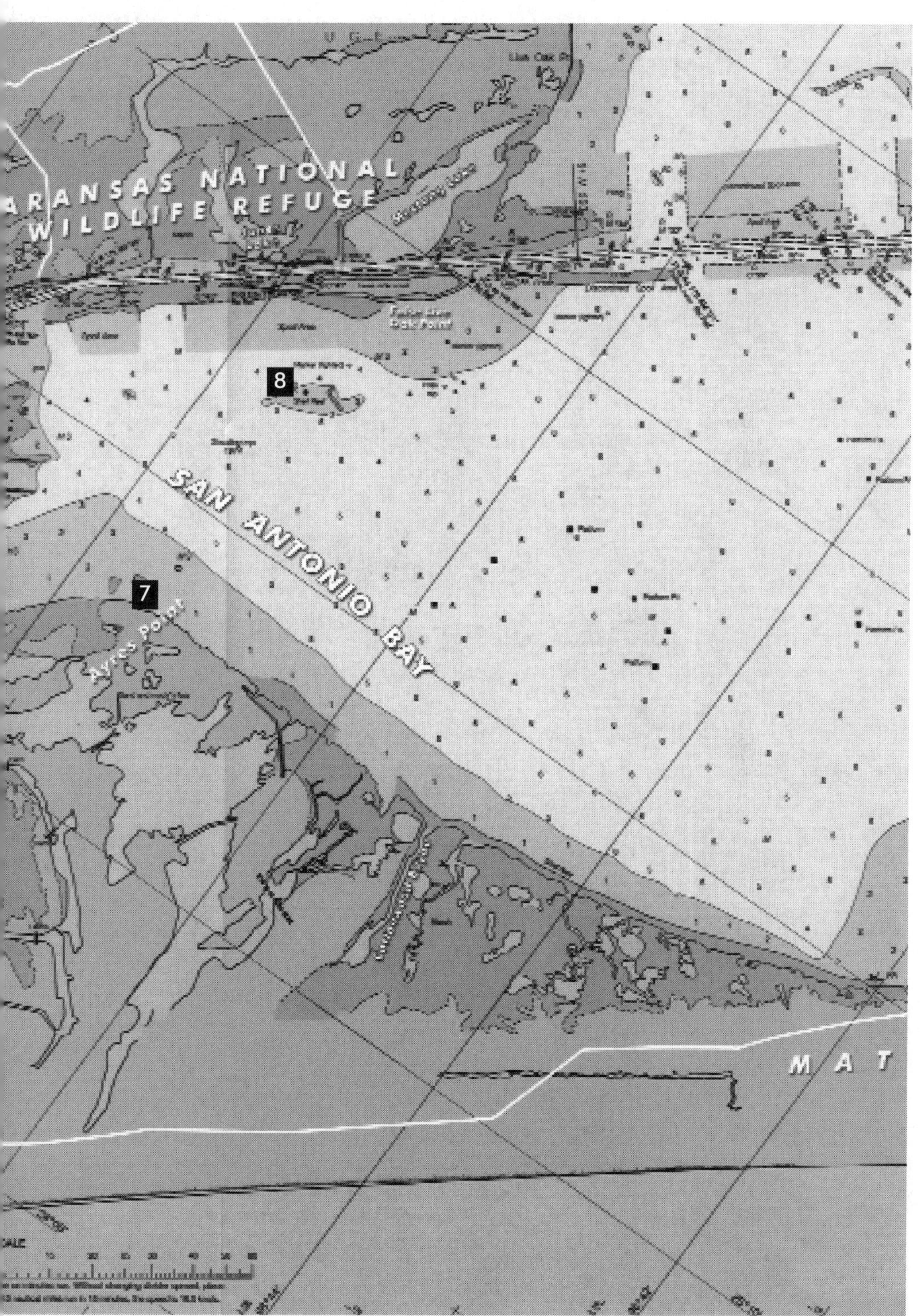
ARANSAS NATIONAL
WILDLIFE REFUGE
SAN ANTONIO BAY
Ayres Point
MAT
8
7

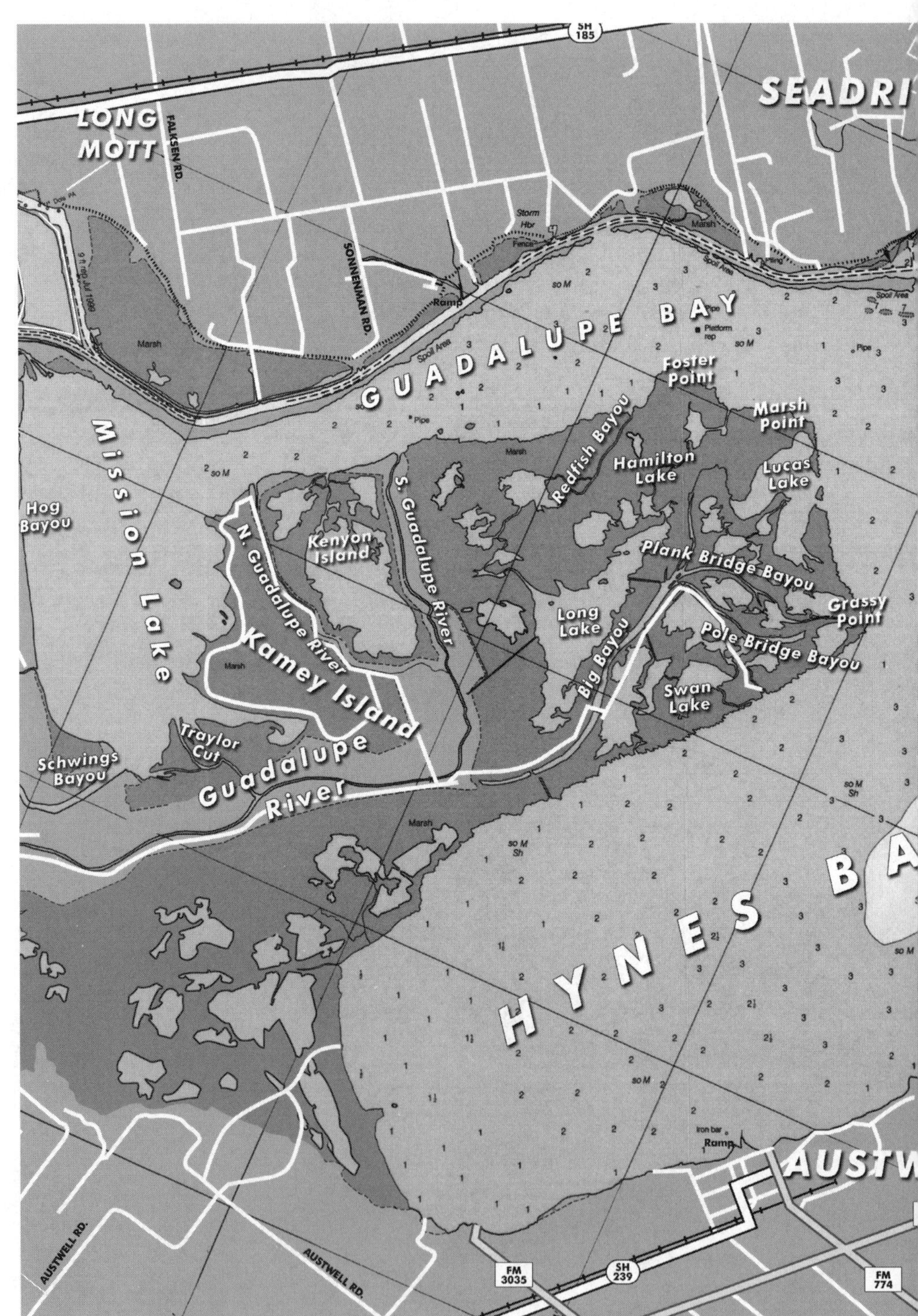
SH
185
SEADRI
LONG
MOTT
FALKSEN RD.
SONNENMAN RD.
Storm
Hbr
Fences
Ramp
Marsh
Spoil Area
Marsh
GUADALUPE BAY
so M
2
3
2
2
2
Spoil Area
7
3
Platform
rep
so M
3
Pipe
3
Foster
Point
Marsh
Point
Pipe
Marsh
Redfish Bayou
Hamilton
Lake
Lucas
Lake
1
Mission Lake
2 so M
2
2
S. Guadalupe River
Hog
Bayou
N. Guadalupe River
Kenyon
Island
Plank Bridge Bayou
2
Long
Lake
Grassy
Point
Marsh
Kamey Island
Big Bayou
Pole Bridge Bayou
Traylor
Cut
Swan
Lake
3
Schwings
Bayou
Guadalupe
River
Marsh
so M
Sh
so M
Sh
2
2
3
3
HYNES BA
2
2
2
2
1½
2
2½
3
3
so M
2
2
2½
3
1½
1
1
so M
Iron bar
Ramp
AUSTW
AUSTWELL RD.
AUSTWELL RD.
FM
3035
SH
239
FM
774

AN ANTONIO BAY
SAN ANTONIO
Mosquito Point
VICTORIA BAR
McDowell Point
HOPPER RD.
Webb Point
Channel to Seadrift
ARANSAS
NATIONAL
WILDLIFE
REFUGE
10
11
12
13
14

There is no denying the voraciousness of a hungry speckled trout.

It is worth mentioning that the Aransas National Wildlife Refuge shoreline from Hopper's Landing to the Intracoastal is sand and grass—a perfect autumn wading spot, especially when the whooping cranes arrive.

AYRES, MESQUITE, & CARLOS BAYS (SEE MAP ON PAGE 82)

These three bays are like navigating a maze to reach. Please follow the channel marker if you are not familiar with the area, and try to travel during daylight. Dark green water means it is deep, and lightens when it gets shallower.

Mesquite Bay is best when Cedar Bayou is flowing from the Gulf. However, in the last few years, it has silted and been cut of from the sweet currents of the ocean. Several groups are lobbying to raise funds to reopen the pass. Let's hope it gets done.

Trout are so thick they sometimes fight over a plug. Such is the case with this pair that was caught on a She Dog by Capt. Lynn Smith.

15 Cedar Bayou Flats (GPS N28 06.741, W96 50.485) and the **16** Bull Haul shoreline (GPS N28 07.592, W96 51.651) are hard, sand-bottomed grass flats adjacent to Cedar Bayou. Obviously, it is best when Cedar Bayou is flowing, yet it does receive tidal movement from the Intracoastal.

17 Bray Cove (GPS N28 08.451, W96 48.210) and the entire southeast shoreline are protected from southerly winds.

18 Ayres Reef (GPS N28 10.560, W96 50.332) is the dividing line between Ayres and Mesquite bays. It, along with **19** Ayres Dugout (GPS N28 10.152, W96 49.937), **20** Second Chain of Islands (GPS N28 11.826, W96 48.846), and **21** Rattlesnake Island (GPS N28 11.773, W96 49.717) are the hotspots.

22 The Third Chain of Islands (GPS N28 08.682, W96 52.463) is the dividing line between Carlos and Mesquite bays. **23** Edar Dugout (GPS N28 08.878, W96 52.940) of Cedar Point holds fish in the winter and spring for jiggers working soft plastics.

Spalding Bight (GPS N28 06.493, W96 53.311) holds clean water and is composed of grass and mud. **1** Jaybird Point* (GPS N28 05.358, W96 55.599) and **2** Jaybird Reef* (GPS N28 05.326, W96 56.115) are good spots for pluggers, and live-baiters tossing croakers in the summer (some consider it the beginning of Aransas Bay). I have spent half a day wading from the point all the way to the end of the reef.

ARANSAS BAY (SEE MAP ON PAGE 90)

I fish Rockport, mostly Aransas Bay, at least three times a year. The Rockport Chamber of Commerce hosts Spring Fling, a gathering of writers and photographers, to showcase this treasure of the Coastal Bend. They sold me on it a long time ago.

I normally trailer my boat down three days before the event to get a full week of fishing. Then, I come back in July and rent a house on Key Allegro and fish for seven days. Then, back again for the Maverick/Hewes/Pathfinder Owner's Tournament. Any excuse is a good excuse to fish Rockport.

3 Long Reef (GPS N28 03.644, W96 57.469) is one of the more popular spots, extending from the tip of Big Island. Nearby **4** Paul's

** see map on page 93*

Capt. Melvin Talasek of Matagorda attempts to land a 30-inch, Port Mansfield speck that ate a black/red-headed Top Dog.

Mott Reef (GPS N28 02.994, W96 56.864) is located in a cove that protects from gales and offers firm footing. I normally catch fish there during summer.

The San Jose shoreline **5** (GPS N28 00.599, W96 58.603) from Long Reef to **6** Allyns Bight (GPS N27 58.530, W96 59.115) is continuous grass beds and guts that hold trout in the spring and summer. Work tight to the shoreline and you will find redfish. Allyns Bight is protected from most winds, but can get boggy in certain spots. Spring and fall tides are best.

7 Cow Chip Cove (GPS N27 58.131, W96 58.903) to **8** Blind Pass (GPS N27 57.002, W96 59.539) is grass and mud. Blind Pass is the boat cut between San Jose Island and Mud Island. The entire **9** Mud Island (GPS N27 58.819 W97 00.788) shoreline (north and south) is grass and offers great wading, especially with croakers and topwaters.

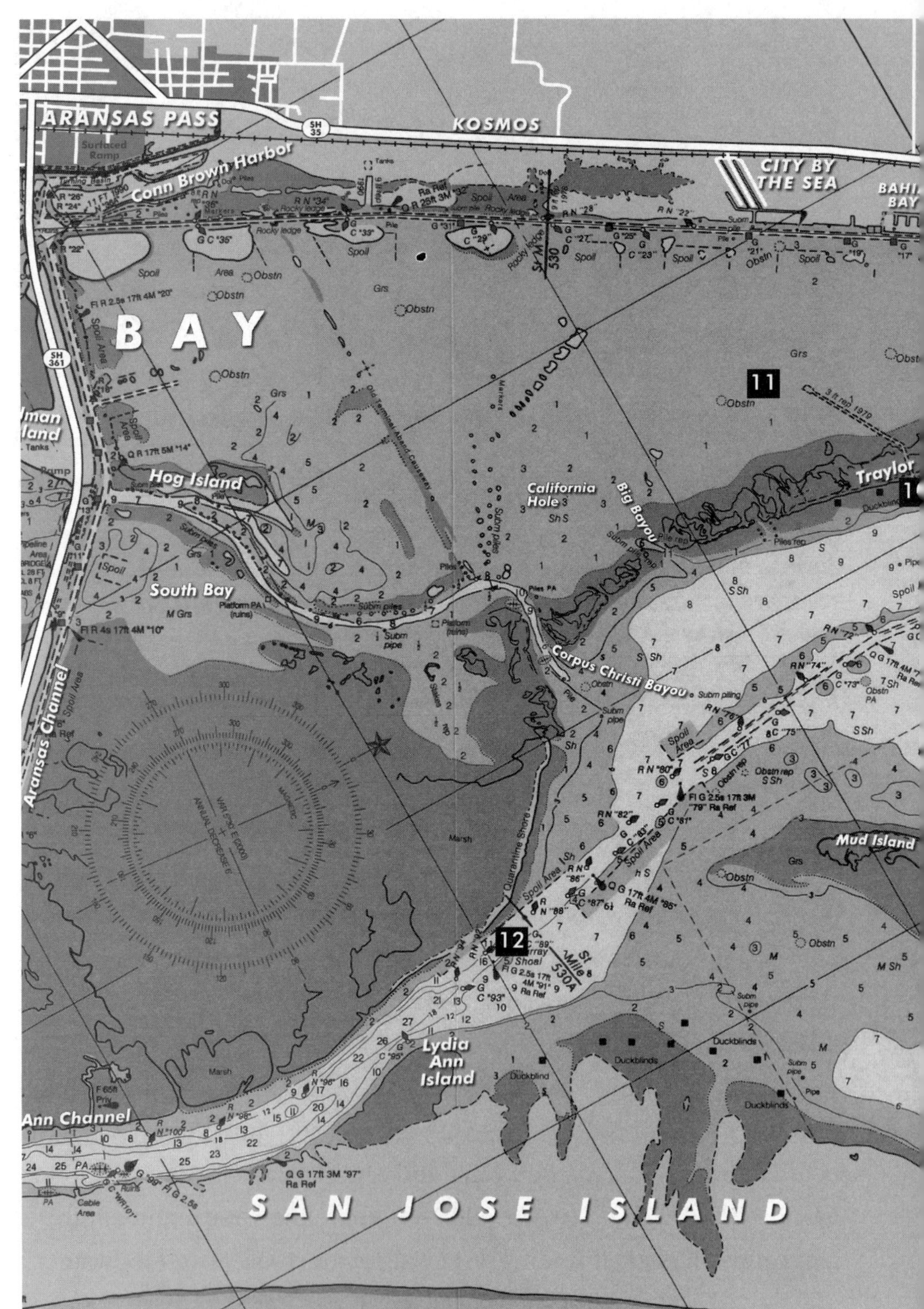
ARANSAS PASS
KOSMOS
CITY BY THE SEA
BAHIA BAY
Conn Brown Harbor
BAY
Hog Island
South Bay
Aransas Channel
California Hole
Big Bayou
Traylor
11
10
Corpus Christi Bayou
Mud Island
Quarantine Shore
Spoil Area
12
St. Mile 530A
Murray Shoal
Lydia Ann Island
Duckblinds
Ann Channel
Marsh
SAN JOSE ISLAND

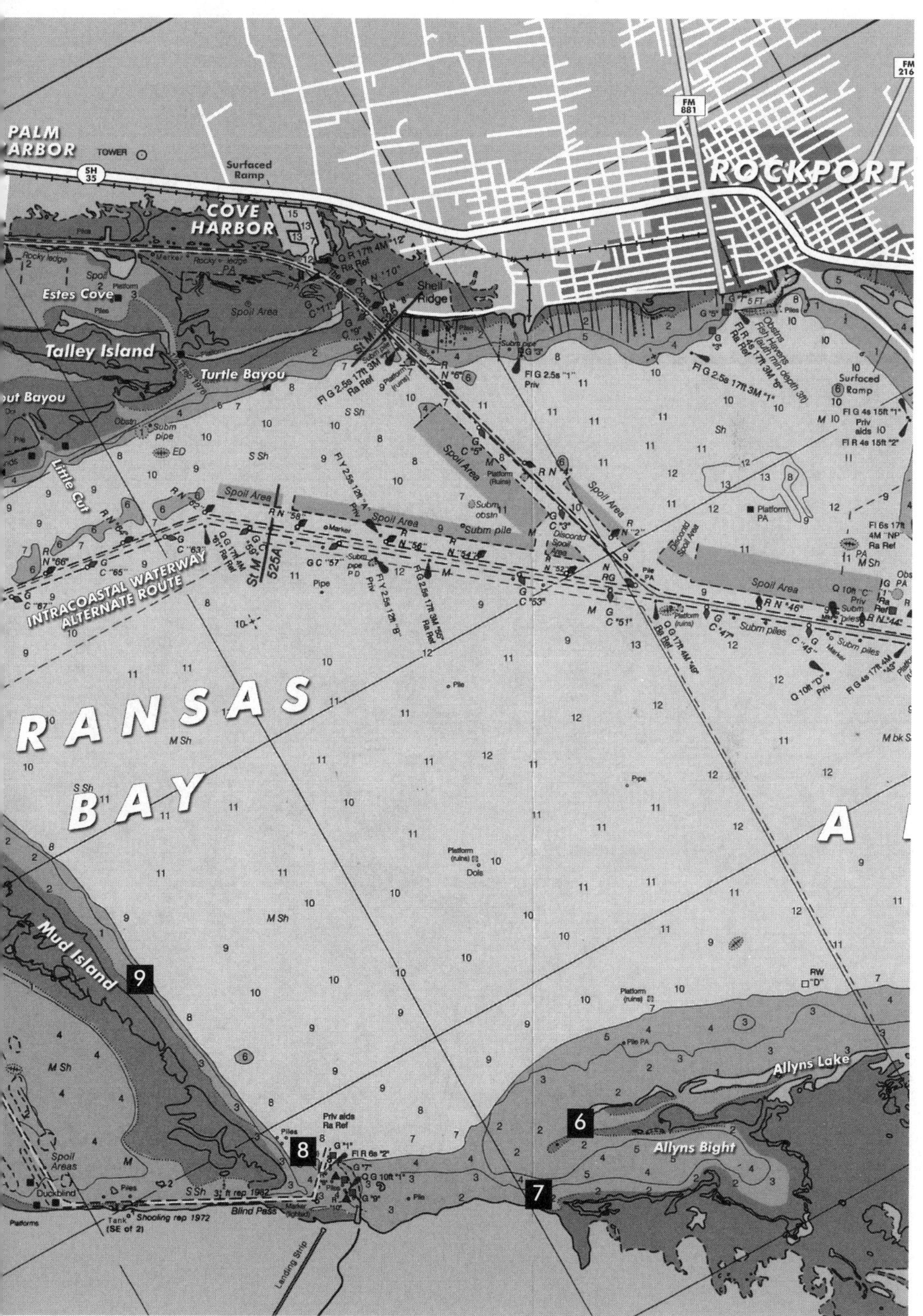

PALM HARBOR
TOWER
SH 35
Surfaced Ramp
COVE HARBOR
ROCKPORT
FM 881
FM 216
Rocky ledge
Spoil
Platform
Estes Cove
Shell Ridge
Talley Island
Turtle Bayou
out Bayou
Little Cut
INTRACOASTAL WATERWAY ALTERNATE ROUTE
Spoil Area
Spoil Area
Spoil Area
Spoil Area
Spoil Area
Spoil Area
Discontd Spoil Area
Platform (Ruins)
Platform PA
Platform (ruins)
Platform (ruins)
Subm pile
Subm piles
Subm piles
Marker
Pipe
R A N S A S
B A Y
M Sh
S Sh
Mud Island
Platform (ruins)
Dols
Allyns Lake
Allyns Bight
Priv aids Ra Ref
Piles
Blind Pass
Landing Strip
Shoaling rep 1972
Tank (SE of 2)
Duckblind
Spoil Areas
Platforms
9
8
7
6
RW "D"
Marker lightstr
S Sh 3½ ft rep 1992

LIVE OAK PENINSULA
FULTON BEACH ROAD
Surfaced Ramp
Live Oak Pt
Obstructions Wells and Pipelines
FULTON
Old Mansion
Harbor Oaks
Little Bay
Key Allegro
Ninemile Point
Grass Island Reefs
Scotch Tom Reef
Shell Reefs
Mack Reef
Halfmoon Reef
Spoil Area
Spoil Area
Spoil Area
Obstructions Wells and Pipelines
ARANSAS BAY
Deadman Island
Long Reef
Pauls Mott Reef
Big Island
Pauls Mott
Area subject to inundation

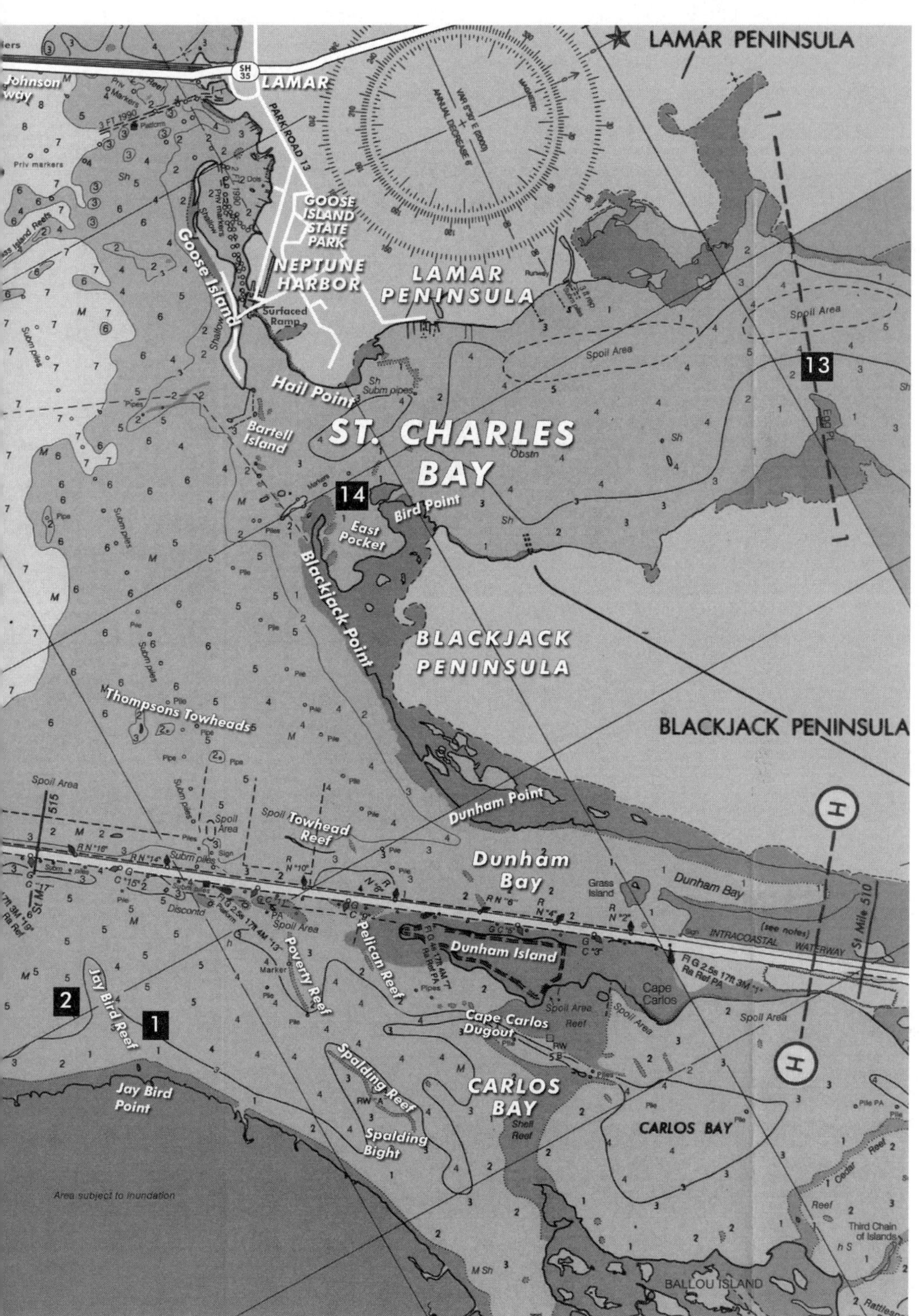
LAMÁR PENINSULA
LAMAR
SH 35
Johnson way
GOOSE ISLAND STATE PARK
NEPTUNE HARBOR
Goose Island
PARK ROAD 13
LAMAR PENINSULA
Surfaced Ramp
Hail Point
Bartell Island
ST. CHARLES BAY
Spoil Area
Spoil Area
13
East Pocket
Bird Point
14
Blackjack Point
BLACKJACK PENINSULA
BLACKJACK PENINSULA
Thompsons Towheads
Dunham Point
Spoil Area
Towhead Reef
Dunham Bay
Dunham Bay
Grass Island
INTRACOASTAL WATERWAY
St. Mile 510
(see notes)
Poverty Reef
Pelican Reef
Dunham Island
Cape Carlos
Cape Carlos Dugout
Spoil Area Reef
Spoil Area
2
1
Jay Bird Reef
Jay Bird Point
Spalding Reef
Spalding Bight
CARLOS BAY
Shell Reef
CARLOS BAY
Cedar Reef
Reef
Third Chain of Islands
Area subject to inundation
BALLOU ISLAND
Rattlesna...

Art Wright, Gulf Coast sales manager for Maverick Boat Company shows the fruits of his springtime labor while fishing with Capt. Lynn Smith in Mesquite Bay.

10 Traylor Island (GPS N27 56.706 W97 04.437 protects **11** Estes Flats (GPS N27 56.783 W97 05.543) and offers firm wading over grass beds on the outside beach. This is a favorite of the locals within five minutes of Cove Harbor Marina.

12 Middle Pass is truly a big trout flat, or as the locals term it, "Super Flat" (GPS N27 53.722, W97 02.380). I have fished it a few times with Capt. Rhett Price, and according to him, it is where the "big girls" hang out in the spring. Super Flat is recognizable by the plethora of duck blinds, and easily accessed from the Lydia Ann Channel. It is a super spot to intercept reds and flounder that use the channel to run to the Gulf.

ST. CHARLES & COPANO BAYS (SEE MAP ON PAGE 96)

This bay is another navigation hazard if you do not know where you are going. It has tons of shell, and locals keep it quiet when big fish eat their bait.

Every shoreline is a potential wading spot, from the north Cavasso shoreline to **13** Big Devil* shore (GPS N28 10.126, W96 57.214) to the East Pocket by **14** Blackjack Point* (GPS N28 07.575, W96 57.871). Get a map if you do not know where you are going. The reefs near the Mouth of St. Charles cost Capt. Melvin Talasek a lower unit when we fished a Bob Sealy Tournament a few years ago.

Copano Bay is wadable on its south shoreline near **1** Mission Bay (GPS N28 08.400, W97 08.952), its west shoreline near **2** Swan Lake (GPS N28 03.031, W97 10.000), **3** Port Bay (GPS N28 01.621, W97 08.732), and its east shoreline near **4** Shell Point (GPS N28 11.083, W97 01.101). However, to me, Copano is best when the wind allows you to fish the open-bay reefs.

** see map on page 93*

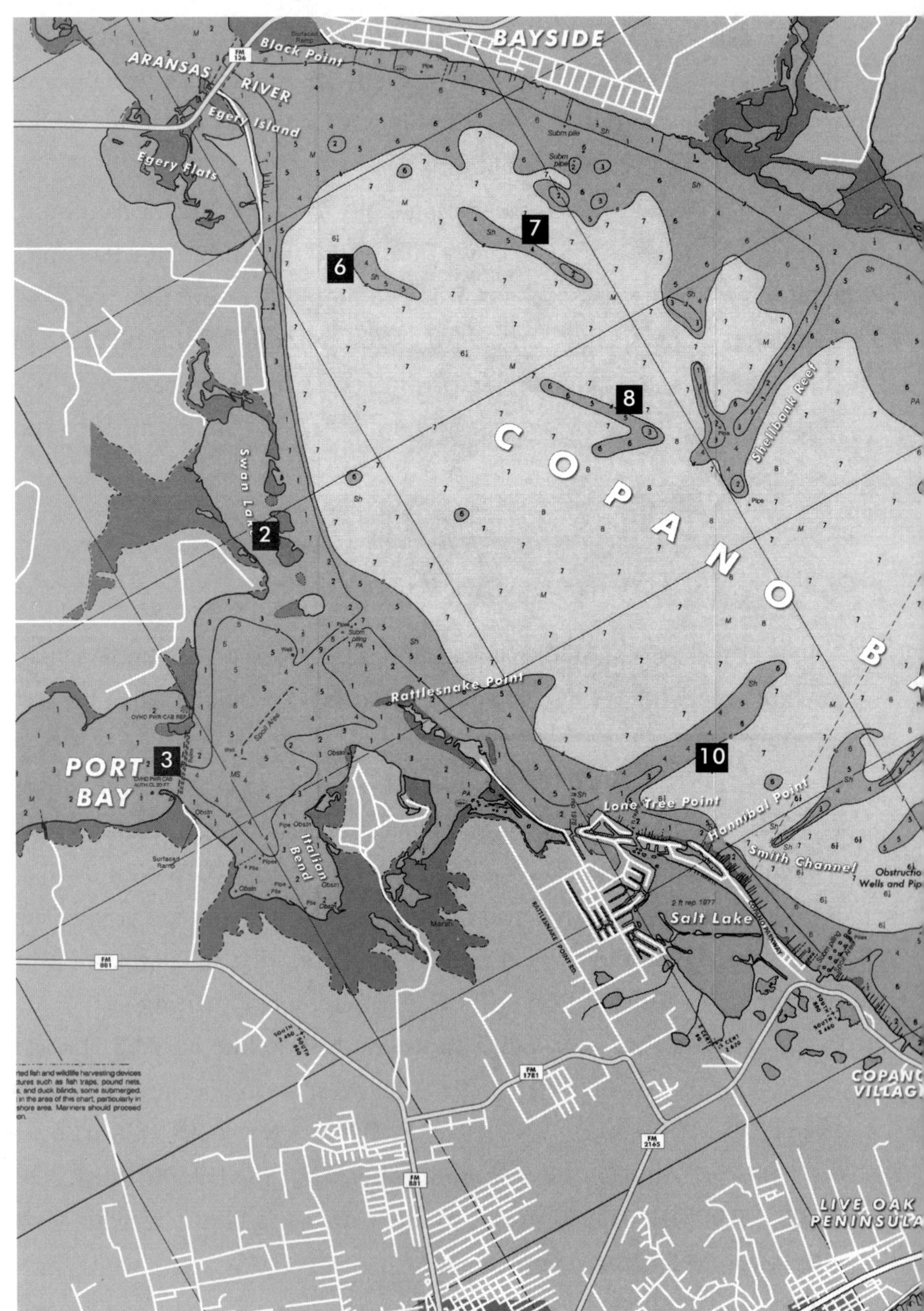

BAYSIDE
ARANSAS RIVER
Black Point
Egery Island
Egery Flats
Swan Lake
COPANO BAY
Shellbank Reef
PORT BAY
Rattlesnake Point
Italian Bend
Lone Tree Point
Hannibal Point
Smith Channel
Salt Lake
Obstruction Wells and Pip
Spoil Area
COPANO VILLAGE
LIVE OAK PENINSULA
2
3
6
7
8
10

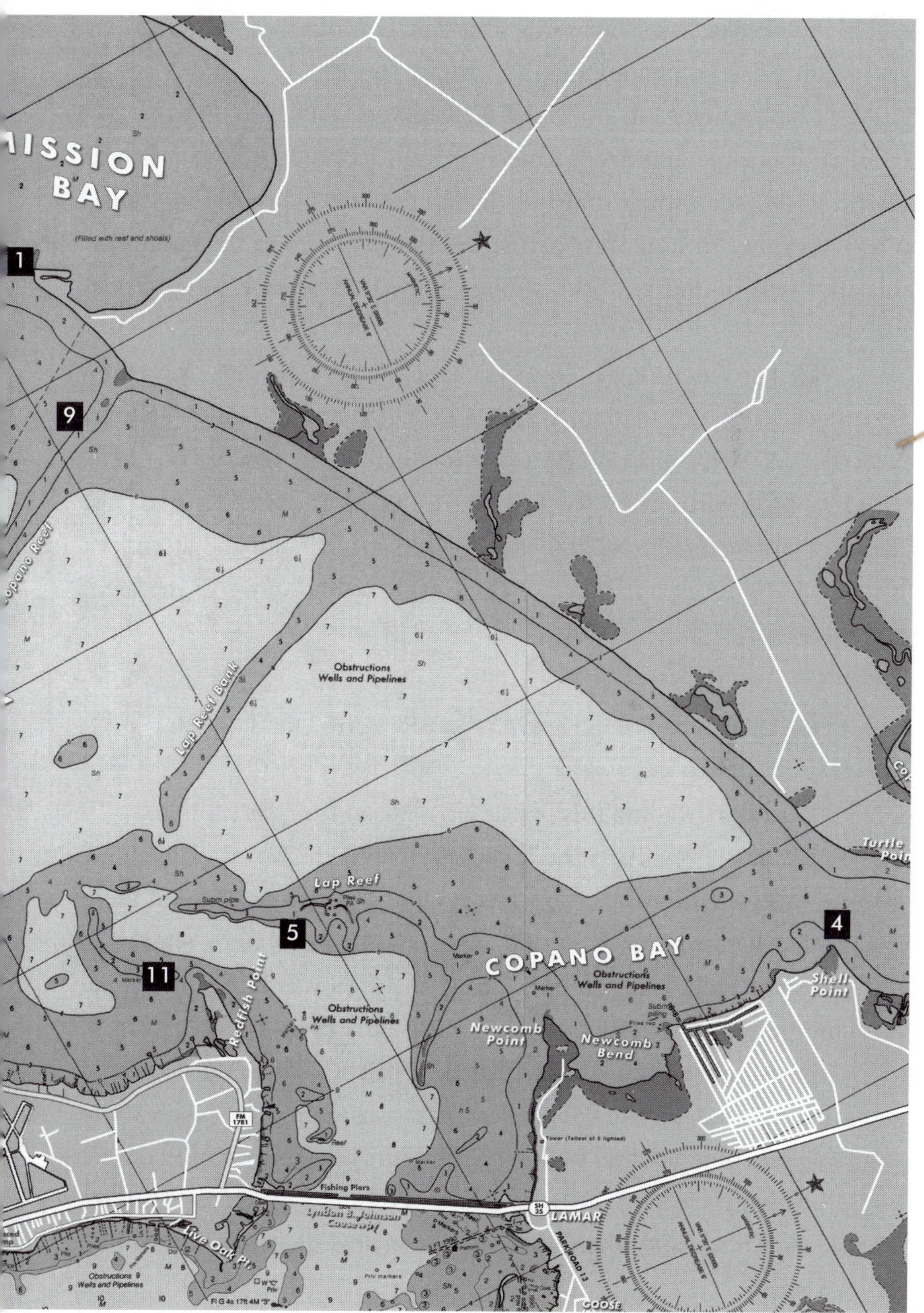

MISSION BAY
(Filled with reef and shoals)
1
9
Copano Reef
Lap Reef Bank
Obstructions
Wells and Pipelines
Lap Reef
Subm pipe
5
11
Redfish Point
Obstructions
Wells and Pipelines
COPANO BAY
Newcomb
Point
Newcomb
Bend
Obstructions
Wells and Pipelines
Subm
piling
Piles
4
Shell
Point
Turtle
Point
Cop
Marker
Marker
Tower (Tallest of 5 lighted)
Live Oak Pt
Lyndon B. Johnson Causeway
Fishing Piers
Reef
Marker
SH
35
LAMAR
PARK ROAD 13
GOOSE
Obstructions
Wells and Pipelines
Fl G 4s 17ft 4M "3"

Much like East Matagorda and San Antonio bays, Copano Bay reef wading can be phenomenal for trophy specks.

I have caught lots of fish off **5** Lap Reef (GPS N28 07.910, W97 03.072). It is large and drops quickly from 4 to 7 feet, allowing fish to retreat to the deep water on low tide and feed on the reef at high tide. A few Rockport Troutmasters participants have placed in the money on this spot year in and year out, though they did not want to be recognized.

6 Forty Acre Reef (GPS N28 04.615, W97 11.257), **7** Three Foot Reef (GPS N28 05.650, W97 10.924), **8** Boomerang Reef (GPS N28 05.762, W97 09.145), **9** Copano Reef (GPS N28 08.001, W97 07.410), **10** Smith Reef (GPS N28 05.251, W97 05.852), and **11** Redfish Point Reef (GPS N28 06.591, W97 03.740) all demand attention. If the fish are not at one piece of shell, pick up and move to the next, and the next.

Corpus Christi Bay (see map on page 100)

Most days wading this bay are logged on the east shoreline.

1 East Flats (GPS N27 48.731, W97 08.220) is one of my favorite spots on the coast. The water is clear as an aquarium, and there is always a chance to catch a wall-hanger. Capt. Chuck Uzzle's first trip to East Flats resulted in a 7-pound trout on a fly. I was throwing topwaters, and he was determined to catch a fish on a fly.

Five minutes out of the boat, I popped a "four." A couple of steps later, I had a "five." The next cast was a healthy "six." Uzzle stopped and contemplated walking back to the boat, but I would not let him. I needed fly-fishing pictures, so I urged him to press on. Minutes later, he had his beauty, then walked tight against the shore and duped 30-inch reds.

"Man, this is like fishing in AstroWorld water," he said in his own one-of-a-kind jargon. "I can actually see my toes. The boys on Sabine would never believe it."

2 Shamrock Cove (GPS N27 44.950, W97 10.001) is another beautiful flat protected from winds, perfect for topwaters and flies. Though many elect to drift it, working tight to the marsh shore and Shamrock Island is always good for redfish.

There are many stingrays in the area. Shuffle slow and take your time.

NAS/Truax Field
OCEAN DRIVE
SEAPLANE RESTRICTED AREA
334.800
Obstructions Wells and Pipelines
CORPUS
CHRIS BA
Spoil Area
Spoil Area
INTRACOASTAL WATERWAY
Obstructions Wells and Pipelines
Boat Hole
Dead Man Hole
Crane Islands
Kates Hole
Grants Cove
Croaker Hole
Water Exchange Channel
Fish Pass
Area subject to inundation
Sand dunes
Mustang
Island
MEXICO
COLREGS DEMARCATION LINE
80.850a (see note A)

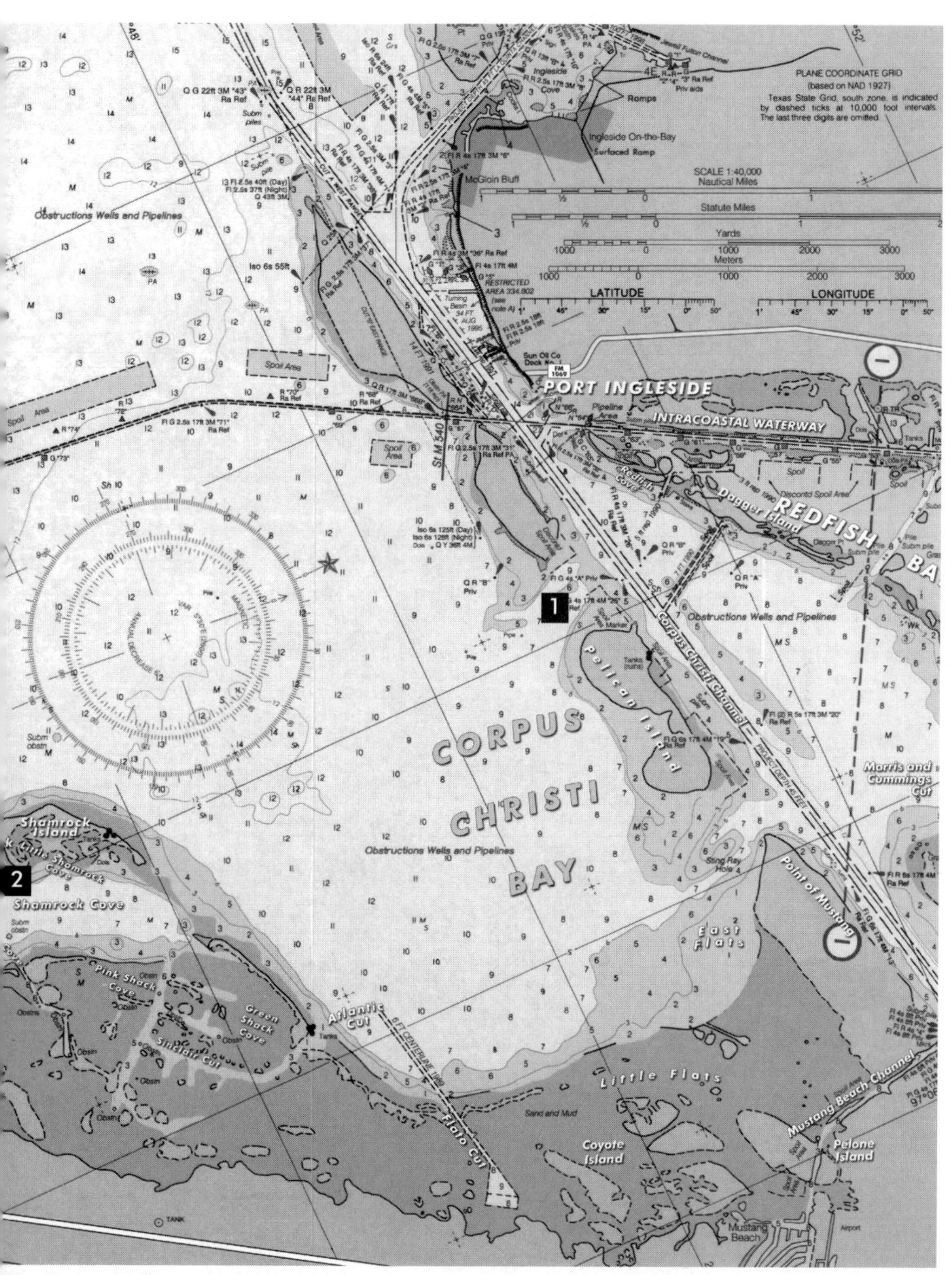
PLANE COORDINATE GRID
(based on NAD 1927)
Texas State Grid, south zone, is indicated by dashed ticks at 10,000 foot intervals. The last three digits are omitted.
SCALE 1:40,000
Nautical Miles
Statute Miles
Yards
Meters
LATITUDE
LONGITUDE
PORT INGLESIDE
Ingleside On-the-Bay
Surfaced Ramp
McGloin Bluff
Ingleside Cove
Ramps
INTRACOASTAL WATERWAY
Obstructions Wells and Pipelines
Obstructions Wells and Pipelines
Obstructions Wells and Pipelines
REDFISH BAY
Redfish Cove
Dagger Island
Corpus Christi Channel
Pelican Island
Morris and Cummings Cut
Point of Mustang
East Flats
Sting Ray Hole
CORPUS CHRISTI BAY
Shamrock Island
Little Shamrock Cove
Shamrock Cove
Pink Shack Cove
Green Shack Cove
Sinclair Cut
Atlantic Cut
Flato Cut
Little Flats
Sand and Mud
Coyote Island
Pelone Island
Mustang Beach
Mustang Beach Channel
Airport
Spoil Area
Sun Oil Co Dock
Turning Basin
RESTRICTED AREA 334.902
1
2

Chapter Six

Lower Coast Hotspots :
Knee-deep in big trout country

A study by Texas Parks and Wildlife Department (TPWD) biologists disclosed that 86 percent of 30-inch speckled trout caught in gill-net surveys on the entire Texas coast during the past 25 years came from Laguna Madre waters.

That is stout.

According to former TPWD Coastal Fisheries Director Hal Osburn, this is attributable to several factors: "You have a fish swimming through a shorter gauntlet. Lack of fishing pressure is a key. There are places in Laguna Madre that fish can go into that cannot be reached by people. It is easy for the fish to hide, like in the mountains of Afghanistan."

Osburn said the hypersaline waters of Laguna Madre, saltier than the Gulf of Mexico, contribute to trophy trout growth: "Trout on the upper coast of Texas work harder to maintain their internal osmotic balance of blood chemistry because the water is fresher, or has a lower salinity level. Trout like saltier environments, therefore they lose some of the nutrients of their food in freshwater due to their bodies working harder to maintain homeostasis. Laguna Madre is very salty, so they can relax and absorb all the nutrients of their food. A trout getting more nutrients grows bigger."

Indeed, lower coast trout grow big. The state record came from Baffin Bay, and another a fly-fisherman took a confirmed 15-pounder in 2002 on fly. It is a fact that if you want to increase your odds of catching a trophy trout, you better head south. That is not to say the upper or middle coast does not produce big fish, just not as many as Laguna Madre.

In my estimation, Laguna Madre begins at the JFK Causeway in Corpus Christi and ends at the Brazos Santiago jetty on South Padre Island. Between there are miles of sugar sand flats and sea grass beds.

This is wading paradise.

BAFFIN BAY (SEE MAP ON PAGE 106)

The lore of Baffin Bay is much larger than the actual square miles of fishing venue. Baffin is a big trout destination for good reason. It consistently coughs up gorilla specks year-round.

I fish out-of-state annually, and writers across the country often ask: "What about Baffin—is it as good as they say?"

I answer: "Yes, it is good, often great."

The one downside of fishing Baffin is its remote location. Actually, it could be a positive aspect with regard to fishing pressure. You do not just head to Baffin on an afternoon jaunt, unless you live in Riviera, and not too many people live in that remote South Texas town.

From Bird Island Basin, you are looking at a 28-mile stroll to the mouth of Baffin. From the JFK Causeway in Corpus Christi, it is 42 miles. It is a long boat ride, especially in the dark. However, if you have a love affair with broad lavender backs like I do, the 50 bucks at the pump is well worth it when a magnum sow crushes your plug. Besides, my Pathfinder is pretty fast, and gets me there in less than an hour.

The thing that sets Baffin's terrain apart from other Texas bays is its unusual rocks. The locals would like you to believe that these rocks are lower-unit eating-machines, but I have never had a problem running on plane between the channel markers. I do, however, idle when outside markers. It may take longer to get to a spot, but at least my engine will get me home.

These rocks, according to some authorities, are attributable to prehistoric worms. Whatever the case, they are abundant and provide structure wherefrom specks and reds ambush prey. You have probably seen the John Dearman prints of giant trout chasing shrimp around the rocks. Well, unless you have teased a fish and actually seen it bound from the rocks and inhale your bait, you have not experienced the majestic mystery of Baffin Bay. Do yourself a favor, and fish this Texas treasure.

If you are reluctant to try new places on your own, hire a guide and learn from the experience. Ask specific questions and take notes. A guided fishing trip is not always about catching a cooler full of fish, but rather, the information learned, which lasts much longer than the fillets in your belly.

The Intracoastal Waterway dissects Laguna Madre, creating endless wading shorelines on the east and west bank. The East Flats (GPS N27 24.502, W97 20.503) just east of Little Bar is hard sand and grass best at high tide for trout, redfish, and flounder. Giggers love it, as flounder move onto the flats on an incoming tide.

The spoil areas lining the Intracoastal are all potential wading haunts. Their proximity to the deep water of the Intracoastal makes all the islands a potential hot spot. There are too many to name, yet, most do not have names. If you see mullet flipping or shrimp jumping, stop

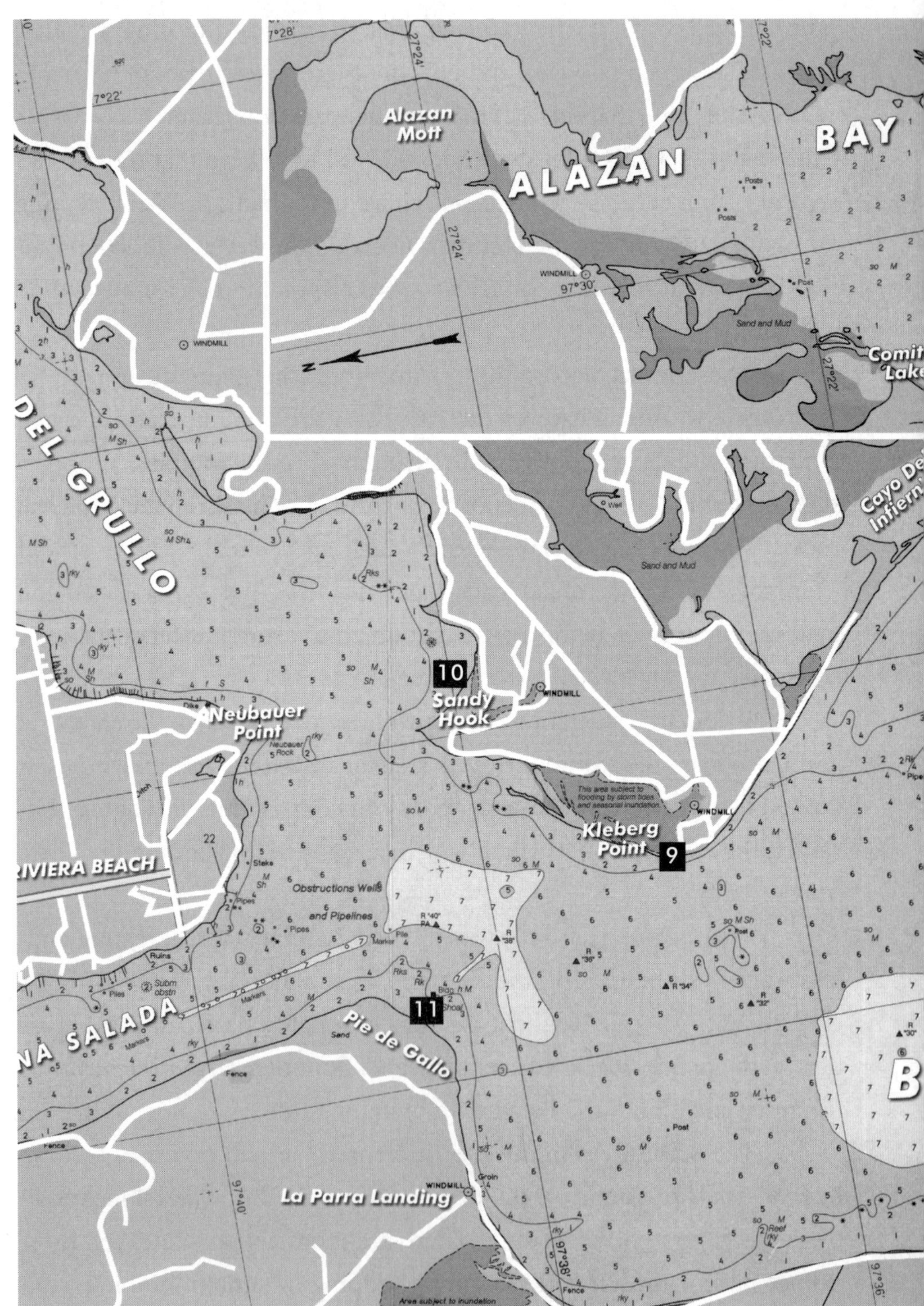
Alazan
Mott
ALAZAN
BAY
Comit
Lake
WINDMILL
97°30'
Sand and Mud
WINDMILL
DEL GRULLO
Cayo Del
Infierno
Well
Sand and Mud
10
Sandy
Hook
WINDMILL
Neubauer
Point
Neubauer
Rock
This area subject to
flooding by storm tides
and seasonal inundation.
WINDMILL
Kleberg
Point
9
22
RIVIERA BEACH
Stake
Obstructions Wells
and Pipelines
Pipes
Pipes
Ruins
Marker
Subm
obstn
Pipes
NA SALADA
11
Rks
Rk
Bldg
Shoal
Pie de Gallo
Sand
Fence
La Parra Landing
WINDMILL
97°40'
97°38'
Fence
Area subject to inundation
97°36'

Sand and Mud
Acetera
Artesian Well
WINDMILL
ALAZAN BAY
Obstn
Pipe
8
7
Starvation
Point
WINDMILL
East
Kleberg
Point
Subm
pipe
PA
R "14"
PA
R "16"
PA
Reef
Rk Tdy
Rk
Rks
Rk
Rk
Rk
Rk
R "20"
R "22"
R "24"
R "26"
R "28"
R "18"
Obstn Wells
and Pipelines
AFFIN BAY
Penas
Rinco
Pipe
Foul
Foul
bk Sh
14
LAS
CORRALLOS
Pipe
12
Fence
Fence
Fence
13
BLACK BLUFF
MOTA
NEGRO
27°14'
97°34'
97°32'
97°30'
VAR 5°45' E (2000)
ANNUAL DECREASE 6'
MAGNETIC

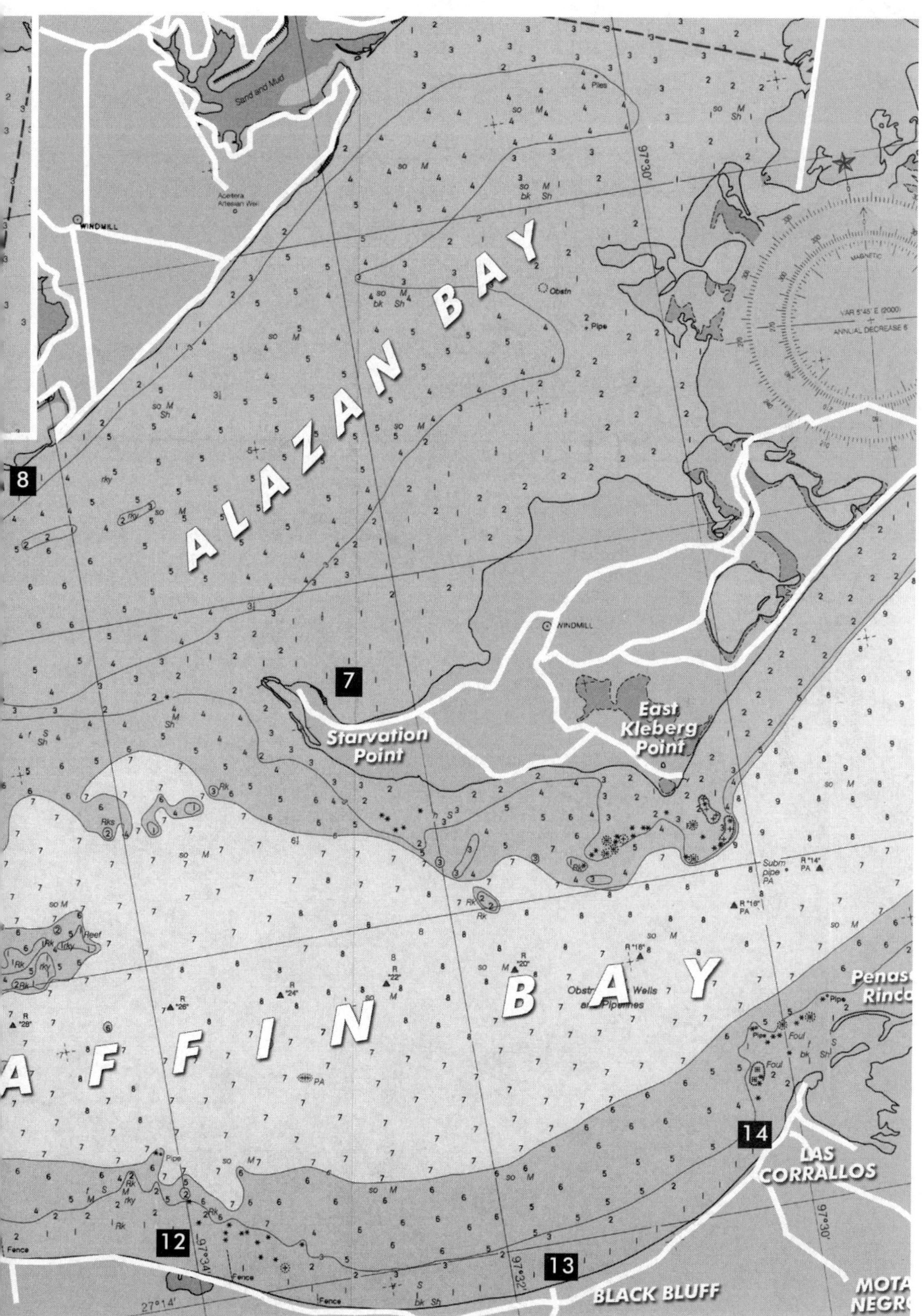

107

Shifting sand dunes
Picacho Nuevo Well
Casa
VAR. 6°45'E (2000)
ANNUAL DECREASE 6'
MAGNETIC
PENASCAL RINCON
Point Penascal
15
INTRACOASTAL
WATERW
Spoil Area
3
Discontd Spoil Area
Spoil Area
Pipeline Area
Discontd Spoil Area
Discontd Spoil Area
Platform
L A G U N A
Obstructions Wells and Pipelines
Area subject to inundation
MURDOCK
YARBOROUGH
2
P A D R E

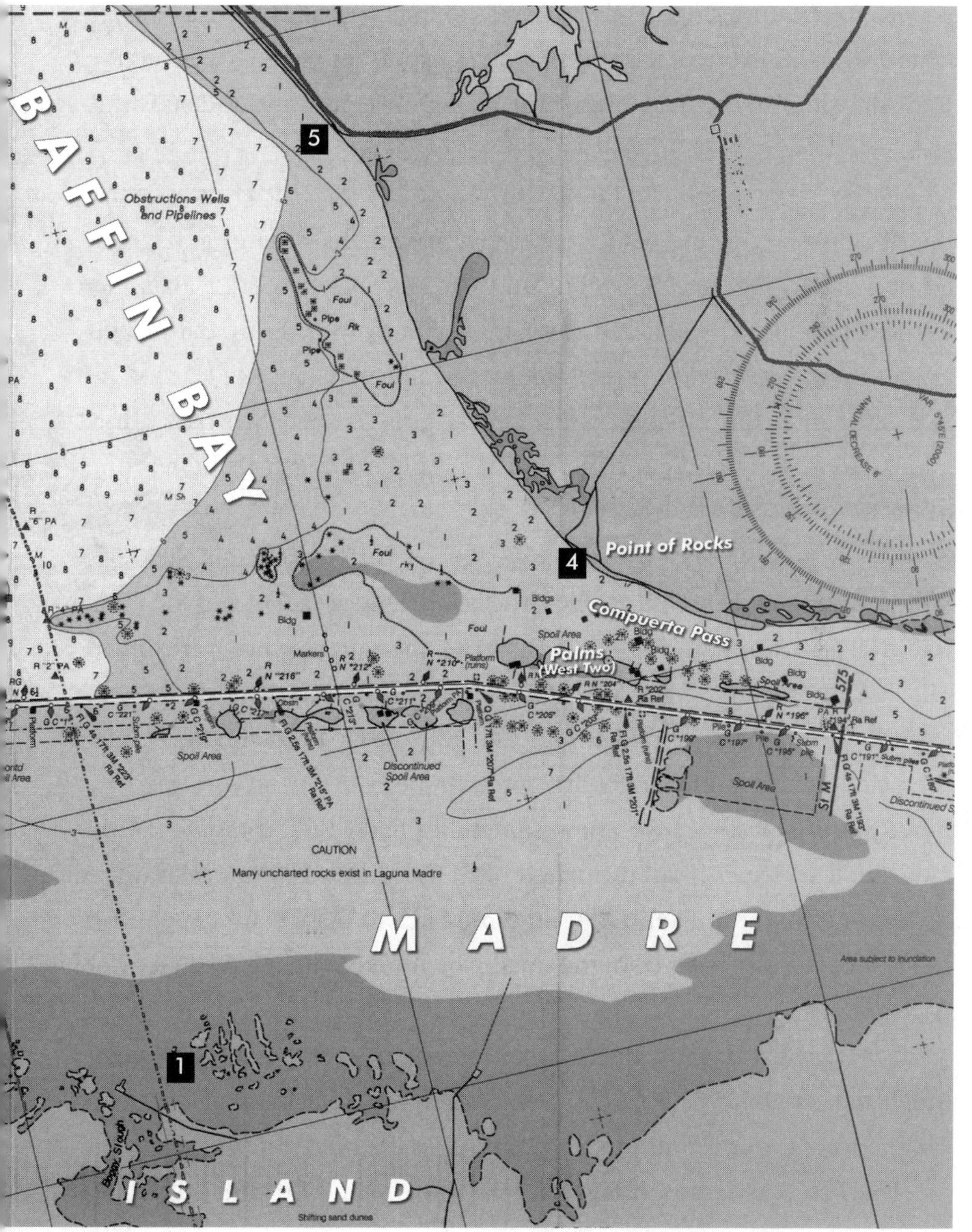
BAFFIN BAY
Obstructions Wells
and Pipelines
Foul
Pipe
Rk
Pipe
Foul
Foul
rkj
Foul
Point of Rocks
Bldgs
Compuerta Pass
Spoil Area
Bldg
Foul
Palms
(West Two)
Markers
Platform
(ruins)
N "216"
N "212"
N "210"
N "204"
N "202"
N "196"
Ra Ref
Spoil Area
Bldg
Bldg
PARK
575
C "221"
C "215"
C "211"
C "205"
C "199"
C "197"
C "195"
C "191"
Spoil Area
Discontinued
Spoil Area
Spoil Area
Discontinued S
CAUTION
Many uncharted rocks exist in Laguna Madre
MADRE
Area subject to inundation
ISLAND
Shifting sand dunes

and wade.

Continuing on the west bank, the **1** Meadows (GPS N27 16.830, W97 22.774) is sand and grass surrounding an island that is superb for floundering. Wade toward the Intracoastal; there are drops from 1 to 3 feet. The area is very shallow in spots, and needs a good tide to push bait onto the flats. Fly-fishing anglers love to wade and stalk this area.

2 Yarborough Flats (GPS N27 13.467, W97 23.283) is south of the Meadows. It is the same basic terrain with hard sand and grass. Some refer to the area between the two points as Flounder Flats. My friend Capt. Jesse Arsola of Bay City regularly travels to Baffin and guides trips. When I do not see him for a while at Matagorda Harbor, he is usually in Baffin tangling with the big girls. Arsola throws a Corky almost exclusively, and consistently catches big trout. Yarborough is one of his favorite spots.

My favorite spot to fish is **3** Rocky Slough (GPS N27 09.755, W97 26.228). As the name implies, rocks litter the area. During the 2000 Baffin Bay Troutmasters, Capt. Talasek, then-high school freshman Michael Briggs, and I found tons of mullet flipping against the east shoreline. Talasek dropped Briggs and me off close to the shoreline, then circled back and made a drift another 100 yards from us. When we heard water splashing, we knew something had dunked his black Top Dog. He lost that fish, an estimated 6 pounds, then lost another at the boat trying to net it. Eventually, he came back to get us. We caught fish the rest of the day, but not of the quality he hooked during his first hour of fishing.

The next day, we invited a friend of ours (who had not caught much the day before in Corpus Christi Bay) to follow us in his boat. That morning, our friend put a 7-pounder in the boat not 50 yards from us. The fish was large enough to win third in the Troutmasters "Big

Trout" category, and send him home with over a grand in prize money. Our boy, Briggs, took home the youth division trophy.

On the north shoreline near the mouth of Baffin Bay is **4** Point of Rocks (GPS N27 19.222, W97 24.845). Some refer to the area as "the Badlands," while others call it "Twin Palms." Whatever your favorite moniker, it is a good spot to wade, especially with a north wind blowing. Idle slowly to the spot and look for rocks; they are everywhere, some hiding just below the surface.

5 Tide Gauge (GPS N27 18.522, W97 27.633) is another popular spot protected from north gales. It is especially good in the winter when north winds persist. The bar is 1 to 2 feet, then drops to 7 feet. Trout hang on the ledge, waiting for the tide to push bait onto the bar. February is a great time to catch large specks.

6 East Kleberg Point (GPS N27 16.505, W97 30.454) is another leeward shoreline in a north wind. Points are especially good structure as they often have guts and bars that hold fish.

Eighty-six percent of trout over 30-inches caught in TPWD gillnet surveys during the last 25 years have come from the Laguna Madre.

Right around the corner is **7** Starvation Pocket (GPS N27 17.703, W97 32.167), which consists of hard sand. Work toward the north shore of Alazan Bay and you can cast into deep rocks. The pocket is protected from southerly breezes.

The entire north shoreline of Alazan Bay is a winter haven for waders. It consists of grass flats, drop-offs, and rocks. The mouth of **8** Cayo Del Inflernillo (GPS N27 18.963, W97 34.442), **9** Kleberg Point (GPS N27 17.054, W97 36.633), and **10** Sandy Hook (GPS N27 18.439, W97 38.150) are protected in the winter. Those launching from Bird Island or the JFK Causeway seldom venture this far in the bay, so it is lightly fished. Riviera Beach launchers can get there in less than 10 minutes.

The south shoreline is more a summer and spring wading locale. Beginning near the mouth of Laguna Salada, **11** Kenedy Point (GPS N27 16.418, W97 38.529) drops from 2 to 5 feet in some places, with scattered rocks throughout. Croaker, live shrimp, and piggy perch are popular natural bait offerings, while topwaters, Bass Assassins, Trout Killers, Corky, and gold spoons are strong hardware selections.

12 White Bluff Rocks (GPS N27 14.541, W97 35.749), **13** South Rocks (GPS N27 14.434, W97 34.317), Black Bluff (GPS N27 13.947, W97 32.884), **14** Los Carrallos (GPS N27 14.808, W97 30.146), **15** Kenedy Shoreline (GPS N27 15.061, W97 27.661), and **16** Penascal Point (GPS N27 16.061, W97 25.556) round out the south shoreline hotspots. Each has its share of rocks, grass, and sand, and holds fish with the presence of bait.

Fish Baffin as you would reef-laden bays like San Antonio and East Matagorda: if the fish are not on one set of rocks, go to the next. Each set you fish might hold the next state record.

PORT MANSFIELD (SEE MAP ON PAGE 114)

Waist-deep on a translucent floor of sea grass and sugar sand, I turned toward the west and peered over my left shoulder at the flags flying on the point.

"Are you sure we are in Texas?" I asked my wading partner, Capt. Bruce Shuler.

"Did you know we are on the same latitude line as West Palm Beach, Florida?" the captain replied. "We like to call it the 'Texas Keys'."

My first excursion to Port Mansfield was a bit of culture shock. I did not know Texas had water like this. I, like so many other Texans, was oblivious to the pristine waters of Lower Laguna Madre. My idea of crystal clear water is a hazy emerald. Fishable water in my home locale might be confused with a large cup of weak coffee.

Texas is a massive state. You do not jump in the car and decide to ride from the northern border and touch the southern border in one day. The same is true traveling from east to west. Most North Texans have never ventured farther south than Houston, and most Houstonians have never traveled past Corpus Christi.

When tires point east on Highway 186 in Raymondville, travelers have one thing in mind: fishing. If strangers roll into town without a rod and reel in the cab, locals think you are lost.

"I tell all my fishing clients: If you have something on your mind other than fishing, you better bring it with you," said Port Mansfield icon Capt. Bob Fuston.

Fuston began running charters in Port Mansfield in 1981 after doctors told him he needed to eliminate the stress of his nuclear power plant job. Known by most as "the Red Bandana," Fuston has made a living wading through rafts of redfish and schools of speckled trout. He did not choose to be "the Red Bandana," the townspeople chose it for

LAGUNA
CAUTION
Many uncharted rocks exist
in Laguna Madre.
St M 620
St M 625
Spoil Area
Spoil Area
Spoil Area
Spoil Area

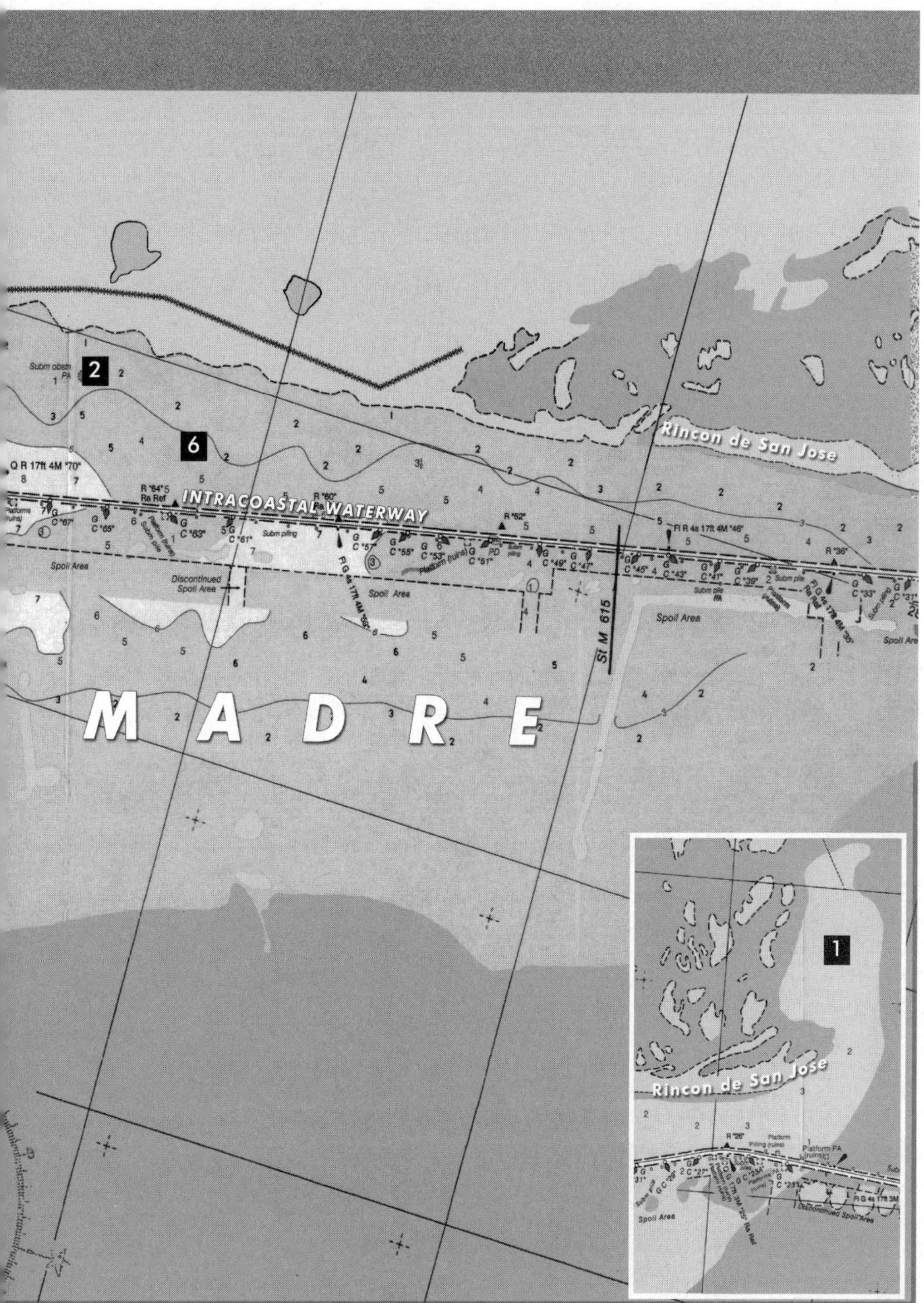
Rincon de San Jose
INTRACOASTAL WATERWAY
MADRE
Q R 17ft 4M "70"
R "64" 5
Ra Ref
R "60"
R "52"
Fl R 4s 17ft 4M "46"
R "36"
Spoil Area
Discontinued
Spoil Area
Spoil Area
Spoil Area
Spoil Area
St M 615
Subm obstn
Subm piling
Subm pile
Platform (ruins)
Rincon de San Jose
R "26"
Platform
Piling (ruins)
Platform PA
(ruins)
Spoil Area
Discontinued Spoil Area
Fl G 4s 17ft 3M

Chubby Island
Four Mile Slough
Sand and Mud
Green Hill
El Sauz Island
Four Mile Slough
PA
R TR
Platform
Spoil Area
Spoil Area
Spoil Area
Spoil Area
INTRACOASTAL WATERWAY
R "150" Ra Ref
R "156"
G "155"
G "153"
C "151"
C "147"
C "145"
C "157A"
G "157" Ra Ref
G "159" PA Ra Ref
G "161"
C "161A"
C "163"
G "165" PA Ra Ref
C "167"
C "169"
R "172"
St M
835
Fl R 4s 17ft 4M "160"
Fl G 4s 17ft 5M "171" Ra Ref
LAGUNA
LAGUNA
MAGNETIC
ANNUAL DECREASE
VAR 5°45'E (2000)
ED
Spoil Area
Spoil Area
Spoil Area Ra Ref
R "18" PA Ra Ref
R "16" Ra Ref
Discontinued Spoil Area

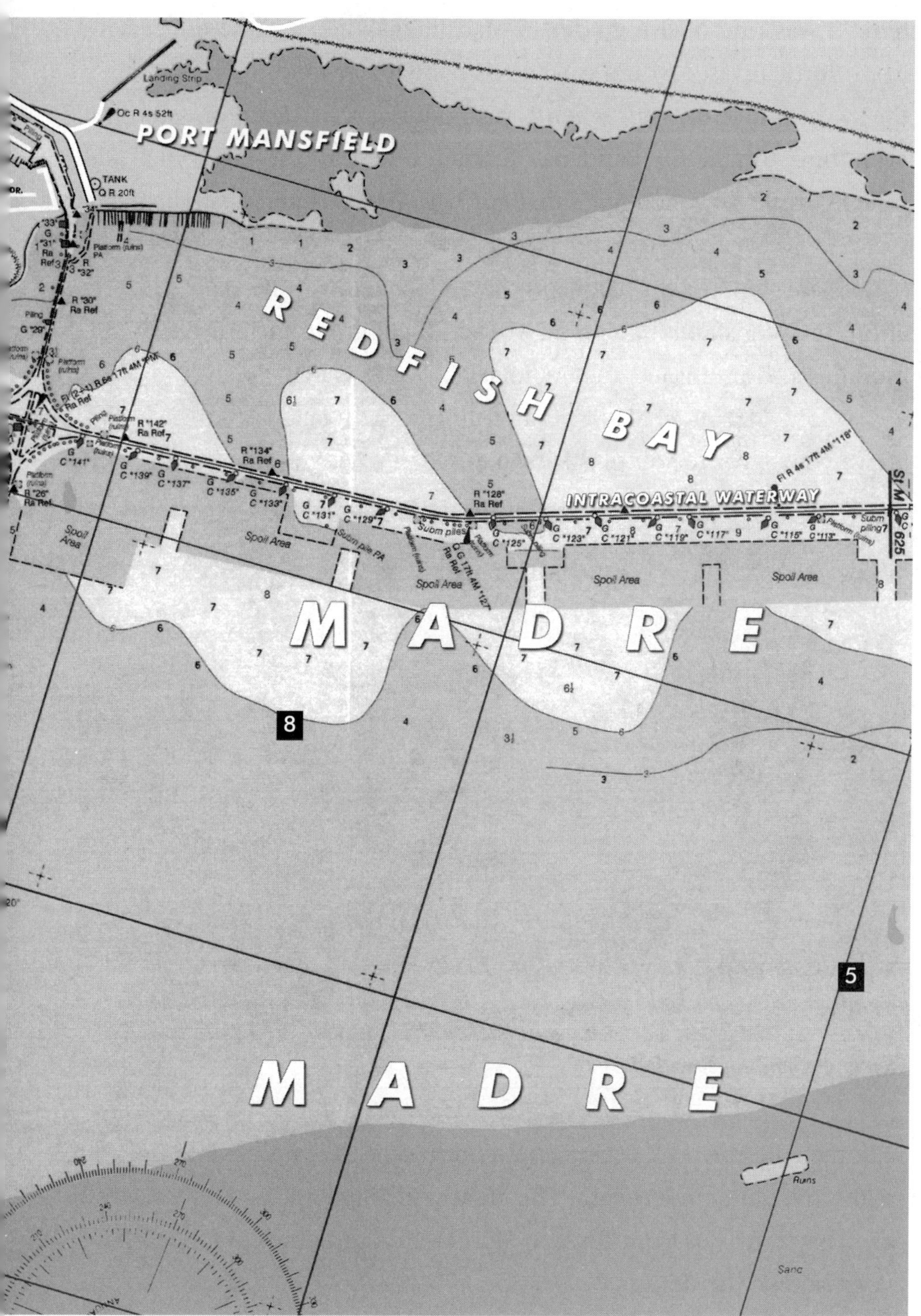
PORT MANSFIELD
Landing Strip
Oc R 4s 52ft
TANK
Q R 20ft
REDFISH BAY
INTRACOASTAL WATERWAY
Spoil Area
Spoil Area
Spoil Area
Spoil Area
MADRE
MADRE
8
5
117

him: "I was one of five guides in Mansfield. When I came down here from North Texas, I would wear a red bandana around by head to keep the sweat out of my eyes when I was building rods. Then, I would not even think to take the bandana off when I went to the post office and people would say, 'there goes that guy with the red bandana.' The name stuck."

You could say Fuston put Port Mansfield on the map. His creation, the Mansfield Mauler, gained national attention in fishing communities and prompted anglers to ask: "Where is Mansfield?"

The Mansfield Mauler is a rattling cork attached 18 to 24 inches above your favorite soft plastic or natural bait. When jerked or popped

Captain Bob Fuston began running charters in Port Mansfield in 1981. Known by most as "the Red Bandana," Fuston has made a living wading through rafts of redfish and schools of speckled trout.

with the rod, the cork causes commotion on the surface while the bait swims and darts underneath. The Mansfield Mauler is a proven method on all bay estuaries from Texas to Florida, though some companies have "copy-catted" the design.

"I came up with the bait because I had a 92-year-old man who fished with me twice a month. He had a hard time working a shrimp tail, so I came up with the Mauler," said Fuston.

The bait got its name in 1985 when outdoor writer Ken Grissom of the now defunct *Houston Post* called the bait "3M" (Marvelous Mansfield Mauler).

"Grissom had some good fishing trips using the bait and got excited about it," Fuston said. "We had a trout eat the shrimp tail then tried to eat the Mauler as well. I shortened the name a little."

Fuston believes the absence of industry contributes to the size of Port Mansfield fish: "Port Mansfield is strictly a fishing town. We have no industry to pollute our shorelines, and no pesticides to run in our water."

Though most travel to Mansfield for its endless acres of grass flats or easy access to blue water, animal lovers can see a petting zoo of Texas wildlife.

Ten hours of wading will wane the energy of any angler. Shuler's Get-A-Way Adventures Lodge hosts a bubbling hot tub for worn legs and aching shoulders. I plopped in the warm whirlpool one afternoon and watched the sun set over the harbor. As I watched the avian activity of gulls diving on baitfishes in the channel, a larger bird glided across the channel.

Surely not," I thought to myself. Yet, when the Rio Grande hen landed in Shuler's yard, my suspicions where confirmed.

"There are turkeys all over town," Shuler said. "The gobblers will strut on the highways in the spring."

Shuler and his wife, Shirley, run an impressive hunting and fishing camp on the waterfront of Port Mansfield. When I say "camp," do not take that literally. The lodge sleeps more than 30 people, prepares three hearty meals a day, provides comfortable sleeping quarters with private baths, has a deck overlooking the water to have your morning coffee, a hot tub to relax and enjoy the sunset, a private dock to moor boats and load anglers, and a lighted pier for night fishing.

The most popular attraction, other than fishing, is the old "Outpost" gas and convenience store at dusk. There, potential Boone and Crockett bucks warily walk out of the brush to browse on a bounty of golden corn fed by the storeowners. Vehicles begin to take a spot in the parking lot 30 minutes before sunset to catch a glimpse of the famed South Texas *Muy Grande*." Photo opportunities abound. For most, this is the closest they will ever be to a wild white-tailed deer.

"Most know how good the fishing can be, then realize how special Mansfield is after seeing the deer and turkey," Shuler said.

Fuston does not see the huge schools of redfish or half-acre pods of mullet like he did in the 1980s. He attributes it to boats running the shallow shorelines, and an increase in fishing pressure. "When I started down here, I ran a 25-foot Robalo. I found every bar out here with my lower unit. Shallowsport scooters and other flats boats have made life easier for the fisherman, though we may be doing harm to the fishing and sea grasses by running so shallow. I used to be able to find herds of redfish, and you could throw a brown paper bag out there and catch fish. I think the boat traffic is scattering the fish."

Still, according to Fuston, a bad day in Port Mansfield can be better than a good day elsewhere. The wind does starch the flags at times, but on more than one occasion, I have caught fish with Shuler during winds in which I would have not even considered hitching the boat on the upper coast.

"With all the changes in the world, we still have a good fishing hole here, as good as anywhere on the coast," said Fuston.

According to Shuler, tarpon in the 4- to 6-foot range gang at the mouth of the channel in the summertime: "We hooked the same tarpon nine times off our pier last summer. There are many tarpon that use the harbor."

Several major airlines service the Harlingen International Airport, less than an hour from Port Mansfield. Though lodging is limited, first-class accommodations are available.

1 Gladys' Hole (GPS N26 48.730, W97 29.400) is a popular wading spot of sand and mud just west of the Land Cut. Fish traveling the Land Cut often use the cove to stage and feed before heading through East Cut to the Gulf of Mexico. Topwaters, Corky, MirrOlure, soft plastic, and live baits regularly take fish. Expect to catch trout, redfish, flounder, and black drum.

The entire shoreline west of the Intracoastal is solid grass beds. When the tide rolls in, work in waist- to knee-deep water. When it heads out, work from your chest to neck and cast as far as you can with soft plastics. Shuler likes glow or bone Trout Killers.

2 The New Fence Shoreline (GPS N26 42.910, W97 27.901), **3** Oak Mott (GPS N26 41.300, W97 27.100), and **4** Little Jack's Hole (GPS N26 40.920, W97 26.853) are great topwater spots. I caught over 30 trout there one morning on a redheaded chartreuse Top Dog Jr. Capt. Talasek's grandson, Blain, coaxed a 9-pounder that same morning. Very seldom have I fished the west shoreline and not caught fish.

5 Butcher's Island (GPS N26 38.125, W97 23.147), **6** Dubb's Island (GPS N26 43.690, W97 25.803), and **7** Wagner Bar (GPS N26 40.952, W97 25.301) are good at high tide. When the water begins to rush out of East Cut, fish the channel running parallel with both islands.

The area north of **8** East Cut (GPS N26 34.620, W97 22.200) is shallow, hard sand and holds fish on the incoming and outgoing tide. It is the first place fish hit on an incoming tide, and the last place it swims on an outgoing tide before reaching East Cut. Fish it as you would San Luis Pass, Pass Cavallo, and Rollover Pass. The area is partic-

My good friends Capt. Sam Heaton of Minn Kota and Bill Wallace of Power Pro grin before releasing a tarpon back to the Indian River on the east coast of Florida. South Padre jetty anglers do get several shots at "poons" during the summer.

ularly good in the fall when bull redfish and flounder roam the flats on their way to the ocean to spawn.

9 South of East Cut (GPS N26 33.601, W97 22.252) is an endless flat where I have caught many redfish on topwaters. Get out of the boat and walk if you see mullet flipping. Eventually, you will find the reds. Let a partner drop you off, take the boat half a mile away, then get out and wade away from you. When you get to the boat, get in, hopscotch another half-mile, and let your partner wade to it. This way, you will not wade a mile from the boat and have to walk another mile to retrieve it.

South of Port Mansfield on the west shoreline is West Bay. All of the shoreline is wadable, though it can get muddy in spots. Most prefer to drift this area. If you wade it, keep your weight on your toes and pick your feet up so not to bog down.

LOWER LAGUNA MADRE (SEE MAP ON PAGE 124) (ARROYO COLORADO TO PORT ISABEL)

There is no telling what you will catch in this South Texas estuary. Snook, tarpon, trout, redfish, flounder, and black drum are regulars. Many choose to drift the ominous grass beds, but for those who like to stalk big trout, this is your place.

The spoil islands lining the Intracoastal are all potential wading spots for trout and flounder. Be aware that some of the areas are boggy and tough to wade. These islands pay big dividends thanks to their proximity to the deep channel. Live shrimp, glow D.O.A. Shrimp, or topwaters produce worked on the drop-offs.

Bronze brutes, are suckers for topwaters in the lower Laguna Madre.

1 Green Island (GPS N26 23.561, W97 19.200) and **2** Three Islands (GPS N26 16.951, W97 16.121) have grass beds and a nearby channel for deep-water jigging. The **3** Cullen Bay shore (GPS N26 13.211, W97 18.751) near Gabrielson Island is sand and mud. **4** Stover Point (GPS N26 11.302, W97 17.101) and **5** Airport Cove (GPS N26 10.151, W97 18.003) are a mixture of grass and mud.

ARROYO COLORADO
Coose Hill
Cayo Atascoso
St M .5.
R "10"
Ra Ref
SM
Spoil Area
Spoil Area
Arroyo Colorado Cutoff
Ramp
Tr
North Point
Laguna Atascosa
National Wildlife Refuge
(protected area: 50 CFR 32.63)
SM
Worth Point
RINCON
BUENA
VISTA
Colorado Island
EL MORRO
Horse Island
R N "8"
G C "7"
Shoaling PA
(10 ft rep June 1990)
Shoaling PA
(7 ft rep June 1990)
R N "6"
Spoil Area
Spoil Area
Spoil Area
Mud Flats
Area subject to inundation
SM
Fl R
Ra Ref
Spoil Area
R "200"
R "204"
R "208"
R "207"
Ra Ref
C "205A"
C "205"
C "209"
C "211"
C "213"
C "201A"
C "201"
C "199"
C "197A"
C "1
Platform (ruins)
Platform (ruins)
Platforms (ruins)
Subm
pile
Subm
pile
Subm
piling
Subm
piling
Spoil Area
Shoaling PA
(9 ft rep June 1990)
QR 17ft 4M "212"
G C "5"
GR "A"
QR 17ft 3M "4"
St M
Platform (ruins)
R "10"
Ra Ref
Subm
piling
G C "13" C "11"
Fl G 2.5s 17ft 3M "9"
645
Shoaling PA
(10 ft rep June 1990)
G C "7"
G C "5"
C "3"
Spoil Area
Spoil Area
Spoil Area
LAGUNA
1
Green Island

R "12"
Ra Ref
ARROYO
CITY
G "11"
Ra Ref
Chubby Island
Mud
Island
Hawk
Island
Mullet Island
INTRACOASTAL WATERWAY
MADRE
Spoil Area
Spoil Area
Spoil Area
Spoil Area
St M
St M
St M
R "192"
G "191"
C "193"
C "193A"
640
G "189A"
C "189"
R "188"
G "185"
C "185"
Subm
piling
FI G 4s 17ft 4M "187"
Platform
(ruins)
G "183"
Ra Ref
C "181"
R "184"
PA
FI R 4s 17ft 4M "180"
Ra Ref
G "179"
Ra Ref
Platform
(ruins)
C "177A"
G "177"
C "177"
G "175"
Subm
piling
C "173A"
G
Subm pile
C "173"
Subm
pile
Platform
(ruins)
R "176"
R "1
FI G 4s
Ra Ref
635
M
M
CAUTION
Many uncharted rocks exist in Laguna Madre.

BUENA VISTA ROAD
OLD RUNWAY ROAD
BUEN
VISTA
Stover Cove
SM
Coyote
Point
SM
Laguna
de los
Patos
BAYSIDE DRIVE
3
Gatlin Island
Gabriel
Island
Barclay
Island
El Rea
Bay
Stover
Point
SM
4
El Realito Peninsula
L A G U N A
Z
Piling
Spoil Area
Spoil Area
Spoil Area
R "50"
Ra Ref
R "58"
Ra Ref
R "68"
Ra Ref
R "76"
Ra Ref
R "84"
Ra Ref
St M
655
PA
Platform
(ruins)
Pile
Subm
piling
3 Subm piles
Platform (ruins)
Subm
piling
G
C "85"
Fl G 2.5s 17ft 3M "83"
G
C "81"
G
C "79"
G
C "77"
Fl G 4s 17ft 3M "75"
G
C "73"
G
C "71"
G
C "69"
Fl G 6s 17ft 4M "67"
Platform
(ruins) C "65"
G
C "63"
G
C "61"
G
C "59"
Fl G 4s 17ft 4M "57"
G
C "55"
G
C "53"
C "51"
Platforms
Fl G
CAUTION
Many uncharted rocks exist in Laguna Madre.

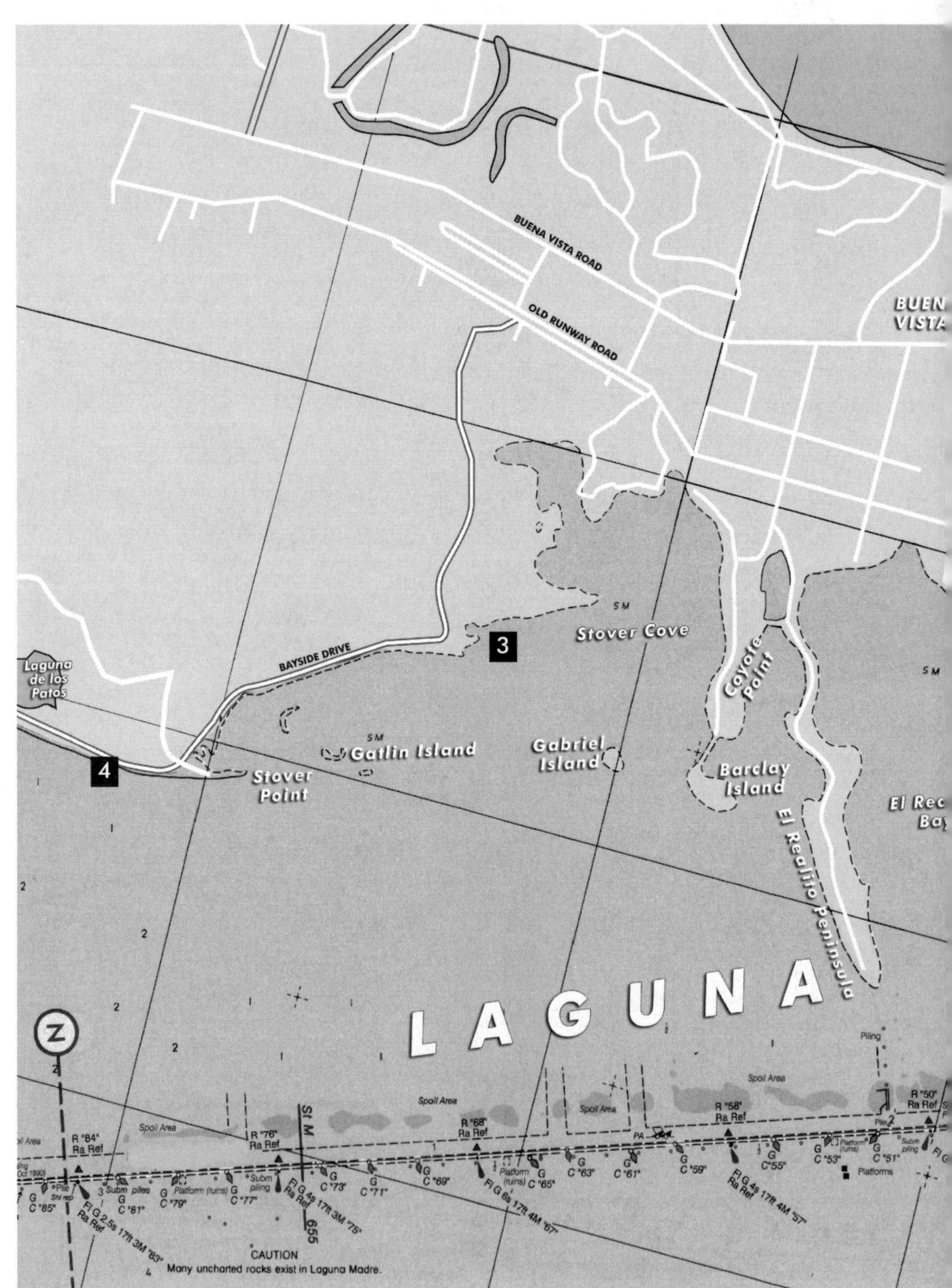

126

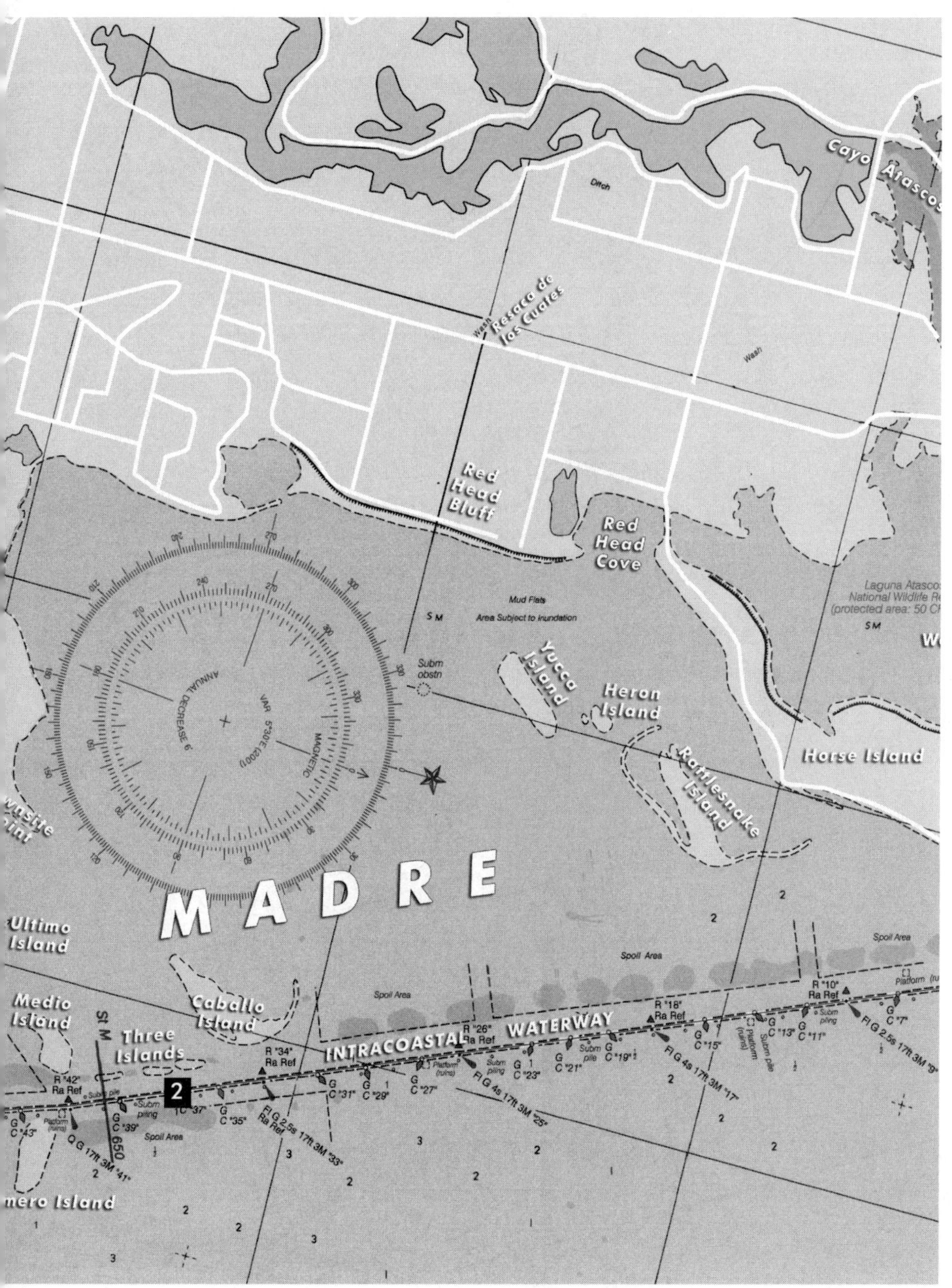
Cayo Atascos
Ditch
Resaca de los Cuates
Wash
Wash
Red Head Bluff
Red Head Cove
Laguna Atasco
National Wildlife R
(protected area: 50 C
SM
W
Mud Flats
Area Subject to inundation
SM
Subm obstn
Yucca Island
Heron Island
Rattlesnake Island
Horse Island
ANNUAL DECREASE 6'
VAR 5°55'E (2001)
MAGNETIC
M A D R E
Ultimo Island
Medio Island
Caballo Island
Three Islands
SM
Spoil Area
Spoil Area
Spoil Area
Spoil Area
INTRACOASTAL WATERWAY
R "10" Ra Ref
Platform (ru
R "18" Ra Ref
R "26" Ra Ref
G "7"
Fl G 2.5s 17ft 3M "9"
G C "11"
G C "13"
Subm pile
Platform (ruins)
G C "15"
Fl G 4s 17ft 3M "17"
Subm G pile C "19"
G C "21"
G C "23"
Platform (ruins)
Fl G 4s 17ft 3M "25"
R "34" Ra Ref
G C "27"
G C "29"
Fl G 2.5s 17ft 3M "33"
G C "31"
2
R "42" Ra Ref
Subm pile
G C "37"
G C "35"
G C "43"
Platform (ruins)
Subm piling
G C "39"
QG 17ft 3M "41"
Spoil Area
nero Island

Isabel-
ron County
rt
TANK
BAYSIDE DRIVE
Sand and mud
5
Sand and mud
Moranco
Blanco
6
Holly
Beach
CENTERLINE
ROAD
HOLLY
BEACH ROAD
City of
Port Isabel
Reservoir
HOLLY BEACH ROAD
Sand and mud
Laguna Vista
Cove
7
Loma de
la Grulla
Platform
FM
510
Platform
El
Tular
SH
100
L A G U N A
CAUTION
Survey platforms, signs, pipes, piles, and
stakes, some submerged, may exist along the
maintained channels. Piles and platforms are not
charted where they interfere with a light symbol.
TANK
Laguna
Vista
Cable Area
Laguna
Largo

INTRACOSTAL WATERWAY
G C "85"
Pile
Subm pile
G C "87"
Subm pile
Subm pile
G C "89"
Platform (ruins)
Shoaling (rep Oct 1990)
"92"
Ra Ref
Subm piling
QG 17ft 3M "91"
Platform (ruins)
G C "93"
Subm piling
G C "95"
Subm pile
Subm pile
G C "97"
Subm pile
Ra
Subm pile
Fl G 2.5s 17ft 3M "99"
Subm pile
G C "101"
Subm pile
Subm pile
G C "103"
Subm pile
G C "105"
R "108"
Ra Ref
Subm pile
Fl G 4s 17ft 3M "107"
Ra Ref
G C "109"
Subm pile
G C "111"
Subm pile
G C "113"
Subm pile
R "116"
Ra Ref
Fl G 6s 17ft 4M "115"
Ra Ref
G C "117"
Subm piles
G C "119"
Platform (ruins)
Subm pile
G C "121"
Subm pile
R "124"
Ra Ref
Fl G 6s 17ft 4M "123"
PA
Sign PA
Cable Area
Subm pile
G C "125"
G C "127"
Subm pile
G C "129"
R "132"
Ra Ref
Fl G 4s 17ft 3M "131"
Ra Ref
Platform (ruins)
CAUTION
Many uncharted rocks exist
in Laguna Madre
so M
MAGNETIC
VAR 5°30'E (2002)
ANNUAL DECREASE 6'
MADRE
PADRE ISLAND
PADRE ISLAND BLVD.
GULF OF MEXICO
Area subject to inundation
Andy Bowie
Park
TANK
Mkrs
so M
Mkrs
5 ft rep 1974
5 ft rep 1994
Mkrs

Though this snook was caught in Stuart, Florida by Capt. Mark Nichols of DOA Lures, anglers in South Texas around South Padre Island do land quite a few line-siders.

6 Holly Beach (GPS N26 08.651, W97 17.302) and **7** Laguna Vista Cove (GPS N26 07.221, W97 17.823) consistently cough up big trout. My friend, Danno Wise, a local scribe and editor of *Coastal Outdoors* magazine, lives in Laguna Vista and confirms reports. You can hear his weekly radio show, including fishing and hunting reports, on FM 95.3.

If you read in your local newspaper the Texas Parks and Wildlife Department Coastal Fishing Report (www.tpwd.state.tx.us), which I have written for the past six years, you will be amazed how many times Holly Beach and Airport Cove have been included in the report.

Incidentally, you can read reports dating back years on the website.

Obviously, these are not all the wading spots available in lower Laguna Madre. There are many more grass beds, sand flats, and muddy-bottomed locales, most unnamed and kept quiet by the locals.

Chapter Seven

Pass It On

Wading the passes

Crystal Beach is a rendezvous point for hundreds of teenagers when summer arrives. Bikini-clad blondes hanging from Jeep roll bars signal the start of a three-month break from the books. Bronze skin, blue eyes, and sand between my toes are all fond teenage memories. However, Bolivar Peninsula is more than just pretty girls and endless beaches. It is the home of Rollover Pass, a consistent rod-bending locale for countless peripatetic anglers.

My parents first introduced me to Rollover Pass in 1980, when they rented a beach house on Bolivar. We sat on lawn chairs and coolers loaded with sandwiches and snacks, and duped blue crabs with chicken necks tied to a string.

Years later, my parents bought me a set of wheels and, as my fishing prowess grew, I began wading the bay side of the Pass. Armed with pearl and red-tailed tandem-rigged Lit'l Fishies that you could buy only from Granny's Bait Camp, Texas Chicken, and pink or white 51M

MirrOlures, I shouldered next to other fishermen standing in the shallows, casting into the deeper gut that funneled the incoming tide.

Toss up-current and let the tide swim your offering through the channel. *Thump!* Two others and I would be bowed up on angry speckled trout when the fishing was good—six or seven at a time when it was great.

Texas passes are fish magnets, aquatic highways for fish entering and exiting the Gulf of Mexico. They are the lifeblood of bay estuaries, providing assiduous flushing of new organisms and marine life. Sabine Pass, Rollover Pass, San Luis Pass, Bolivar Roads, and Pass Cavallo are all established wading venues ready to cough up a bounty.

SABINE PASS

Sabine's extensive jetty system is the boundary line between Texas and Louisiana. Access is by boat-only, though the outside beaches adjacent to the pass provide ample wading opportunities.

Huge redfish and black drum fall to finger mullet and cracked blue crab. The rocks give up sheepshead up to double-digits on live shrimp under a popping cork, or free-lined deeper in the water column. Sharks are an option for hooks baited with fish or cut-bait.

Specks are often the main attraction on the rocks. Boaters will utilize a trolling motor and work parallel to the granite. Glow and pumpkinseed Bass Assassins, Trout Killers, Sand Eels, Hogies, Cocahoe Minnows, and Mister Twisters are solid soft plastic choices. Chrome Rat-L-Traps, Hoginars, slow-sinking MirrOlures, and Corky are good for suspending fish.

Topwaters such as Top Dogs, She Dogs, Super Spooks, and Skitter Walks provide quite a bang. That's right, surface plugs in the deep waters of the pass. Cast as close to the rocks as possible then dog-walk it back to the boat. If the current is moving and baitfishes are present, trout will surge from the depths to engulf your rattling fake.

If you wade the east side of the pass, a Louisiana license in required. Stay on the west side of the pass if you have only a Texas license.

Bull redfish use the pass throughout the year. Big black drum show up in the spring and regularly eat crab and mullet. Do not be surprised to catch a big speck if you toss a feisty finger mullet or pogey near the rocks.

Directions: From Houston, take IH-10 east to Winnie, then Highway 73 to Port Arthur. In Port Arthur, take the Martin Luther King exit (Highway 82) and go over the bridge to Pleasure Island. Head south to the causeway bridge. There is a public boat ramp there.

ROLLOVER PASS

Rollover cuts right through Highway 87. The pass is accessible by ferry from Galveston, and by way of High Island from the mainland. Anglers can drive their car over the pass then pull into the parking lot and fish. A fence borders the deep channel to prevent people falling in and getting swept out to sea.

Mud minnows and bright-colored jigs tipped with shrimp are effective flounder bait in spring and autumn. Redfish and black drum are year-round players on finger mullet and crab.

Waders work Rollover Bay, a section of East Galveston Bay divided by the Intracoastal Waterway on the incoming tide and the Gulf side of the pass on the outgoing. Beware of swift currents associated with a falling tide. Rollover Pass is a narrow gut, and just like pinching a water hose, when you constrict the flow, water pressure increases. Extreme caution is advised and a life preserver should be worn at all times when fishing the Gulf side.

Waders tossing tandem-rigged Little Fishies or D.O.A. Shrimp usually score in the spring and summer on specks and reds. Let it sink to the bottom and give it a jig. Flounder will attack in the spring and fall.

Bull redfish work the pass throughout the year. Cracked crab, finger mullet, live shrimp, Carolina-rigged croaker, mullet, or pogies normally get eaten.

Directions: From Houston, take IH-10 east. Take the Highway 73 exit (No. 828) then head south on Highway 124. When you reach High Island, head west on Highway 87. There will be a sign that says, "Rollover Pass." From Galveston on FM 3005/Highway 87, turn onto Ferry Road/Highway 87N and take the free ferry to the Bolivar Peninsula. Continue on Highway 87 until you see the "Rollover Pass" sign.

BOLIVAR ROADS

When the Gulf is right, the Bolivar Pocket is as good a wading spot is there is on the Texas Coast, especially for large trout. Just this past summer, my friend Mike Wille duped a 9-pounder with a topwater, then released it back to the brine. There are countless other reports of big fish over the years. This spot is particularly popular because it is easily accessible by vehicle. Wille likes to take his kayak to cover more ground. "I caught my fish in off-colored water," he said. "I have had some good days there over the years, throwing topwaters."

By boat, you can launch at the ramp near the north jetty and head through the boat cut, then anchor in the Pocket and wade. The area is composed of mud and grass, and is best on an incoming tide. Pluggers do well with MirrOlures, Corky, She Dogs, and Super Spooks.

Live-baiters better hang on when popping a live shrimp or free-lining a golden croaker.

On the south side of the jetty is Fort Travis Flats. This, too, is easily accessible by tires, and is best on an incoming tide. When tide is falling, work deeper with soft plastics and diving plugs. These spots are especially good when nagging westerly winds muddy up your favorite spots in the bay.

Directions: From Houston, take IH-10 east and take the Highway 73 exit (No. 828), then head south on Highway 124. When you reach High Island, head west on Highway 87. When you see the ferry signs, you know you are close. From Galveston on FM 3005/Highway 87, turn onto Ferry Road/Highway 87N and take the free ferry to the Bolivar Peninsula. When you get off the ferry, look for the road leading to the boat ramp. If you are on foot, get out of your vehicle and start wading.

SAN LUIS PASS

More anglers frequent San Luis than any pass in Texas, probably due to its proximity to a major metropolitan city like Houston, and easy access from Galveston, Freeport, and nearby Lake Jackson. Its waters are the life of West Galveston, Christmas, and Bastrop bays, offering superb wading in the spring and summer.

When tides run green in the summer, pelagic species like kingfish and ling will strike a gold spoon or 808 MirrOlure. Flounder, redfish, and black drum take natural baits, and trout are suckers for topwaters, jerkbaits, and live shrimp beneath an Alameda cork.

San Luis Pass claims more lives due to drowning than any other locale on the Texas coast. Wear a life preserver and know the area you are shuffling. If the current is too strong, retreat to shallower water. No fish is worth your life.

Friend and fellow scribe Doug Pike makes the drive regularly when the ocean is calm: "I can get there from downtown Houston in an hour and 15 minutes. I will dial up the 'surf cam' on my computer and take a look at the waves, then make my decision to head south. I have had some great days at the pass."

Directions: From Houston, take Highway 288S toward Lake Jackson, then merge onto Highway 332E. Look for the signs that point to Surfside. Go through Surfside and look for the bridge connecting Surfside to Galveston Island.

PASS CAVALLO

Cavallo is a boat-access-only pass near Port O'Connor that feeds West Matagorda and nearby Espiritu Santo bays. Once a premier tarpon spot, the pass has since silted and is not navigable for large boats with deep running skegs. However, bay boats have no problem entering the pass when light winds allow.

The beach surrounding the pass is awesome when emerald tides persist in the summer. Trout gang up in the first and second guts, and will eat an array of hardware. Natural baits, including croaker (a Port O'Connor favorite) do not last long in the brine foam.

The bay side of the pass is equally impressive. The south shoreline of Matagorda Island divides the Gulf and the bay. It is littered with grass pockets and sandy undulations. Consistent tide flow ushers mullet and menhaden onto the flats—and where there is bait, there are usually fish.

A few summers ago, my friend Rodney Corporron jumped a 4-foot tarpon on the flats while wading for specks. The area holds so much summertime promise I regularly trek from my home port of

Matagorda Harbor to Pass Cavallo, a 32-mile boat ride one way. By land, it is an hour and a half journey, but in my center-console Pathfinder, it takes a little over 50 minutes

Directions: From Houston, take US-59S to El Campo, then turn left onto Highway 71. When you get to Highway 35, take a right and head toward Palacios and Port Lavaca. Take U.S. 87 to FM 1862, then take it to Port O'Connor. There are many boat ramps in town.

TIDES ARE THE KEY

Whether you wade, drift, or walk the rocks, degree of tidal movement plays a key role in fishing success when plugging a pass. Generally, the pros work the channel side (inside) of a jetty on an outgoing tide, and the Gulf side (outside) on the incoming. However, passes like Rollover, San Luis, and Pass Cavallo do not have a jetty. For these, work the bay side on the incoming and the Gulf side on the ongoing.

Tide times listed in various tide prediction charts usually have a number indicating how much water will move at high or low tide. A number of 0.8 or better indicates vigorous tidal movement. Lunar phases dictate the tides, and days that fall five days either side of a full or new moon witness the strongest water fluctuation.

Texas passes are exceptional saline venues, Nevertheless, at times these spots are treacherous to fish on foot. Water is a powerful beast. Know when to take a dip and when to cancel the trip. You want to make it back to shore to boast to your friends.

Wading a pass as opposed to a placid bay requires different gear. For starters, a life vest is cheap insurance if shifting sand and an angry ocean engulfs you. If the bulkiness of a preserver is a turn-off, try a CO_2 vest that inflates with the pull of a cord. They are less restrictive and fit over the shoulders or around the waist like a fanny pack. Stearns and SOSpenders are popular brands.

Wading belts with pliers or your favorite fish tool attached are also a plus. Try the 5-inch NuMark or Wade-Aid belt for better back support on daylong wades. Ditch the cord-like stringers with the float on the end and the plastic tackle box in the pouch. With as little as two fish threaded, stringers become fish-ka-bobs for sharks. If you wade a bumpy surf, there is a good chance a breaker will come crashing down on you, loosening the reins of the pouch. I lost $50 worth of plugs once to an agitated surf. A better choice would be a floating donut-type net to protect your fish. Most come with a small box attached to the float to carry extra plugs, jigheads, and leader material.

If you don't enjoy country and western music, learn the Texas two-step anyway. Passes are loaded with stingrays and one false, clumsy step could send a bacteria-infected barb through your lower extremities. Shuffle and take your time. Invest in a pair of stingray boots (ForEverLast or Hodgman). Though they are not 100 percent "stingray proof," often they deflect or soften the blow.

Chapter Eight

Wading the Surf:

...to the ocean, white with foam

My first heart-pounding, water-thrashing, toilet bowl-flushing, surf-fishing blowup was eight miles down old Highway 87 near High Island. I was a teenager on that summer day in the mid 1980s, devoid of a powerboat and the greenbacks for its upkeep. Yet, I did have wheels—all ambitious anglers need when the ocean calms and turns emerald.

While long-boarders pray for steady, southerly winds, surf-fishers begin tinkering with casting equipment when the weatherman forecasts light northerly winds and beach water temps reach 75 degrees. When the surf is right, go. Put off mowing the yard, reschedule the doctor appointment, or come down with an overnight sickness. The Gulf of Mexico may not be flat tomorrow, and not bearable again for several days. The surf-running angler is at the mercy of the wind and barometric pressure.

Days when winds are light yet the surf is bouncy and rough coincide with a low barometer. Offshore ground swells build and form waves on the beachfront sandbars. Catch a day when winds are still and the barometric pressure is higher than 29.80, and the Gulf becomes a huge, tranquil pond.

Determining which stretch of beach to fish is tough unless you know where to look. At high tide, comb the first gut. Flipping mullet and hopping shrimp are strong indicators of fish in the area. Birds hovering over millions of schooling menhaden are a safe bet, too. Low tide conditions pull baitfishes past the first bar and into the second and

My friend and fishing buddy, Eddie Sullivan, attempts to land a seven-pound trout in the Matagorda surf at sunrise.

third guts. Follow the bait and you find the fish.

Breaking waves tell you where the bars are located. The swells build in the deeper guts and crest on the shallower humps or sand bars. If the ocean is dead calm, look for the lighter spots in the sea of green that mark the bars. Darker hues indicate the guts.

Go-to baits for the surf are a matter of opinion. Throw what gives you the most confidence. My preference is a She Dog—all day. Others with less patience opt for jerk-, swimming, or natural baits like live shrimp or croaker.

"I will throw the topwater at times in the surf, but the bait that catches most of my fish is the Bass Assassin. It's hard to beat red shad," said Capt. Bill Pustejovsky.

Trout Killers, Hogies, Norton Sand Eels, D.O.A. Shrimp, and spoons also catch fish consistently. Popular colors include pumpkinseed/chartreuse, plum, fire tiger, glow, electric chicken, lime-treuse, and pepper/chartreuse.

Pack light for the beach. A shirt with double pockets will hold extra jigs and soft plastics. A cap or shoulder box will settle your plugs. Tackle boxes put in the pouch of a wading belt are just one crashing wave away from becoming property of the sea. It took me one trip and the loss of a dozen of my favorite topwaters to brand that into my brain. I made some angler happy at high tide the following day.

GIVE A RIP ABOUT RIPS

A word to the wise: When tides and currents are so strong they hinder your mobility in the surf, retreat to the beach. An angry sea has no conscience. A limit of specks or a shot at a 30-incher is not worth risking you life. Trust me. I have first-hand knowledge. The Almighty mercifully gave me a pardon on consecutive days two years ago.

My wife worries when I plunge into the Gulf of Mexico or wade close to a pass, vowing to block the door if I cannot find at least a partner to accompany me. At times, she wonders if she should put on violet costume and dot her back with spots to garner the attention I give speckled trout.

I made a vow: Never again will I jeopardize our marriage or

At high tide you can literally stand in shin-deep water and cast to the first gut and catch speckled trout.

make her a widow with my wide-eyed, foolish ambitions of tide-runners. Never again will I plunge into the saline foam without a life-preserving device.

I intend to keep my promise—although, I would like to see her in that suit.

Anytime the surf is green to the beach, if your heart pumps saltwater like mine, you sprint to the sand with plugs a-flying and soft plastics a-wiggling. Something innate tells you that you must drive or fly down the beach in your jeep or four-wheeled drive truck going "ninety to nothing." You can't help it.

When you get there, you are like a gunslinger, fastening your wading belt and stringer with your surface-running bullets attached around the hip. Then, like the beloved soldiers that stormed the beach at Normandy, you paddle for the outer bars to tangle with your favorite marine life, not giving the slightest concern to the mood of the ocean.

The sea's attitude at Matagorda Beach five summers ago was full of cross currents and riptides, characteristic of a low and dropping tide. Hurling my black Top Dog as far as the spool would allow, the plug would always return to my right as the currents moved in the direction of Mitchell's Cut in Sargent.

To lighten the wading workload, I worked the beach with the current as the occasional afternoon blowup kept my attention. Commotion on the surface caught my eye when schools of nervous mullet began flipping and bounding from below the water line. I edged in that direction.

Slurp! Then I felt the weight of the fish and the bend of rod as a wave blocked the view of the hookup. Not a bad 22-inch trout, but I wanted more. I got more. More than I could handle. Suddenly images of arm-length sea trout angrily engulfing an artificial mullet imitation were not of prime concern. Instead, getting back to a sandy, hard bottom without swallowing half the Gulf was now my main concern. My wide-eyed, big trout ambitions had led me into a riptide, with my father watching the whole thing from 20 yards away. I should have recognized the signs: no waves rolling, ripples, wakes moving from all directions, and the distinct drop-off or hole my feet felt as they shuffled across the ocean floor.

I began sidestroking with my left arm and scissor-kicking with my legs, trying not to panic and draw the attention and boiling blood pressure of my father. I knew what he would do if he thought I was in trouble: come after me. Then there would be two in the rip.

I used only my left arm because my right was keeping my reel out of the salt. That was very dumb and could have cost me the battle. Consequently, the water floated my hat a few times. Relaxing my body, I let the current float me out of the rip and then I swam back to higher ground.

Close call.

You would think I learned something. The next morning on the west beach of Matagorda, I saw bait activity again. Casting amid a pod of finfish, my topwater met a bang after only a couple of twitches. The current was again moving to the right, this time toward the mouth of the Colorado River. Naturally, my body adhered to the current and went with the flow as I fought the fish.

Oblivious to anything besides landing the fish, I didn't notice the water pushing me into another riptide. This time, I felt the drop-off and was able to fight the current and keep one foot on the higher bar while working astern to avoid the calamity of the deeper hole

Another close call.

Once again, the good Lord was watching over me. He was probably thinking: *How many times will I have to reach out and save you before you take a few precautions?* It is security to know that you have the Creator on your side, but He gave me a brain with the intent I would use it.

Inflatable suspender-type life preservers, mentioned in another chapter, are sufficiently comfortable and unobtrusive to do away with whatever excuses you might have for not wearing one in the surf. Nonetheless, if you just refuse to wear a life saving device, purchase a floating Styrofoam donut stringer, sometimes called a Do-net. It will keep your catch out of the mouths of sharks, while serving as a life buoy if you get into trouble.

If you prefer a wading belt, the Wade-Aid belt (1-888-WADE-AID) has foam back support that is also buoyant. Although the belt is not Coast Guard Approved, it works like the old water ski belt that fits around the waist.

The surf does get this flat at times, but not very often.

Water is a powerful animal. If it does grab you and takes your footing away and you are not wearing a flotation device, the best thing to do is stay calm, relax, and let the buoyancy of your body float you back to the top. I learned this first hand in the rapids on a tubing trip during my college years.

Surf-waders or anglers wading near a pass should always take precautions and wear life saving flotation devices. I was blessed and got a second chance two days in a row. However, my baseball mind of playing percentages tells me that three strikes and I could be out. You can bet I will be protected the next time the surf turns flat green.

The best advice is to use common sense. If crosscurrents and tidal exchanges are too strong, do not fight it. Get out of the pool. No speckled trout or bull redfish is worth a life. The ocean does not always practice catch-and-release.

BE PATIENT

Body functions slow in darkness. This is due primarily because the eyes are our guide. When a human cannot see clearly, he is cautious of what lies ahead. Hence, many a dog-walking aficionado's downfall is working the plastic mullet too quickly.

Tossing topwaters , like this MirrOlure She Dog, makes up 99 percent of my fishing in the surf.

Eyes relay messages back to the hands and arms when working a bait in the daylight. The impatient's eyes tell him to speed up, while the relaxed angler's eyeballs say to methodically work the imitation.

It has happened to each of us at one time or another: A trout emerges and thrashes your Top Dog, spraying water like a fat kid doing a belly-buster from the high dive. Startled, your first reaction is to jerk back and set the trebles. Yet, when you heave, all you feel is the weight of the heavy salt air. Pros will say to wait stoically until you feel the weight of the fish in your hands, then yank the rod. Let the fish hook itself before driving the hooks deeper. This calls for extreme patience, and at times a barbiturate-like demeanor.

In the dark, there is no feedback from the eyes. The ears relay movement and motion by the melodious sound of the round ball bearing banging inside the plug. The fisherman learns to rely on his tactile senses.

It still gets my heart pumping in the predawn darkness to hear the toilet flush on my topwater, then feel the line peeling from my drag. Trust me, it is worth the "way too early" alarm.

MILES AND MILES OF SAND

The appealing attribute of summer surf-fishing is the endless miles of beach accessible by foot. When the ocean is right, the playing field is level for peripatetic anglers and those with center consoles.

The upper coast from Sabine to San Luis Pass is the easiest to reach by foot. The entire stretch is accessible by four wheels, except a few miles of private beach in Galveston.

Old Highway 87 runs parallel with the beach from High Island to Sabine Pass. Though Hurricane Alicia closed the road in 1983, it remains drivable at reduced speeds. When traveling under headlights, be aware of massive holes in the already eroded pavement. Do not get in a hurry. Allow time for safe driving when working this stretch of beach.

Take a right (west) turn at High Island, and Crystal Beach runs all the way to the Bolivar Ferry. Sandwiched between is Rollover Pass, an established wading mecca. On an incoming tide, fish the bay side. Work the surf side on the outgoing.

Jeeps and other 4x4s are a great vehicles to run the beach and jump out and wade.

Cross the ferry and there is foot-friendly beach from Galveston to Surfside. San Luis Pass, which feeds West Galveston Bay, is another wading hotspot. Strong currents make fishing treacherous at times. Play it safe. If tides are moving too swift, back up and get in shin-deep water.

Middle coast beaches extend from Sargent to Port Aransas. Anglers can drive to the beach in Sargent and work to the east and west. Mitchell's Cut is a couple of miles to the west. This stretch of beach is not always groomed and maintained; a 4X4 is essential.

Highway 60 runs through Matagorda and ends at the mouth of the Colorado River. This is the last stretch of Texas beach accessible by vehicle until crossing the ferry at Port Aransas. The east beach of Matagorda is almost 19 miles long, ending at Mitchell's Cut. The county maintains the first 2.4 miles, but a 4X4 is critical to fish past this point. High shell banks and deeper guts appear farther down the beach, providing cleaner, greener water. Historically, the Mitchell's Cut area hosts bigger trout.

Beaches from Port Aransas to Padre Island are frequent stops for surf-pluggers on foot. Once your tires leave Highway 361, the beach is not accessible by car until South Padre Island.

If anglers are crowding your favorite ocean spot and a boat is at your disposal, the beaches from west of the Matagorda jetty to the north jetty of Port Aransas, and the Padre Island National Seashore in Corpus Christi to East Cut in Port Mansfield, are often desolate.

When tides are falling and riptides persist, fishing the surf from a boat is the ticket. Here, Capt. Melvin Talasek nets a fish for a customer while drifting the surf.

"There are some good fish in our surf," said Capt. Bruce Shuler of Port Mansfield. "It is untouched by light tackle anglers because our fishing is so good inshore during the summer."

Working the beachfront by boat never crossed my mind until I moved to Bay City and made Matagorda my home port. Thirty-year pro Capt. Melvin Talasek took me to the surf by boat six summers ago. Two hours into the trip, I was hooked.

I admit seasickness is one of my weaknesses. I have had some nauseating days when seas were rolling with 2- to 3-foot swells. Yet, several trips I have hung my head over the starboard side to evacuate my insides, then anchored and wade-fished. It is hard to leave the surf when the fish are shoulder-to-shoulder thick.

"I like to throw the Top Dog in the surf to find the fish," Talasek said. "If trout are there, they are going to bang it."

Respect the limits of your vessel. When seas are too rough, turn around. An angry sea can have its way with any boat, regardless of the captain's experience. Other days, the ocean turns into a tranquil pond and a 16-foot flatbottom can roam the big water. Regardless, do not venture past the jetty without consulting the marine forecast.

Chapter Nine

A Shore Thing

Drive-In Wade-Fishing Hotspots

Before the days of my 22-foot Pathfinder, encounters with saline marine life were on foot. I caught fish in those days, too. Conceivably, because I gave the particular drive-in venue all my attention for that particular morning or afternoon—good fishing or bad. Where was I going to go? I could not get in a boat and shimmy to another shoreline. This was the spot. So, I worked every inch of scattered shell or mud repeatedly until my shoulders were fatigued from casting. These episodes in my fishing life taught me patience and how to work a shoreline thoroughly—traits many center-console-driven anglers are lacking.

Sure, a bay boat is enjoyable, yet the $400-600 monthly note is not. Combine fuel, oil, grease, upkeep, and registration, that is an expensive price tag for the average angler. Still, if time and money do not justify purchasing a boat, miles of walk-in, inexpensive, and often-free shore-access fishing spots pepper the vast Texas coast. (The surf and passes are discussed in another chapter).

SABINE LAKE

Pleasure Island has prime bay access from the rocks of the north and south revetment wall. Drive your car down the wall of rocks and pick a spot. I have watched anglers walk up and down the rubble casting topwaters and drawing vicious strikes from Sabine trout. Covered piers are scattered about every mile along the wall.

Some choose to grab a bucket or lawn chair and use live shrimp or shad to catch reds, trout, and flounder. Yet, if you are a plugger, a Top Dog or Super Spook will draw plenty of blowups and strikes as will soft plastic red shad, plum, or pumpkinseed Bass Assassins and Norton Sand Eels. A Rat-L-Trap rolled parallel to the stones will draw attention from trout, reds, and flounder.

The Walter Umphrey State Park Pier is the most used public pier on the lake. Located on the south end of the lake, the pier comes to life at night as fishers pull wagons with aerated coolers full of feisty live shrimp. Trout, redfish, flounder, black drum, croaker, sand trout, and whiting are common species that hit the deck of the flat boards after dunking a popping cork. The pier is user-friendly and has easy access from the parking lot. Right across the street, Causeway Bait and Tackle is a reliable bait source. Artificials that consistently yield trout are tandem-rigged lures in the glow and pumpkinseed variety.

Directions: From Houston, take I-10 East. Take TX-73 exit toward Winnie, merge onto TX-73, take the TX-82 South ramp toward M.L. King Dr., merge onto TX-82 South. Go over the bridge and look for signs at the stop sign (Walter Umphrey Pier-turn left, north and south revetment walls-turn right).

EAST GALVESTON BAY

There are plenty bank-fishing spots and shores to wade at Rollover Pass on the Bolivar Peninsula. Some anglers crab, others drown fresh dead shrimp for croakers and other panfish. Redfish and flounder are abundant in autumn as both start their migration to the Gulf of Mexico. Best baits are live finger mullet, cut bait, and live shrimp. Beware of dangerous currents and strong tidal movements that are unique to ocean passes.

Anglers using artificials line the flats of Rollover Bay and cast into the channel. Tandem-rigged Lit'l Fishies have been a summertime trout catcher for years. Chartreuse and white No. 51 and No. 52 MirrOlures work, along with pepper/chartreuse, pumpkinseed/chartreuse, and black/chartreuse plastics on a 1/4-ounce jighead. When the tide is really pumping, try a 3/8-ounce head to get the bait on the bottom quicker. Southerly winds are conducive to good fishing.

Directions: From Houston, take I-10 East, take TX-73 (exit 828) toward Winnie. Turn onto TX-124 South in Winnie. Turn right on old TX-87 South and drive until you see the signs.

Frozen Point on the banks of the Anahuac National Wildlife Refuge is the best spot on the entire Galveston Bay complex for shore-access waders who want to catch a trophy speck. The Wildlife Flats have shell, mud, and marsh—all the amenities that attract baitfishes, thereby attracting predator game fish. Best conditions are northerly winds.

By far, my favorite bait to use on this trout-infested bank is a topwater. Top Dogs in black, bone, or 808 color (black/gold/orange) put trebles in yellow-mouthed trout year-round. Super Spooks in woodpecker (red/white), bone, and mullet colors also draw plenty of bangs. If your arms or rod are not made to walk-the-dog, gold spoons or plastic jerkbaits and swimmers also get your line stretched. Northerly winds or light southeast are the best conditions.

Directions: From Houston, take I-10 East, take exit 812 (Hankamer, TX-61). Turn right on TX-61 and stay straight to go onto FM 562. Take left on FM 1985 ("Y" in the road) and travel approximately four miles until you see the Anahuac National Wildlife Refuge sign on the right. Take the gravel road and stop at the check-in station.

TRINITY BAY

You can access the North Flats, along with the Houston Lighting and Power (HL&P) Spillway, through McCollum Park. The opportune time to fish is on strong tide days when abundant water pushes shrimp, shad, and mullet close to the bank. The flat is strictly a wade-fishing area, as high bluffs prohibit bank fishing. Miles of grass-infested sand and humps make wading easy and effortless. Topwaters, soft plastics, and spoons catch fish. Live bait is available only if you bring a cast net. There are no bait camps near the park.

The HL&P Spillway has harbored many 10 pounds-plus trout, including the Coastal Conservation Association (CCA) Star Tournament Upper Coast winner two years ago. Pluggers stand in the shallows and cast from the rocks into the deeper channel with subsurface plugs and soft plastics. Live-baiters take troll buckets with mullet, piggy perch, or shrimp and get plenty of wiggles from redfish, croaker, sand trout, and black drum. Best wind direction is north or northwest.

Directions: From Houston, take I-10 East to exit 800 near Mont Belvieu. Turn right on FM 1187 and stay straight to go onto Tri City Beach Road. After crossing the bridge over the canal, start looking for McCollum Park Road on the left. Turn left and follow the road to the park.

GALVESTON BAY

The east shoreline of the Kemah Flats to San Leon offers road accessible wade-fishing. Scattered shell along the flats provides fishable structure parallel to the Houston Ship Channel. Like fishing any flats area, sufficient water is needed to push baitfishes to the shoreline so that trout, redfish, and flounder will follow. The area's proximity to the Ship Channel also makes it a prime winter fishing venue. Fish hold in the deeper, warmer water when the thermometer is low, and head to the shallows as the air heats. Bayview Reef, along with Parker and Humble reefs, provide structure on Kemah Flats. The reefs are on the ledge of a drop-off that goes from 2 to 6 feet and fishes well during the dreaded westerly winds of summer.

April Fool Reef, Todd's Dump, and San Leon Reef are within wading distance of San Leon, as is the Bacliff HL&P Spillway, which draws baitfishes to its sauna-like waters in the fall and winter. Best months for trout and redfish are January through March. Flounder are good April through October.

Topwaters; glow/chartreuse, plum, pumpkinseed, firetiger, and red shad soft plastics; spoons, and rattling sinkers are great artificial imitations. If live bait is your thing, summertime croaker-soaking is fabulous on these reefs; just check the lines at the local bait camps. Other times of the year, a shrimp or live finger mullet will coax a bite and put a bend in the rod from flatfish and other species with spots.

Directions: From Houston to Kemah, take I-45 South to the NASA Road 1 exit (FM 528). Go over the Interstate and travel on West NASA Road 1. Turn right on TX-146 and turn left on FM 646. Stay straight until you come to Bayshore Drive (turn left on W. Bayshore Dr. to go to the Kemah Flats, then turn right on E. Bayshore Dr. to go to San Leon).

The Texas City Dike is the most used foot- or car-accessed fishing spot on the upper coast. This spoil area is surrounded by acres of sandy, hard-bottomed humps and holes along the flats. Artificial anglers have best results with topwaters, spoons, and soft plastics. Live-baiters who wade can pull a bucket full of shrimp, piggies, or croaker (in season) and draw strikes. The Dike has several bait camps along its nearly 12-mile stretch of bank that offer live or fresh dead bait.

Several piers line the Dike, including some illuminated at night. Nocturnal fishing under the lights is fabulous throughout the year for trout, redfish, black drum, sand trout, whiting, croaker, and flounder. Best baits for night fishing are live shrimp, speck rigs, glow plastics, and tandem-rigged beetles. Redfish and flounder are very good in the fall and winter. Black drum show up in the spring. Speckled trout are good throughout the year with moderate winds and a moving tide. This area is best on a southeast or westerly wind.

Directions: From Houston, take I-45 South. Take the FM 1764 East/Emmett F. Lowry Expressway exit (Exit 16) toward Texas City. Turn right on Bay St. Turn left on Dike Road.

Pelican Island is accessible via Galveston Island and is home to Sea Wolf Park (N 29 19.88', W 94 46.72'). The park is the flatfish spot during autumn and winter as flounder make their run to the Gulf. The north shoreline of the island is wadeable and prime for trout, redfish, flounder, black drum, sand trout, croaker, and shark.

Throw a live finfish on a green tide and you are likely to catch pelagic species that have meandered through the North or South Jetties. If you do not want to get wet, fish off the rocks with fresh dead or live shrimp. Topwaters are good in belly-deep water, casting to the deep and working the bait over the ever-changing ledges of the channel. Jigs tipped with peeled shrimp are good for flounder. The area is best on a southeast or due west wind.

Directions: From Houston, take I-45 South to Galveston, turn left at 51st Street, which runs onto Sea Wolf Pkwy., then follow the road until it ends.

MATAGORDA BAY

Most of the south shoreline of East Matagorda Bay is accessible by truck—as long as it's four-wheel-drive. Many trails over the dunes lead to the bay from the beach. When I have only a few hours to fish and do not want to mess with the hassle of a boat, I drive down in the afternoon and make a wade.

Boiler Bayou, Hog Island, Kain Cove, Oyster Farm, and Brown Cedar Cut are accessible by truck. For first-timers, navigate during daylight. Pack a GPS, too, just in case the marsh becomes one large chunk of salt grass to your internal compass.

Most anglers who drive in to fish these spots throw hardware, for the simple reason it is too difficult to keep live bait alive in the back of a pickup that is bouncing and shifting. These roads are not paved, and most are bumpier than bumpy. Go slow and do not get in a hurry. If you see a hole filled with water, inspect it before you go through. Calling a wrecker to dig you out of the mud is expensive in the marsh.

Three Mile Cut is about 2.4 miles down the beach. Hurricane Claudette opened it to the Gulf in July 2003, but it has since silted. Turn left, and go through the opening of the dunes to the bayou and shallow ponds fed by East Matagorda Bay. On good tides, big trout and redfish feed on rafts of mullet and shrimp. When extreme low tides persist, redfish tail in the back lakes vulnerable to a fly, small topwater, or soft plastic.

Directions: From Houston, take U.S. 59 south to Wharton, then take TX-60 south to Matagorda. Optionally, take Highway 288 south, then turn on TX-35 south and take it to Bay City. Get on TX-60 south to Matagorda. Once in Matagorda, take a left at the blinking light and go over the swing bridge to get onto the peninsula. Follow the road until it dead-ends at the beach. Get on the beach and proceed.

Oyster Lake Bridge between Bay City and Palacios is a popular spot to wade shell and mud. The area is particularly strong in the spring and fall when shrimp dump out of Oyster Lake. The area is good even when easterly winds blow. Many people camp overnight and set out lights to draw bait and game fishes.

Oyster Lake is a redfish hangout, and many bruisers succumb near the bridge in the fall. Best baits are live shrimp under a popping cork, cracked crabs, topwaters, and red shad plastics.

Directions: From Bay City, take TX-35 to Tidehaven (El Maton). Turn left at the high school and head toward Collegeport. Proceed to Oyster Lake Road and follow it until you come to the bridge.

TRES PALACIOS, KELLER, AND LAVACA BAY

The Palacios Pavilion in Tres Palacios Bay is a winter haunt for waders. Scattered reefs and drop-offs hold cold fish. Jigging with Corkies, 51M MirrOlures, and soft plastics scores regularly.

The entire west shoreline of Tres Palacios from Grassy Point to Turtle Point at the mouth of Turtle Bay is wadeable and accessible by vehicle. Abandoned piers provide structure for fish like sheepshead and black drum. These fish have a tough time turning down live shrimp.

Directions: Take TX-35 to Palacios and proceed to Main Street and Palacios Harbor.

Keep heading south on TX-35 to Olivia and the north shoreline of Keller Bay. Grass, shell, and mud litter the shoreline beginning at the state park area. Keller Bay has long been a trophy trout destination, but its remote location keeps the traffic to a minimum.

Directions: Take TX-35 toward Port Lavaca, then get off on TX-172 and keep going until you run into water. From U.S. 59, take the TX-172 exit in Ganado and head south.

Heading toward Port Lavaca on TX-35, there are wade-fishing opportunities just before you get to the causeway bridge over Lavaca Bay on both sides of the bay. Cross over the bridge and take a right on FM 1090, then take a right on East Maxwell Road and follow it to the water. The entire west shoreline of Lavaca Bay north of the causeway is good wading with scattered shell and mud.

South of the causeway on the west shoreline near Magnolia Beach is solid wading for trout, redfish, and flounder over grass beds. To get there, stay on TX-35 going out of Port Lavaca and take a left on FM 2433. Take a left on Highway 238, a right on Highway 316, and a left on FM 2717 and follow it to the water. To Magnolia Beach, stay on Highway 316 and follow the signs.

ARANSAS, REDFISH, AND CORPUS CHRISTI BAY

Little Bay, in the heart of Rockport near Key Allegro, is one of the most popular drive-in wading spots on the entire coast. Trout, redfish, and flounder are the usual quarry and the entire bay floor is composed of sand and grass.

Bait camps within a stone's throw make it easy to transport live bait such as mullet, croaker, piggy perch, and live shrimp. Nearby hotels have piers with lights that help dupe nighttime trout on topwaters.

The entire shoreline paralleling Fulton Beach Road is wadeable hard sand and grass, provided you park on the shoulder on the water side. Just be careful not to venture onto private property.

Directions: Take TX-35 into Fulton. Once you cross over the Copano Bay Bridge, take a left on any through street and it will take you to Fulton Beach Road. Once you find a spot to fish, safely park, get out, and wade.

From Aransas Pass to Port Aransas on Highway 361 is eight miles of wading in Redfish Bay. The Aransas Channel runs on the east side of the road, but the best wading is on the west side. Deep channels and flats provide adequate structure to fish, even in the cold of winter. There are no named roads off the main highway; look for worn routes in the sand to direct your path. Be aware of duck hunters from November through January.

Cross the ferry to Port Aransas and stay on Highway 361 for 21 miles heading toward Corpus Christi. There are many roads on the north side of the highway that lead through the marsh to the southeast shoreline of Corpus Christi Bay.

Anglers targeting tailing redfish will enjoy this stretch of the coast with its crystal clear, sandy grass shores. Undulations and drop-offs provide structure that holds fish consistently. Shamrock Cove is a popular locale.

Following Highway 361 toward Corpus Christi, you come to a stoplight. Go left and head toward Bird Island Basin on Park Road 22. Turn right and head toward Corpus Christi by going over the JFK Causeway. You are now on South Padre Island Drive (SPID 358).

Once you cross over the bridge, the water on your left and right is wadeable. In fact, you will probably see many anglers in the water, from pluggers to live-baiters. Vast grass beds with humps and guts provide structure that holds a variety of game fishes. It is not uncommon to bag a limit of trout with a bonus redfish.

Stay on SPID and you cross Oso Bay. Sure, many times it looks like a mud hole when the wind is howling, but locals know it produces big trout. A local group of waders without boats call themselves "Team Oso." These guys are good and prove there are heavy fish in dirty old Oso Bay.

The farther south you travel, the more remote Laguna Madre becomes. Baffin Bay is surrounded by private property, namely the King Ranch, and the waters near Port Mansfield border the Kenedy Ranch.

Port Isabel does have a few spots—namely, Laguna Vista—but be sure you obtain permission to access the water when on private property. Trespassing is still against the law in Texas.

Chapter Ten

Wading Into Danger

Fastening my wading belt and boots, I plunged from the stern and slid my feet across the sandy shell bottom. My buddy, Blair, was hesitant to venture from the boat after hearing tales of aggressive aquatic life within these waters. "Shark Week" on the Discovery Channel did not help matters, either.

I tried to ensure him that all was safe. Most anglers do not realize it, but you have a better chance of a being involved in a car wreck than a shark attack. Don't get me wrong, I do take precautions. A shuffle of the feet (we call it the "Texas two-step") as you walk across the bay floor usually alerts bottom-feeders like stingrays and sends them scurrying out of your path. That's all it takes—until you spot one.

Redfish were rooting in the mud with the tip of their turquoise tails waving like flags just above the surface, feasting on small blue crabs and shrimp. Another step, and a 3-foot rust-colored ray gingerly glided in front. Redfish and rays are common bedfellows in Texas. Most artist renditions of a Lone Star coastal scene involving redfish usually have a stingaree somewhere in the print. Both species are there for a reason: food is abundant.

Adjusting my mindset from redfish to barbed marine life, I began picking up my feet a little more. One more futile cast and I headed back to the boat. Halfway there, I caught myself before actually stepping on another ray. Never before in all my days on the coast have I seen so many stingrays in one fishing trip.

So much for being a tough guy.

Getting up close and personal with fish on their terrain is one of the thrills of wade-fishing. However, precautions are in order to ensure safety and many more days of traversing your favorite saline shoreline.

A Ray of Hope

As water temperatures climb into the 60s in spring, stingrays will be present. Although many waders go a lifetime without getting stuck by the razor, toxin-rich barbs, encounters with these bottom-feeders do occur.

Walt Wendtland fondly remembers his brush with a ray. He and friend Floyd Cirutti were wading a shell bank, casting for redfish feeding in a gut between a reef and a bayou. Wendtland said he always shuffles his feet to avoid stingrays; nevertheless, as he waded toward the reef, the water became shallower and off-color. As he approached the reef, he had to step up on a shell pad with his right foot. When the weight of his foot hit bottom, it rested right on top of a small ray. According to Wendtland, he knew right away: "It felt like a hot nail going through by foot. It actually went through the arch of my foot and broke off. I did the wrong thing when I got to the boat. I put my foot in ice and it began to throb in unbearable pain, so I took it out. It kept me from wading for two weeks."

Wendtland recalled going to the emergency room right away and getting several numbing injections in the affected area before letting his doctor extract the barb.

Stingray slashes produce some of the most excruciating pain known to man. If you are so unfortunate, doctors say that the best remedy until you can make it to the emergency room is to put the wound under the warm discharge from your outboard water pump. Immerse the foot in the warm water and let the solution draw the proteins out of the venomous wound. This will sooth the pain somewhat and keep circulation in the affected areas.

Like any injury, one would think that ice would help the situation, but not with stingray barbs. Ice causes the affected area to crystallize, and doctors say that makes matters worse. Doctors also advise to leave the barb in the skin—do not try to remove it yourself—and seek medical attention immediately.

Wearing protective equipment never crossed my mind, until I finally woke up one day. Coming from a baseball background, "percentages" control my lifestyle. If you participate long enough—like wading soggy shallows—every time you venture out, the percentage favoring an accident goes up. It may be minuscule, but the chance is still there. So, like any good player and coach would do, I reduce the percentage by protecting myself.

As with anything in life, confidence is everything, even with fishing. If you spend most of your mental energy worrying about avoiding injection of poisonous bacteria, there is not much brainpower left to concentrate on fishing.

A pair of quality stingray boots can calm the senses and deflect the blows. I have a pair of Hodgman Reef Boots and ForEverLast Ray-

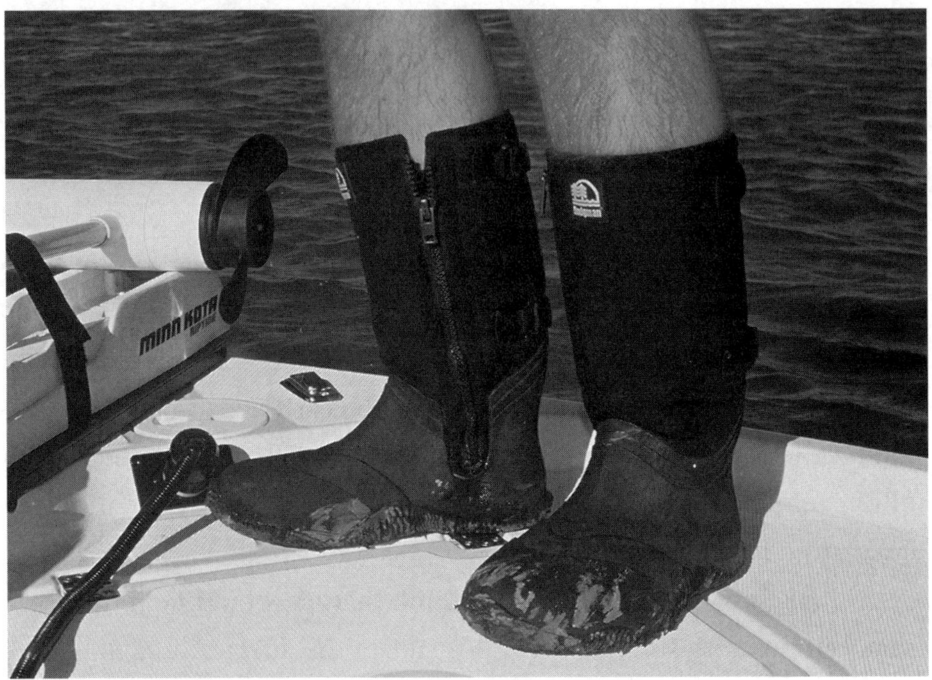

Hodgman Reef Boots

Guard Wading Boots. Both are excellent choices, but neither is totally "stingray proof."

I have been hit twice since donning a pair four years ago: once at the Oyster Farm in East Matagorda Bay, and once while wading the Indian River in Jensen Beach, Florida. I would have the scars to prove it had I not been wearing the boots.

WOLVES OF THE SEA

If you wade often, chances are you have probably had an up-close and personal meeting with a shark, especially if you are catching fish and sliding them down a floating stringer. Passes, inlets, oceans or bays with high salinity levels are almost certain to inhabit big fish with teeth and a protruding dorsal fin.

A floating stringer with fish is easy pickings to a shark. Although most wading encounters with sharks harm only the fish, there are documented instances of a bull shark or blacktip mistaking a flailing leg for a wounded mullet. If a shark does decide to pay you a visit and begins to dine on your catch, let the thing have it. Attach your stringer so that you can easily let it loose if something grabs it and takes off. Many of the wading belts today have a little slit on the side so that the metal prod can fit snug, yet be released with one finger.

Do not affix a stringer around your waist with a knot. A knot might prove too time-consuming and cumbersome when seconds really count. I have seen a few waders dragged down the beach by a shark while trying to untangle the knot around their waist.

A donut stringer is a better choice. It consists of a round float with a net attached. Waders can plop their catch through the round hole and into a net. Some use the net to hold live shrimp, mullet, or threadfin herring. The net does not allow the fish to swim freely, so predators do not locate the meal as easily and attacks are minimized. The net does not alleviate shark attack altogether, it just reduces the percentages.

Sharks were so thick one recent summer in West Matagorda Bay, Capts. Tommy Countz and Bobby Gardner invented another contraption to deter the carnivores. The two pros took a brown tow sack and sewed it around the existing net, making it tougher for the sharks to see the fish and even tougher to rip it apart.

"It was really bad around Green's and Cotton's Bayou," Countz said. "There were some 6- and 7-footers on the bar, and they were coming after your fish. One ripped apart my Do-Net. I got tired of it and tried a burlap sack around the Do-Net and it seems to work.

"You know, I have never worried about sharks too much, but

when a 6-foot bull shark begins to circle me, I become concerned. You can never tell what bull sharks are thinking."

TOAST, JELLY, AND MY ACHING BACK

Warmer mercury readings breathe life into things that burn. Longer daylight hours in the spring and summer make waders more susceptible to sunburns while spawning a new crop of jellyfish and cabbageheads.

The right attire can protect you from both. A long-sleeved, light-colored shirt and hat combined with sun block protect the skin from irritations caused by ultraviolet rays, both direct and reflected off the water. Long pants keep jellyfish from coming in contact with exposed skin. Jellyfish will not kill you, but wade into a wad of them and it feels like someone is sticking you with hundreds of straight pins.

Wading gear has improved tremendously. Long days of combing shorelines strain the lower back. New wading belts, much like weightlifting belts that support the lower lumbar region, have revived many "stove-up" anglers. Five-inch wide belts by NuMark and Wade-Aid add needed support for daylong wades—and waders who feel better spend more time in the water. More hours in the water result in a greater opportunity to test your drag.

MICROSCOPIC MAYHEM

According to the Center for Disease Control, *Vibrio vulnificus* is a warm seawater bacterium in the same family as cholera. It is part of the vibrios family called "halophilic" because they require salt. Eating contaminated seafood such as oysters, or exposing an open wound in infected seawater often causes infection with the bacteria.

Common symptoms are vomiting, diarrhea, and abdominal pain, but in immunocompromised persons, especially those with liver disease, *V. vulnificus* can infect the bloodstream, causing a severe illness characterized by fever, chills, septic shock, and skin lesions. Bloodstream infections are fatal 50 percent of the time, according to CDC. Persons with pre-existing medical conditions are 80 times more likely to develop bloodstream infections.

The risk for waders is direct contact with open wounds in waters where the bacterium persists, or getting pricked by the horn of a shrimp. The bacterium is often found in oysters and other shellfish in warm coastal waters during the summer. Though the disease is rare, it is often underreported. Between 1988 and 1995, CDC received reports of 300 *V. vulnificus* infections, mainly from Gulf Coast states like Alabama, Florida, Louisiana, Texas, and Mississippi.

The ounce of prevention is to keep all open wounds dry and out of the water. If you have an open sore on your leg, wear waders. Breathable waders are bearable during the summer months, as opposed to 3mm neoprenes. If any of the above symptoms persist after a day wading, see a doctor immediately. The infection can be treated with antibiotics such as Doxycycline without long-term consequences.

These precautions are not scare tactics against wading, just a better understanding of what lies below the surface. For me, the thrill and joy of wading far outweighs the risks.

TEXAS HEAT

The beginning of my senior year of high school, I had my first serious bout with the summer heat after staying late at football practice for extra running. After a mile in full pads, I was done, literally.

On the way back to the field house, I hurled, then sat motionlessly in front of my locker trying to garner enough energy to make it to the shower. I had overheated and was exhibiting all the signs of heat exhaustion: nausea, dizziness, clammy skin, and dementia. Never before had I felt that way, and not since have I come close. Had I become unconscious or stopped sweating, I could have slipped into a deadly heat stroke.

I vividly remember the day so well because it was my eighteenth birthday, and a party awaited me when I arrived home. Remembering how I drove home is the scary part; I do not recall much. When I got home, a few of my friends were there waiting to eat birthday cake. I walked in, hit the living room floor, and woke up the next morning. Party pooper!

Since that episode, I have had two bouts with the heat in a dozen years. Five summers ago in the Matagorda surf, I became nauseated due to seasickness early in the morning. Nevertheless, I kept fishing. The more I pumped fluids back into my body, the more I spewed. I could never catch up to the amount of water needed to cool my body in the Texas sun. Finally, I made it back to the dock around 5 o'clock that afternoon, but had trouble keeping my balance while cleaning fish. That's right, my partner and I caught lots of fish, but I paid for it. Had the fish not been so thick, I probably would have come in earlier and suffered less.

As I grow older, I like to think I have become wiser. At least I am trying. Nonetheless, that same summer, the surf seduced and the heat attacked again.

My partners and I waded mid-bay reefs in East Matagorda Bay until noon, then made a phone call to the Sargent swing-bridge to ask the attendant what the surf looked like.

"It is as flat and greener than I have seen it in a long time," the friendly man said. "I have already heard of a few guys who caught their limits this morning."

Well, that was a no-brainer.

I promptly yelled at my buddies, Eddie Sullivan and Randy Stacy, to head back in the boat. They were halfway across Long Reef when they heard me. After a short detour at Rawling's Bait Camp for more ice, we were in the surf and drifting by 2 o'clock. Note we were "drifting." The reason: tides were falling and the fish were stacked on the second and third bars in 6-7 feet of water. We did try to make a wade, but a quick look at my feet while I was fighting a burly redfish quickened my heart as hundreds of blacktip sharks littered the water. Some over 8 feet prowled the first gut.

To make a long story short, three hours floating in a boat during the heat of the day did it to me again. As before, if the fishing had not been so good, I would have left hours before. Such is the determination of a Texas angler. However, when the day was over, I did not feel like fishing for the next 10 days.

Summer 2003, after a morning wade in East Bay, the wind became calm and "slicked off" by noon. Sullivan, Walt Wendtland, his two kids, and I headed for the Gulf. This time I draped a towel under my hat to shield the sun from my neck, and consumed a 2-liter bottle of water before I reached the ocean.

The fishing was as "good as it gets." Yet, amid all the fish hitting the deck, I continued to drink water and worked on knocking out another 2 liters. I did not overheat that day, but did recognize something valuable: From the time we left the bay at 11:30 a.m. until we reached the dock around 5:00 p.m., not one of my four friends in the boat that day had the urge to urinate. They all were drinking as much as I was, but we were excreting all the fluids through our sweat glands before it could reach the bladder. Had we not sucked down so much water, we all would have felt like we had baked in a kiln.

"I try to run all of my August trips at night," Capt. Bill Pustejovsky said. "I have suffered from heat exhaustion before, and it set me back two weeks. I just can't fish all day in this heat."

If someone displays symptoms of heat exhaustion or stroke, seek shaded shelter—no matter how well the fish are biting. Until you can get the victim to medical attention, try to cool the body temperature by immersing in cold water. Try, if conscious, to get the victim to drink water or other fluids loaded with electrolytes.

If you begin to feel the sun beating you, get off the water, especially if you are alone. You could be far away from the nearest dock, and if you get dizzy or disoriented, the trip could turn disastrous.

Be smart and preempt the risk factors. Begin drinking water early in the morning. If you are fishing from a boat, go early or late in the evening, well before or after the sun gets high above. If you insist on staying out all day and do not wade, take a dip every hour to keep the body's core temperature at a safe level.

I have learned my lesson. I am never too cool to respect the summer heat.

USE YOUR HEAD

Rarely will you hear negatives cross my lips concerning a day on God's saline estuaries. Unless, of course, I witness some knucklehead abusing game laws, mistaking the bays and ocean for a landfill, or operating a motor vessel while under the influence of alcohol.

However, if relaying my personal bad fishing experiences to readers can steer them in the opposite direction and make for a better day on the water, I think it is worth the pessimistic ink.

Traditionally, I do not choose to drift-fish during scorching summer months. I choose to work belly- to chest-deep water, occasionally dunking my entire frame beneath the surface to keep cool. One day, opportune tides forced me to remain in the boat. Incoming tides were in the dark, early morning hours when the first or second guts pay off.

By dawn, tides had already started to fall, and with low tide conditions, trout move to the deeper waters of the third bar. The outer reaches of the last bar are treacherous for surf waders, especially with an outgoing tide that produces rips and undertows. The only way to reach the fish was by boat.

The only downfall when fishing out of a boat in the ocean is my inner ear's propensity to spin. My sea legs are about as strong as a strand of fettuccini, and it does not take long for nausea to ruin my day. Nevertheless, I seem to forget bout after bout of seasickness in my past when angry specks are bashing topwater plugs.

The particular morning was no exception. By 8:30 a.m., I was hanging my head overboard and releasing breakfast in 2-foot seas, then made more casts after gathering my bearings. I could not just turn the key and head back through the jetty to placid waters. I was in a friend's boat and we had already made a 15-mile commitment down the beach. We were here for the long haul.

We caught scattered fish throughout the morning. I hurled in half-hour intervals then loaded back up with fluids to stave off dehydration, hoping my partner would give up waiting for the specks to show in epic proportions.

The trout finally began engulfing our plugs by mid-afternoon, but I was done—make that well done. I convinced my partner to drop me off on the solid ground of the beach so he could work on the fish. Two hours later, the blather of his outboard woke me and I dizzily stumbled to the boat and headed inland.

That unforgettable day has not been duplicated since, thankfully. Yet, it could have been avoided with a little common sense.

The severe sunburn I received could have been prevented before the sun came out and the internal melee commenced. I had Smartshield Sunscreen on board, the absolute best sun protection I have ever lathered on my extremities. Still, with all the up-chucking and wave-riding that morning, it never occurred to me to apply the lotion; I too busy trying to keep from coughing my insides overboard.

Protection from harmful ultraviolet rays is often of little concern to summertime anglers. According to the American Cancer Society, 50 percent of Americans who live to age 65 will have skin cancer at least once.

To avoid excess exposure to the sun, use the best quality sunscreen products with the proper SPF (Sun Protection Factor) level. According to SmartShield, one SPF is the amount of time in minutes that it takes your unprotected skin to become lightly reddened or irritated from being exposed to the sun.

Each person has a different SPF based on skin type, amount of skin pigment (skin darkness), existing tan, and prior sun exposure. SmartShield says the SPF number on sunscreen products indicate approximately how many times your normal SPF time is multiplied by correctly applying that product.

If your personal SPF is 30 minutes and you choose an 8 SPF product, you would extend your time to reach the sensitivity to the sun as described above by eight times. The time would be calculated by multiplying your personal SPF time of 30 minutes by the SPF number on the sunscreen product, which was 8.

The total, in the example, is 4 hours (240 minutes). That means the sun would have the same effect on your skin using properly applied SPF 8 sunscreen in four hours as it would in 30 minutes without sunscreen.

The sun's greatest UV exposure is between 11:00 a.m. and 3:00

p.m., so wear a hat and covering clothing during these peak times. Use shade when available, and reapply sunscreen when perspiring or swimming. I have invested in a $20 beach umbrella that easily folds and fits in the rod locker of my boat. When resting in the boat after a wade, I break out the umbrella and slide the pole in one of my upright rod holders. You will be surprised how much relief that small amount of shade provides.

My dizziness on that dreadful day was a symptom of heat exhaustion. Losing all my fluids from nausea combined with extreme heat tapped my body of the water it needed for internal cooling. When these symptoms persist, get to a cooler environment, regardless if the fishing is superb, and rehydrate with water and other fluids loaded with electrolytes (sports drinks). Heat exhaustion is the stage before heat stroke when your body tells you it is about to burn up inside.

No fish is worth that.

BOATING SAFETY IS OF THE UTMOST

"Whoa, did you see that?" yelled the tugboat captain on his VHF radio upon entering the Colorado River Locks in Matagorda.

"You don't know how often we see that down here," responded the swing bridge keeper. "Pretty scary."

The captain's disbelief was prompted by the dangerous chance taken by a boater. The small fishing boat crossed the big tug's bow with only a few feet to spare between the dingy, tug, and bridge. Instead of safely waiting for the tug to pass, the boater's lack of patience almost cost him his life.

Big boats have the right-a-way, and what many boaters do not know is that those tugs do not have brakes, cannot stop quickly, and do not bend when something like a 22-foot fiberglass vessel collides with them.

According to the Texas Parks and Wildlife Department (TPWD), there were 61 boating-related fatalities in 2003 on Texas public waterways, up drastically from the year before.

"Even one fatality is a tragedy. Everyone must do everything possible to do their part in making Texas waterways safer," said Dennis Johnston, chief of TPWD marine law enforcement.

Boat collisions, even minor ones, often end tragically due to occupants not wearing a life jacket. When a minor accident occurs on the road, you can step out of the car and walk away. In a boat, you must swim or try to stay afloat, and this is what hinders most.

Boaters are reminded that all passengers 13 or under in a motorboat under 26 feet in length must wear a U.S. Coast Guard approved life vest while underway.

Last year, a 12-year-old passenger was dumped from my boat. We were fishing the wells and buoys in West Matagorda Bay when the wind kicked up and roughed the water. The youngster, with minimal agility and maximum clumsiness, stepped onto the bow just as a swell rocked the boat. Like jumping from a springboard, the wave tossed the juvenile into the drink. The father laughed it off since his boy was wearing a life jacket.

Most accidents or "man overboards" do not end so humorously, especially when alcohol is involved. What baffles me is the "Open Container" law. It is illegal to have an open container of alcohol when driving or riding in a road vehicle, but for boaters, though the stakes are higher, the practice is lawful. Go figure.

Texas game wardens have been commissioned to crack down on intoxicated boaters, and have, since stiffer penalties were enacted that carry the same consequences as Driving While Intoxicated (DWI). The loss of mental or physical faculties, or a blood alcohol content of .08 or higher defines Boating While Intoxicated (BWI).

A first conviction is punishable by a fine not to exceed $2,000, confinement in jail not to exceed 180 days, or both. A second conviction is punishable by a fine not to exceed $4,000, confinement not to exceed one year, or both. A third conviction is punishable by fine not to exceed $10,000, and imprisonment for not more than 10 years or less than 2 years. Failure to submit a specimen to determine blood alcohol content can result in suspension of your driver's license.

A successfully completed TPWD certified boater education course and photo I.D. is required for any person born after September 1, 1984 to operate on the public waters of Texas in a vessel powered by a motor of 10 horsepower or more or a windblown vessel over 14 feet in length.

In addition, all boats must have the following required safety equipment:

U.S. Coast Guard Type I, II, III, or V wearable Personal Flotation Device (PFD) for every occupant in the boat. A Type V PFD is acceptable only if used in accordance with the specific instructions on the label of the device.

Vessels 16 feet and longer, excluding canoes and kayaks, are required to be equipped with one Type IV throwable PFD in addition to the Type I, II, III, or V PFD for each person on board.

Any vessel less than 12 meters in length (39.4 ft.) is required to carry a whistle, horn, or some other means to make sufficient sound to signal intentions and positions in periods of reduced visibility. Vessels 12 meters or more in length are required to carry a whistle or horn, and a bell.

Every motorboat towing a person or persons on water skis, aquaplane, or similar device must have an observer, other than the operator, 13 years of age or older, or be equipped with a rearview mirror of a size no less than 4 inches in measurement from bottom to top and across from one side to the other.

All vessels, including motorboats, canoes, kayaks, punts, rowboats, rubber rafts, and other vessels when not at dock must have and exhibit at least one bright light, lantern, or flashlight visible all around the horizon from sunset to sunrise in all weather and during restricted visibility. In addition, a red port light and green starboard light is required.

Outboard motorboats less than 26 feet in length are required to have a U.S. Coast Guard approved fire extinguisher.

Though it is not a requirement, boat operators should always wear their kill switch when the vessel is underway.

While waders must avoid the pitfalls of marine life, they must also give caution to those aluminum and fiberglass bullets that seem to know only one speed: wide open. Boaters should give proper distance to waders, and show genuine etiquette and courtesy for those inhabiting the shorelines. Reduce speed when inspecting prime shallows so not to damage vital sea grasses, oyster shell habitat, or a fellow wader.

DO NOT GO ALONE

Choosing to share my outdoor excursions with friends who value the same principles and love of wildlife bodes well with my wife. She would not allow it any other way. She is gracious in approving of my countless trips to the bay or marsh, but realizes the risk involved every time I step from the land and make a floating piece of fiberglass my refuge, or a firearm my instrument of pleasure for that day. There is safety and protection in numbers. She knows this, and hunting or fishing with a buddy is not an option in my household—it is a mandate.

Safety issue aside, sharing outdoors experiences with a friend always makes them better. Besides, how do you describe an unbelievable shot on a passing greenhead, a topwater explosion from an angry speck, or an omni-colored sunrise silhouetted with tailing redfish? Friends will never be able to understand your passions unless they have shuffled across a bay floor and muddied their boots with you.

My friends, Capt. Chuck Uzzle and the late Sammy Noland, were there one June day in 1999 on Sabine Lake when we all lost our wit to a huge harem of gorilla trout. A healthy 24-inch speck met Sammy's first cast of the morning. Four hours later, we had caught and released 27 trout, the smallest that first fish of the morning; nine were 28 inches or better. One in particular, which I lost at my feet, was conservatively 33 inches. We still talk about the commotion that fish made when it hit my black Top Dog. I have not had a day like that since, and may never again.

There was the day I parked my boat on top of the second bar in the surf. My companions jumped out and waded to the west while I headed east. Easing my way with the current, an hour of futile casts provided no takers. As I headed against the current back to the boat, I found myself fighting just to gain a yard of ground. Twenty minutes later, legs exhausted and head drenched from waves breaking over, the tide began to have its way with me. I was helpless until another fisherman at the boat saw me and relayed relief. It is scary to think what might have happened had I been alone.

A summer morning wading the grassy flats of Espiritu Santo Bay tested my first-aid skills. The incoming tide was ripping through Pass Cavallo, and with it came many marine species, most notably stingrays. As we fished, stingrays flooded the shallow flats along with dingy water from the Gulf of Mexico. The one thing wade-fishers fear, other than a shark attack, occurred. My friend had to step over a submerged piling. When his foot hit bottom, he felt the sand move and a sharp, agonizing pain run through his veins. The ray left a 3-inch barb lodged in the Achilles tendon region. He yelled and hobbled back to the boat.

Blood turned my Pathfinder crimson as his lifeline gushed out of the hole with every pulse of his rapidly beating heart. I quickly started the engine and draped his ankle beneath the hot discharge of the water pump, I tied a tourniquet lightly above the foot to control the bleeding until the ambulance met us at the dock and took him to the emergency room.

My father and I were buzzing down the ship channel at Sabine Pass in the predawn darkness en route to the jetty. We were fishing a tournament, so were in a hurry to get there so that we could begin fishing at the legal hour. Without warning, the motor went dead and the steering cable locked up. Dad tilted the motor up and there, wrapped around the propeller, was a 5-inch diameter mooring rope. I put on a life preserver and Dad tied the anchor rope around my waist. I plunged overboard to try to work the kink off the prop.

Picture it: pitch dark with massive ships plowing and making *Hawaii Five-O*-class waves. Needless to say, our 18-foot flatbottom rocked and swayed violently. It took a fillet knife to saw the rope in half, and the nylon finally broke free and allowed the engine to run again. Dad and I were late, but it did not matter due to a midday bite. We still earned a paycheck for our efforts.

If for no reason other than safety sake, take a friend or companion on your next outdoor activity. Choose someone who is compatible and shares the same outdoor convictions. If you have kids, there is never an excuse to go alone.

Chapter Eleven

Seasonal Wading Hotspots

The beauty of wading Texas is you can do it year-round. Sure, it does get cold here in the winter and the wind blows ferociously at times, but choosing to focus on the positives, which I have tried to do most of my life, I think we have it pretty good.

Fish move from season to season—tides, bait, and moon phases dictate it. Following is a four-season wade-fishing pattern I have noticed since I began gathering and writing the Weekly Coastal Fishing Report for the Texas Parks and Wildlife Department in 1998.

SPRING

Bright Texas sunlight warms the spring shallows and rejuvenates

Wading reefs payoff, especially in the spring and summer when baitfish move to the shell for refuge.

the fishing soul. Transitional winds from winter to spring can be the variable responsible for bent rods or lackluster luck. Try to get out on a day when gales subside. If time does not permit, find a leeward shoreline and tighten your cap another notch.

The Louisiana shoreline of Sabine Lake comes alive with waders lining its mullet-infested banks. Hearty specks and reds gobble slow-sinking MirrOlures, Corkies, and Catch 2000s. By late April and early May, topwaters like She Dogs, Top Dogs, and Super Spooks provide a bang.

Hodges Reef in Trinity Bay is a spring hotspot. Waders drag plastics along the shell and coax trout pushing 5 pounds. Frozen Point on the north shoreline of East Galveston Bay is an awesome walk-in spot from the Anahuac National Wildlife Refuge. The shoreline is scattered with shell and mud, and has consistently produced sow trout on dog-walkers and slow-sinkers.

The annual spring black drum run occurs in the channels near the Texas City Dike and Sea Wolf Park. Large drum have a tough time turning down a cracked blue crab or cut mullet.

April anglers in West Matagorda Bay can hit the snooze button several times before hooking up the boat. Afternoon fishing is best on south shoreline grass beds like Green's and Cotton's bayous. Incoming tides are persistent late in the day and the currents flood the shallows with this a new crop of glass minnows. It is not uncommon to see large schools of redfish and trout gorging in the skinny water. A school of bronze-back bullies knocked me off balance one spring afternoon when they bumped into me while frantically feeding.

Swelling spring tides push fish in the back lakes of Espiritu Santo Bay near Port O'Connor. Spawning trout like the soft mud bottoms. Waders who like stalking big fish in shallow water frequent Pringle, Contee, Power, and Fifth lakes. If water temps reach the high 60s, a topwater elicits blow-ups. Failing that, Corkies, MirrOlures, and live shrimp will work. When winds subside, wade the vast reefs in San Antonio Bay. Trout pushing double-digits are there if the weather cooperates.

The reefs in Rockport's Copano Bay and St. Charles Bay are established spring wading for big trout. Estes Flats in Redfish Bay will be full of the copper-scaled fish, hence the name. Crabs, mullet, shrimp, Red Killer plastics, and topwaters get your line stretched. Black drum migrate through nearby Lydia Ann Channel, and again blue crabs and mullet are the ticket.

The rocks of Baffin Bay hold large trout for waders tossing Corkies, Catch 2000s, 51M MirrOlures, and She Dogs. The Landcut and lower Laguna Madre are good for trout, redfish, and black drum on live shrimp and soft plastics. As temperatures and tides rise and fall, fish jockey from the flats to the Intracoastal Waterway. Shrimp, mullet, and bone- or plum-colored plastics provide action.

SUMMER

The beachfront from Sabine Pass to South Padre comes alive in summer as water temperatures reach and exceed the magic mid-70-degree mark. When calm seas allow, Gulf Coast pluggers migrate to the surf for what most consider the best speckled trout fishing of the year.

If the region does not get swelling rains, the north end of Sabine Lake is good for waders tossing MirrOlures and Corkies around the tip of Pleasure, Stewt's, Sydney, and Rabbit islands. Redfish and flounder are steady in the Neches River on Carolina-rigged live shad.

Live-baiters in the Galveston Bay Complex work the Ship Channel and pieces of shell adjacent to the channel with live croakers.

The east shoreline of Trinity Bay is good for topwater enthusiasts around Little Hodges and Hodges reefs, provided summer rains are minimal. Walk-in waders can access Frozen Point on the north shoreline of East Galveston Bay from the Anahuac National Wildlife Refuge—an established gator trout haunt.

The Bolivar Peninsula surf is good from High Island to Crystal Beach. Limits of trout come on soft plastics and topwaters. Key on mullet and diving brown pelicans.

The Surfside jetty near Freeport is a crowded place during the summer; there are lots of fish to catch. Trout, redfish, sheepshead, black drum, whiting, croaker, Spanish mackerel, and the occasional kingfish or ling (cobia) can be duped from the granite. Shrimp free-lined or under a popping cork are strong natural presentations. D.O.A. Glow Shrimp, TerrorEyz, and Baitbusters are solid artificial offerings.

With light winds, Matagorda anglers have a tough choice: East Matagorda Bay reefs, or the surf. Drull's Lump, Long Reef, Three Beacon Reef, and Halfmoon Reef are all clumps of shell in the middle of the bay surrounded by deeper water. Speckled trout fall on and off the reefs with the tide.

Surf-fishers can drive down the east beach, get out anywhere, and wade the first and second guts. At high tide, trout roam the first gut. As the tide falls, schools slide into the deeper water where a long cast with a topwater can reach them.

The grass beds on the south shoreline of West Matagorda Bay are good around Green's and Cotton's bayous, the Cedars, and the Hump. Elevation changes and undulations on the bay floor provide ambush points for specks.

Redfish and trout fill back bay lakes in Espiritu Santo Bay near

Port O'Connor on swelling June tides. As southwest winds persist in July, tides drop and the mouths of these lakes will be prime.

Croaker soakers in Rockport and Corpus Christi earnestly wait for summer. Locales like Traylor Island, Mud Island, Copano Bay, and Allyn's Bight hold quality trout. Take redfish by drifting or anchoring on Estes Flats with finger mullet, gold spoons, and Top Dog Jr's.

The rocks of Baffin Bay, particularly Rocky Slough, are good for topwater aficionados. Point of Rocks, Penescal Point, Tide Gauge, and the Badlands are spots for trout and reds on Bass Assassins, gold spoons, and Corkies.

Grass beds adjacent to the Intracoastal are the pattern for Lower Laguna Madre anglers. The Kenedy shoreline near Port Mansfield, Laguna Vista near South Padre, and the Brazos Santiago Pass jetty near Port Isabel teems with plenty of predatory jaws ready to bend rods.

FALL

White shrimp beginning their exodus from the marsh through the bays and on to the Gulf of Mexico will set the tone for the finest fishing Texas has to offer. Find gulls milling, diving, and fighting for surface-bounding shrimp, and 90 percent of the time there are hearty autumn speckled trout and redfish under them.

"Fishing the birds" is a rite of fall, giving even the most novice of anglers a chance to enjoy a fresh fish dinner. Live bait is not needed; any fake that wiggles, darts, or floats gets hammered.

Another rite of fall is the migration of ocean-spawning bull redfish and flounder. Every cut, pass, or inlet leading to the Gulf will teem with bronze and brown.

Autumn wading can still be done in shorts, provide you can stand the chill. In the fall, shrimp exit the marsh and fill the bay before continuing their migration to the Gulf.

The north end of Sabine Lake comes alive with bird action near Pleasure Island and Coffee Ground Cove. Flounder at the mouths of marsh drains fall for any soft plastic tipped with fresh shrimp.

The East Ridge near the mouth of the Trinity River in Trinity Bay is solid for waders working Bass Assassins, Norton Sand Eels, and Trout Killers. Pumpkinseed, plum, and red shad are all proven colors. Hodges Reef consistently coughs up trophies for waders tossing Corkies, She Dogs, and Super Spooks. Bird action is good in the same areas as well as on the north shoreline near the Spillway.

East Galveston Bay holds working birds with light boat traffic, though waders on the north shoreline around Frozen Point can watch trout bash plugs against a beautiful autumn sunset. Big Pasture Bayou and Yates Bayou on the south shoreline are good choices as well.

Rollover Pass, the Galveston jetty, and San Luis Pass are good locales for bull redfish. Finger mullet, ribbonfish, and crabs are the baits of choice. Sea Wolf Park is the fall flounder spot in Galveston Bay. Finger mullet, mud minnows, and jigs tipped with shrimp are the ticket.

Arguably the finest fall fishing in Texas, East Matagorda Bay has the potential to produce trophy specks and reds under the birds or on mid-bay reefs like Long, Three Beacon, and Drull's Lump. Though West Matagorda Bay often misses notice for its autumn outlook, the northeast corner near Shell Island holds working birds. Best baits are glow Corkies, Bass Assassins, Sand Eels, and Trout Killers.

Chickenfoot Reef, Panther Reef, and the Chain of Islands in San Antonio Bay are solid wading venues for trout and redfish. Back lakes like Pringle, Contee, and Long hold burly reds on swelling equinox tides. Look for flounder near Pass Cavallo.

Reefs in Copano, St. Charles, and Mesquite bays hold trout and reds for waders working topwaters and suspending MirrOlure Catch 2000s and Corkies. Estes Flats in Aransas Bay and East Flats in Corpus Christi Bay hold trout, redfish, and flounder.

Redfish gather in large schools on the grass flats of Lower Laguna Madre. Gold spoons, topwaters, and pepper/chartreuse Red Killers, Trout Killers, Bass Assassins, and Norton Bull Minnows do the job.

WINTER

When Old Man Winter takes a deep breath and exhales, tides drop well below normal in Texas. Though the Lone Star State's coastal latitude lends itself to a milder winter than most, we still get cold here. However, barring a major fishing-killing freeze (not since 1989), receding water levels should congregate fish in deep bayous, rivers, and channels, and provide easy fishing for those willing to brave the cold.

On Sabine Lake, the Neches and Sabine rivers hold trout, redfish, flounder, and black drum if winter floods do not flush the rivers' brackish content. A Carolina-rigged live shad gets thumped quickly in holes in 8-14 feet of water. On cold mornings, sleep in and wait for the sun to warm the water a few degrees, then try a Bass Assassin, Norton Sand Eel, or Trout Killer. Bull redfish roam the Sabine Pass jetty year-round, and fall for cracked crabs or live finger mullet. You can wade the beach side and walk adjacent to the rocks.

The HL&P Spillway in Trinity Bay is always a wintertime haunt due to the warm water discharge from the power plant. Trout, redfish, and black drum seldom turn down a fresh peeled shrimp or live mullet. Winter fish are often sluggish and the bite can be subtle. If you feel the slightest tug or tick on your rod tip, set the hook.

Offatts Bayou in Galveston Bay is a traditional spot for winter waders. The Blue Hole in the bayou drops to 20 feet, and waders work red shad, black, or plum soft plastics on the drop-off to score large trout.

Rollover Pass, Bolivar Roads, and San Luis Pass are good redfish and flounder locales. Cracked crabs for the reds and jigs tipped with shrimp for the flatfish garners plenty of strikes.

The lower the tide the better for redfish in West Matagorda Bay. Green's and Cotton's bayous and the Middle Grounds hold hordes of redfish that congregate in the guts. Gold spoons, topwaters, and your favorite soft plastics get the job done. The Army Hole and Saluria Bayou in Port O'Connor is a black drum and redfish hangout as well.

In Espiritu Santo Bay and San Antonio Bay, mid-bay reefs will be the ticket, as long as oyster farmers have not drug their cages on the shell that day. The mouths of Contee Lake and Pringle Lake are good for flounder, trout, and redfish on a falling tide. Corkies, Catch 2000s, and soft plastics are best bets for success.

California Hole and the Morris Cummings Cut near Rockport hold winter redfish and trout that eat free-lined shrimp and glow Bass Assassins, Trout Killers, and Sand Eels; live shrimp can be hard to find at bait camps during winter.

Baffin Bay's Tide Gauge, Penescal Point, and Rocky Slough hold fish when the wind is not whipping.

Take note that duck hunters use these same areas during the winter.

Chapter Twelve

On Top of the Game

The Topwater Craze

I have a problem. I am a topwater freak. There, I admit it.

I yearn for water-thrashing, toilet bowl-flushing, white water-dunking blowups. I can't get enough of it. I am a plugger.

Some folks consider me narrow-minded. You see, when water temperature creeps above 65 degrees in the spring, I tie on a topwater and fish it exclusively until frigid mercury readings force me to jig. Although at times jiggers and suspenders get more bites than my dog-walker, seldom do they coax the same caliber of fish, and never enjoy the same merriment.

Topwater aficionados are a different breed, blessed with a sense of patience that allows them to cast and cast for only a handful of bites some days. Then, persistence is rewarded on that day when "everything is right" and trout and redfish fight to eat their plug on every cast.

Tons of theories exist concerning the efficacy of topwater plugs. Those theories are based on countless variables that often result in slight or slam. Here is what I have gleaned from a decade of surface plugging.

DOG-WALKERS VS. CHUGGERS

Dog-walking plugs are mullet imitations that exhibit a side-to-side, left-to-right motion called "walking the dog" when worked. Most have clamorous rattles that cause commotion to attract fish from afar. Popular dog-walkers include MirrOlure Top Dog, She Dog, He Dog, and Top Pup; Pradco Super Spook, Super Spook Jr., Spit'N Image, and Jumpin' Minnow; Rapala Skitter Walk and Skitter Prop; Producer Ghost and Mega-Ghost.

Chuggers are floating baits, usually with a cupped nose, that pop or spit water when jerked. Most do not employ loud rattles; the "chugging" and water commotion draws attention to the bait. Popular chuggers include Storm Chug Bug, Rapala Skitter Pop, and Pradco Tiny Torpedo and Pop-R.

Dog-walkers work best in a chop when their melodious clanking helps fish locate the fake. Chuggers, often smaller than walkers, produce on calm estuaries when little ripples exist.

Capt. Bruce Shuler of Port Mansfield, Texas, likes the Chug Bug when the wind lays in late summer and early fall: "I fished them back in my bassin' days. I had success with them then and have caught plenty of trout and redfish here on the flats."

Shuler agreed that a loud dog-walker produces better when the wind whips: "Chartreuse TD's and TD Jr's (Top Dog) work great when it is rough. It blows down here, a lot of times over 20 knots. Those fish can find that loud bait in rough water."

SHALLOW VS. DEEP

Some theorists say topwaters only work in waist-deep to knee-deep depths, and for the most part, they are right, but not always. My

A pink topwater on a calm day duped this trout in Rockport.

largest trout, a 31-inch Calcasieu Lake gorilla, was caught in 7 feet of water. The boys on Calcasieu south of Lake Charles, Louisiana, and Sabine Lake on the eastern border of Texas, regularly catch trout and redfish on plugs in water that would float your cap.

"We throw She Dogs against the rocks at the Sabine Pass Jetty," said Capt. Chuck Uzzle of Orange, Texas. "The water is 14 feet against the granite, but those trout come up and bang it."

When the redfish gang in West Cove, no topwater is safe. Uzzle and I endured mammoth blows from burly bronzebacks measuring 27 to 34 inches one day in June. As we eased each fish to the boat, a few friends were always swimming with it in a show of support. Nevertheless, all were released to bang another plug.

Though I have had some monumental mornings tossing topwaters from a boat, most adrenaline-pumping blows have come while wading East Matagorda Bay reefs, humps in Port O'Connor, and grass beds in Laguna Madre.

The key to wade-fishing with topwaters is knowing your tides. An incoming tide will push new water onto the flats, and with it baitfishes, shrimp, and other seafood. Trout and redfish hang out in the locale of their next meal. Hence, when tides are high, the fish move shallow. When water begins to fall off the flats, so do the fish.

Shallow or deep, where baitfishes go, so go game fishes.

LIGHT VS. LOW LIGHT

Topwater naysayers claim floating plugs only work early in the morning, late in the evening, or under cloud cover. This is true if the only time you throw a plug is in these conditions. The truth is, most anglers only toss plugs the first or last few hours of daylight. Then, impatience sets in and the knot is cut and tied to a gold spoon or their favorite soft plastic.

"You just have to tie one on and leave it on all day," said Capt. Melvin Talasek of Matagorda, Texas. "If the fish are there they will hit it. They may not eat it right away, but they will hit it. The rattles bother them. Then, when feeding time begins, they will kill the topwater."

Some of my most memorable topwater sessions have occurred at midday. A few summers ago, Talasek and I had fished the Gulf of Mexico surf all morning, with not the slightest hint of a blowup.

The August, sea foam green ocean barely produced a ripple on the first bar—perfect topwater conditions. Around 11 o'clock, someone must have rang the dinner bell. For the next three hours, we caught solid 4- to 6-pound trout on chartreuse, redheaded Top Dogs as sweat poured from our brows.

The Calcasieu trophy mentioned earlier in this piece was caught a few minutes before noon in the heat of a Louisiana summer.

Those holding onto the myth that topwaters only work in low-light situations are, indeed, missing the light.

FAST VS. SLOW

There are two speeds to retrieve a plug: fast and slow. Some like to rip the rod tip up and down and burn the bait across the water. Others, like me, choose to slow the presentation and give the fish a chance to find and size up its quarry.

"Trout want it different everyday," said Capt. Mickey Eastman of Galveston, Texas. "I can't work it fast enough some days, then again, I can't work it slow enough some days."

Eastman said you have to work the bait fast at times and cause as much clatter and commotion as possible to make specks strike: "When trout come up and hit it but miss, I work it even faster so they will think their meal is getting away. You have to make them eat sometimes."

TROUT VS. REDFISH

Compare the mouths of trout and redfish. Trout have agape jaws that allow them to ambush prey from below. Often, when a trout eats a plug you hear a distinct slurping noise made by their wide mouth, much like a largemouth bass. If I closed my eyes and listened to a fish hitting a topwater plug, more often than not, I could tell you if it was a trout or redfish just by the sound of the strike.

Redfish, on the other hand, have smaller, down-pointing mouths positioned to root out crabs and shrimp in the mud and grass. Though their anatomy is not built for classic topwater blows, reds are voracious feeders and will try to wrap their lips around anything moving, no matter how large. Topwater strikes by redfish are often the most thrilling, due to the redfish pouncing on top of the bait in order to get it in their bottom-feeding mouths. If the blow occurs near the boat, you better have a raincoat or you might get wet.

When fishing for both species, a plug that is not too large and not too small is a good choice. Four-inch baits like the She Dog, Top Dog Jr, Super Spook Jr, Skitter Walk, and Chug Bug will do in normal conditions. When fishing for trout in rough conditions, go with the oversized Super Spook, Top Dog, or He Dog. I have fished these baits in 2- to 3-foot waves in the surf and have watched trout ride a wave and crush the plug at the crest. When strictly fishing for reds, downsize your mullet imitation. Smaller baits like the Top Pup, Spit'N Image, and Pop-R are easier to get down a redfish's mouth

EQUIPMENT

Fishing topwaters is laborious to most anglers due to their equipment. The consensus on the brine is a 7-foot, medium to light action rod, perfect for 1/8- to 1/4-ounce leadheads, but painful when twitching and jerking a 1/2-ounce plug.

A stiffer, shorter rod will ease your forearm pain. I like a 6-foot, 6-inch medium action rod with a short handle. Longer 9-inch handles seem to always find my gut, and a stiffer rod cuts down on the buggy-whip motion from a limber stick.

Braided line is a good choice as well. With its limited stretch components, a short movement of the rod is all it takes to work the plug. Monofilament has as much as 25 percent stretch at hookset. Once you have fished a braid like Power Pro, monofilament feels like a rubber band.

COLOR

I will not deny that some shades of topwaters garner more bouts with angry fish, but I think color is less crucial than presentation. Above all, fish a color that gives you confidence and stick with it. If you have had success with chartreuse, fish chartreuse. If pink, fish pink.

"I think the darker lures work better in low-light conditions because they cast a shadow," said Capt. Bobby Gardner of Matagorda, Texas. "When the sun gets high, chrome is hard to beat, but an all-around bait is the pearl, chartreuse-backed She Dog. It catches fish in all conditions."

Whatever your theories on topwater might be, chances are they were formed because whatever you did worked. One thing is certain: if you don't fish a topwater, you won't catch fish on a topwater. The majority of anglers are missing the excitement of topwater by holding to the ageless myth that surface plugs only work in a few situations.

My passion for working dog-walking surface plugs developed when I was a teenager in the foam of the old Highway 87 surf near High Island, Texas. I did not have a boat. Four wheels and two feet were all I needed when light north winds transformed the Gulf of Mexico into a placid lake. Leaving the house by 4:00 a.m., my high school buddies and I would be dancing Jumpin' Minnows on the second bar at least an hour before dawn. The anticipation of the next strike drove us wild. We were like junkies needing a fix. Trout bashing a topwater was our dope—and still is.

Today, the plugging craze is booming. Look on tackle shelves and in tackle boxes. New noisy mullet and finfish look-alikes are hitting the fishing market weekly. More anglers are walking the dog, creating a bigger demand for baits. It is easy to see why; once you have experienced a fish crushing a topwater, you want more.

Fishing a topwater demands patience. There are going to be days when everything clicks and fish fight each other to eat your bait. There are few things more exciting. On the other hand, there will be days when you go an hour, two, or three without even a hint of a blowup. Will you snip the knot and opt for a soft plastic?

Most salts miss out on what topwater angling has to offer by adhering to age-old myths. Too hot, too rough, too deep, and too clear are all illegitimate excuses. For most, I say, "too impatient." Hey, if that is how you like to fish, fine. The old Hank Williams Jr. song has merit: "Old habits are hard to break." Yet, if you truly want to become a topwater aficionado, dispel the notion surface-runners only work in a few situations. The only way to do this is to plug away.

"I have caught them in 50 degree water and 100 degree water on topwaters," said Capt. James Plaag of Galveston. "I have caught them all day long in the heat of the summer in 9 feet of water. I have caught fish in all conditions on the topwater."

Let's dissect a few of the more common myths.

Myth: Topwater fishing is only good in the morning, late in the day, or in low light conditions.

Every time I hear someone say this, I chuckle and chalk it up to inexperience. Anglers do not know what they are missing. The fact is, most topwaters only catch fish in the morning, late afternoon, or on a cloudy day because that is the only time anglers fish them. Keep a plug tied on all day and you will be surprised.

"It is an old wives tale," Capt. Mike Mosley of Matagorda said. "Most anglers will fish the first two hours of the day with a topwater and then give up for a soft plastic. As guides, we have to fish all day and see what a topwater can do if presented right."

Three summers ago in the Matagorda surf, Capt. Melvin Talasek, teenager Michael Briggs, and I were cruising the beachfront in my Pathfinder. We had fished several miles of beach from Mitchell's Cut to the mouth of the Colorado River since sunup without a bite. About 11:00 a.m., we fired the Yamaha and headed west. Talasek wanted to work a deep gut near the Cullen House. The ocean was a huge sheet of glass, not a breath of August wind in the Caribbean-like brine. After Briggs set the anchor, Talasek motioned his deckhand to wade out and tell us if any fish were stacked in the trough.

An angry speck dunked Brigg's first cast, mistaking his black Top Dog for a finger mullet. Talasek and I quickly dove overboard and began sticking trout in the first gut. As the tide began to fall, so did the fish into deeper water. Instead of facing the beach from the second bar, we turned and faced south to the expanse of the Gulf and met herds of attacking trout. As we fought fish, other specks would follow the hooked fish all the way to us. The action was uninterrupted for the next two hours as we coaxed 3- to 5-pound fish in 100-degree weather.

"If fishermen would just tie one on and keep it on all day, they would be surprised at the fish the topwater will catch," Talasek said. "For sure it is not going to catch fish if you take it off."

I could go on and on about the stringers of fish I have been blessed to catch on topwaters in the heat of a sunny day in coastal haunts from Sabine Lake to Port Mansfield. Some say when the sun gets too high, the trout go deep and do not come to the surface and hit a topwater because the light hurts their eyes. Hah! I hope those guys enter the same big trout tournaments I do.

"The pattern with a topwater is there is no pattern," Capt. Jerry Norris of Sabine Lake said. "You have to have a situation where the fish are feeding on mullet or other traveling baitfish. The ideal opportunity is when bait is working the surface. When in doubt, throw a topwater."

Capt. Chris Martin of Seadrift believes misconceptions were bred in freshwater.

"A lot of that mentality came from bass fishers," Martin said. "Bass anglers like working topwaters in the low light conditions of morning and afternoon. If the bait is present and the topwater is presented appropriately, topwaters will work throughout the day in saltwater."

Myth: Topwaters do not work in rough water.

Why not? Does it really matter to the fish? Ever thrown a Super Spook in the surf with 1- to 2-foot rollers? Many times, it gets inhaled. I have had fish jump out of a wave and eat my plug as it rides the crest of the swell.

One summer, I was field-testing the MirrOlure She Dog prototype while waves crashed over my head. The water remained sandy green and the trout engulfed the rattler throughout the afternoon.

Winds were blowing 15-20 miles per hour from the south as Sammy Noland and I fished Long Point on Calcasieu Lake. Two-foot swells rocked my boat, but it did not matter to the trout, evident by the 28-incher Noland duped on a Christmas-tree pattern Mega-Ghost.

"Charlie (Capt. Paradoski) and I catch fish all the time in a rough chop," said Capt. Don Wood. "You want to use a big plug with a loud rattle like a Super Spook."

Desperate times call for desperate measures. I learned something in the 2000 Troutmasters Port O'Connor Open. Winds were puffing at 35-40 mph on the first day of the two-day event. I tried to find some seclusion on a leeward shoreline of Keller Bay. To put it in perspective, my Top Dog looked like a surfer riding a giant tube on the North Shore. Nonetheless, the trout did not mind. If the fish are there and hungry, the topwater will work.

"Cast it in the bumpy surf and the fish hammer it," said Martin. "I have caught good tournament fish in Port O'Connor with the wind howling. If the bait and fish are there, it does not really matter."

Myth: Topwaters only work in shallow water.

Not too many pluggers in southeast Texas and southwest Louisiana, particularly Calcasieu Lake, will agree with that notion. Guides on the Big Lake and neighboring Sabine Lake make a living walking the dog over deep shell and mud. The sister lakes are meccas for huge speckled trout. Drifting over deep-water structure is the preferred means of catching one.

Capt. Erik Rue introduced me to a hefty spotted beauty on Calcasieu Lake in May 2001. Rue and I took turns throughout the morning catching 3- to 4-pound specks on Super Spooks and Top Dogs while drifting south shoreline oyster beds. Around midday, Rue followed his GPS coordinates to a spot in the middle of the lake in 7 feet of water. Easing the anchor overboard, Rue murmured: "I have caught them here on topwaters before."

I took a break from the morning of constant casting to grab a soda, click some frames for a feature story, and reapply sunscreen. Twenty minutes later, I made my first cast. When the wall of white foam subsided and my Curado's drag cooled off, I was extracting the trebles of my black/chartreuse Top Dog from the mouth of a 31-inch trout. The hand-held digital scale read 9.4 pounds. The fiberglass replica of the gorilla with spots greets me daily in my living room, reminding me fish will bash a plug in deep water.

"That is how we do it here," said Rue. "Topwater fishing is becoming a craze in Calcasieu, and most of the structure is at least 5 feet deep. We will get masses of shad schooling in the middle of the lake and hammer the fish in the summer on topwaters throughout the day."

"In Calcasieu and Sabine I think you will catch more fish on top-waters than tails," said Plaag. "There is so much shad and shrimp that ball up because the fish push them to the top. You can drift right out in the middle and get crushed."

Norris works surface plugs around the rigs just off the beach of Sabine Pass: "We throw big Super Spooks around the rigs in 14 feet of water. Those trout will suspend and come up and blow the bait out of the water."

Norris said a topwater is his go-to bait when nothing else will work. He said the sound will get fish to feed: "A topwater has a calling effect in deep water. You have sound and sight working for you. Fish will travel a long way to find out what the commotion is all about. Fish will not do that with a soft plastic because they do not make the noise a topwater will. A topwater will call fish to you; it is a great fish locator."

Mosley has caught fish on topwaters in up to 30 feet of water: "I have caught them in the Colorado River in the deep holes. Read your electronics to see if the fish are suspended. All you have to do is fish it and you will be surprised."

Still an unbeliever? Tie on a topwater and fish it all day. Find out for yourself what all the hype is about. Dispel the age-old myths. A heart-pounding, water-thrashing blowup is just a cast away.

Chapter Thirteen

The Eyes Have It

Fish eyes provide targets

Stroll down the saltwater aisle of your favorite tackle provider. A kaleidoscope of jerking, swimming, diving, suspending, and surface-running baitfish imitations line the shelves. Anglers whose hearts' pump brine are left with a choice much like that of a perspiring child trying to pick one of the innumerable snow cone flavors during the heat of summer. Candy-apple, grape, plum, lime, and strawberry titillate the human pallet and show up as colors on saltwater plugs; but, do fish see underwater what humans see above the surface?

BELOW THE SURFACE

Like human eyes, fish eyes have a cornea, iris, lens, and retina full of rods and cones. These rods and cones give rise to the notion that fish see colors, since vertebrates use these color receptors to distinguish all facets of the color spectrum.

Fish eyes are perfectly spherical, which enables them to see underwater due to a higher refractive index that helps them focus. The round lens is much denser than a human lens, reflecting the heavily refracted light onto the retina to focus clearly underwater. Fish focus by moving in and out instead of stretching the lens like humans.

In humans, the cornea is not as good at bringing light to focus underwater as it is on land. That is due to refraction, which is the changing of direction of light rays from one medium to another. Normally, light passes from air to the fluid in your eye, but underwater, the light passes from fluid to fluid. Refraction does not occur nearly as well in humans underwater. Focusing is difficult and objects appear distorted or as a blob, according to scientificsonline.com. If you want to see what a fish sees underwater, put on a pair of goggles and have a look.

The Hue For You

Choosing the best color for your excursion should emulate what the fish are feeding on at the time. If white shrimp is on the menu, try something in white or glow. If summertime brown shrimp are filtering through the bays, pumpkinseed or smoke colors work well. When the buffet consists of finfish, a light-colored bait with dark back closely represents a mullet, piggy perch, croaker, shad, or glass minnow.

At night, in low light conditions, or dingy off-colored water, dense colors such as red shad, black, purple, and blue cast a shadow that hungry fish will intercept. The theory is that these colors provide a distinct profile when silhouetted against the lighter backdrop of the surface.

"I have always accepted the theory that in low light or stained water situations, throw something dark," said Capt. Chuck Uzzle of Orange. "I am a believer in black baits, especially on my home waters of Sabine Lake. Dark baits in black, red, and purple cast a large profile and silhouette in murky water, and give trout a better opportunity to find and eat them."

Red is the most common color used by artificial aficionados along the Gulf of Mexico. Anglers prefer red lures in very dark or stained water because red is the last hue to disappear in deep, dim water.

"Red over white is by far the most popular color along the coast," said Capt. Mark Nichols of Stuart, Florida, lure maker and owner of D.O.A. Lures. "There is a good reason for it. Red is that dark color that appears in dirty or low light waters and white is a light color that appears in clear, bright waters. The two colors together make a perfect contrast, and that is what you should look for in a lure, something that gives a flash for the fish to see."

With clear water and sun overhead, go with light, translucent colors such as glow, chartreuse, hologram, motor oil, and firetiger green.

"Chartreuse, bone, and white are all good colors for clear water," said Capt. Bill Pustejovsky of Matagorda. "My favorite topwater in green water is the Okie Shad Super Spook, and gold with chartreuse back She Dog. I have had good results with them and have confidence throwing them."

BULL'S EYE

Though vision is vital for fish to seek food and refuge, a fish's own eyes can give its location away to larger predators. There is no mistaking that big fish eat their prey head first. The eye provides a target at which hungry assailants aim with mouths agape. Game fish use the eye of their prey as an archer uses a bull's eye target.

"I have yet to see a big speckled trout eat a mullet tail first," said Uzzle. "Every time you see a huge speck with an oversized mullet stuck in its throat, the tail is always hanging out of its mouth."

Summer is the season for catching trophy trout using golden croakers. Though the speckled trout and croaker are of the same family, trout love to attack the golden grunters. Croakers prompt sea trout to attack even when they are not feeding, increasing the chances of a successful harvest. Inexperienced fishermen using croakers set the hook on the initial strike, but pros tell you to let the trout assault the bait, then wait; the fish will come back and try to swim away with the bait. Those who prematurely bury the barb reel in a lifeless croaker with two fang marks near the eyes.

Brown and white shrimp are popular members of the bay community, but they would prefer to be a recluse or the kid chosen last for the team. Not many salty swimmers turn down a feisty crustacean if it appears at dinnertime.

A shrimp's eyes are its demise, and a glowing mark for glutton snook, redfish, trout, and tarpon to attack. Ask you local bait camp operator to let you see the live shrimp in their tank at night. Notice their eyes gleam in the darkness and reflect when hit by light.

Pseudo Eye

If you still have doubts about the validity of eyes, look at the dot or multi-dots on the top posterior portion of a red drum. The black oval is not there for aesthetic purposes. It is a mark to elude predators.

Redfish are ocean spawners. Though they spend their juvenile days growing in the friendly confines of bay estuaries, by age four, they migrate between the bay and the Gulf of Mexico. Sharing waters with the wolves of the sea such as sharks and barracudas is toil for survival. Reds use the dots on their tail as a mimicking eye. They have a better chance of living if an adversary swipes a piece of tail rather than a chunk of head. On several occasions, I have caught redfish with a blunt caudal fin.

THAT LOOK IN THEIR EYES

Artificial bait manufacturers are cashing in on the lure of the eye. Black, red, chrome, and chartreuse eyes make up the marketing ploys of over half the topwater and subsurface imitations on the marine market.

L&S Bait Company, maker of the MirrOlure, identified the eye as the foundation for its bait's popularity and success.

"My grandfather made the eyes on our lures to be oversized and three-dimensional," said Eric Bachnik, sales manager for L&S and third generation lure maker. "The big red eyes imitate a mullet's eyes and provide a big target."

The three-dimensional effect seems to radiate when sunlight hits the eyes. The red in the eyes can be mistaken for a wounded baitfish as well, according to Bachnik: "When crawled on the bottom, I believe fish think our 51 and 52 baits are shrimp by the way the eyes of our baits look underwater."

Nichols of D.O.A. agreed that fish respond better to red eyes: "I tried black, white, chartreuse, and gold when I was testing my jigheads for the TerrorEyz baits. Red eyes dominated."

"I use both lures regularly (D.O.A. and MirrOlure). The huge red eyes are what make these baits work," said Capt. Melvin Talasek of Matagorda. "Any time you give an ambush feeder like a trout, redfish, or snook a target like that, they are going to bang it."

Talasek knows well the importance of eyes and takes his baits one step farther. By dressing the back trebles of his She Dogs and Top Dogs with a chartreuse and orange teaser, he gives fish another symbolic eye to attack. The teasers are made by dipping thin aquarium tubing in Colorite dye and then cutting and sliding the small pieces of plastics over the shank of the hook.

Yogi Berra once said: "You can see a lot just by looking." For fishermen and fish looking for a bait to bend a rod, the statement could not be more true.

Chapter Fourteen

Tricks of the Trade:

Customizing your favorite lure

Normally, I do not drive two hours to the airport, spend another two hours in the air, then rent a car and drive another hour to catch gafftop "sail cats"—I can do that in Texas. Nevertheless, as Capts. Mark Nichols, Ray Markham, and I drifted at Hell's Gate in the St. Lucie River near Stuart, Florida, there was plenty of "meowing" going on.

They were impressive slimers—all 3 to 6 pounds—consistently thumping our D.O.A. TerrorEyz and deep-running Bait Busters, but we were not there to dupe catfish. The more glamorous tarpon was our target species. Two dozen had already shown their emerald backs, yet not one had felt the urge to suck down our swimming fakes.

"Here kitty, kitty," Markham mocked as I growled like a canine toward a feline as my drag labored against yet another gafftop.

"One thing I have learned," added Nichols. "When there are lots of gafftop, there are normally lots of tarpon, too. They hang out together many times."

Mid-morning, as beads of sweat began to form and attention waned, Nichols' slow retrieve was interrupted. With two quick vertical jabs of his rod tip, Nichols proclaimed he had stuck his Swimming Mullet deep in the jaw of a tarpon.

The 80-pounder bound to the surface in typical tarponesque form, complete with fanatical headshake and gill flare. Three more jumps and the beautiful beast finally frayed enough of the 60-pound leader to end the battle.

Nichols smiled.

"You might want to try some of this stuff."

Without telling us, the crafty captain had added a smelly attractant to the belly of his 6-inch mullet imitation. It might have been the added scent, it might have been his expertise at fishing his own creation; whatever, his tweak resulted in the only poon hooked that morning, proof enough for me to pinch my nose and add a spritz of the magic potion.

Every angler looks for an edge—a hot tip from a guide buddy, a super secret GPS mark, or a special lure that gives you the confidence to fish long and hard. There are many tricks of the trade than can turn a slow day to fair, fair to good, and good to great.

Here are a few lure tweaks I have learned from seasoned captains:

ARTS AND CRAFTS

Five summers ago, Capt. Melvin Talasek and I stood shoulder to shoulder, casting along a drop-off on the edge of Boiler Bayou in East Matagorda Bay. We were catching fish, or I should say, *he* was catching fish.

Our MirrOlure topwater plugs were exactly the same shade, yet my Top Dog was getting slighted while his consistently got hammered. Confused, I asked to inspect his lure.

"What is this?" I asked, pointing to an object attached to the back treble.

"Homemade teasers," he said. "I'll make you some."

The teasers are quite simple to make. Go to any pet store aquarium section and pick up some standard airline tubing. The tubing I buy at Wal-Mart costs less than two dollars for 8 feet. Next, you need two bottles of colored tail dip or worm dye. I like the Colorite chartreuse and fluorescent orange colors, but green, pink, or red will do, whatever your preference. Cut off about three inches of tubing and dip one half in one color and the other half in another. Allow a few minutes to dry. Remove the back treble hook from your lure. Cut a thin sliver of each color of tubing, then slide both

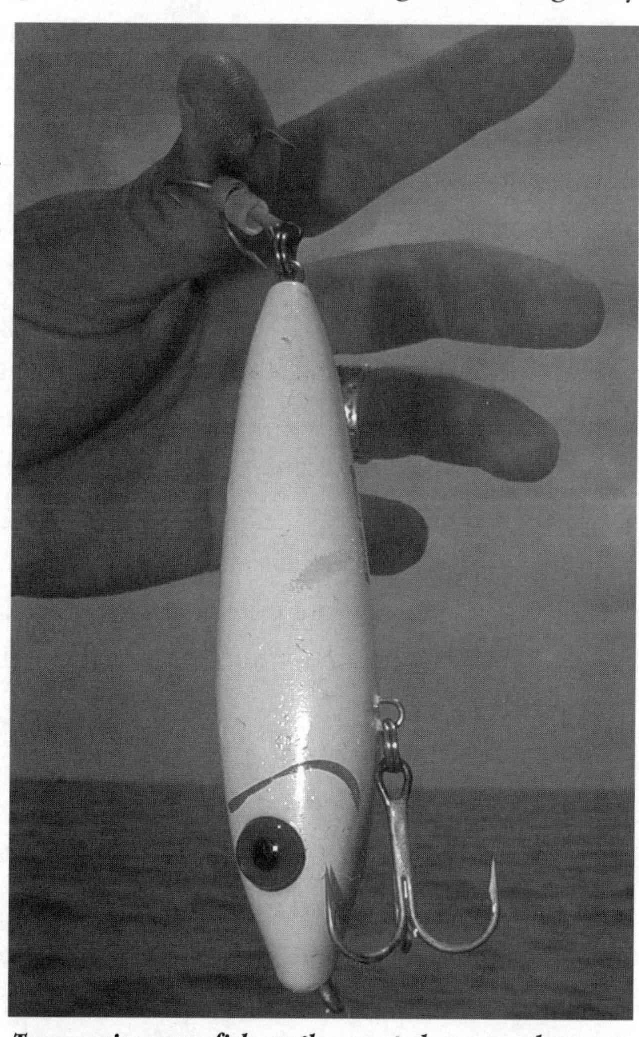

Teasers give game fish another eye to home on when feeding.

over the shank of the treble hook. Reattach the hook to the lure, and you are done.

The teasers work by giving fish another target to hit. Speckled trout, redfish, and snook always attack their prey headfirst, using the eye as a "bull's eye." Teasers give game fish another eye to home on when feeding. All my topwaters are tweaked this way before getting wet. Some anglers customize their plugs by marking a dot with a permanent marker that resembles an eye, like the dot on the tail of a redfish—more eyes, more targets, more strikes.

When the wind blows and the fishing slows in the winter and early spring, Talasek breaks out the paint can and gives his old, rusty lures a new look. Call it boredom or call it art, his creations have prompted a few lure manufacturers, including MirrOlure and Texas Tackle Factory, to concoct new colors for their regular product line. The popular redheaded Nightstalker (black) Top Dog was his idea. At one time, the bait was the hottest color on the Texas coast until the chartreuse-headed She Dog came along—another spawn of Talasek's paint can.

An original chartreuse-headed Dog duped the largest trout of my life (31 inches) before ever hitting the assembly line. Another redheaded paint job on a pearl and chartreuse She Dog put my dad in the "30-inch club."

KEEP OFF THE GRASS

Lone Star speckled trout anglers from the far western reaches of West Matagorda Bay all the way to South Padre frequent the undulating shoal grass shorelines. Ditto on Florida's east coast along the Indian River and the west coast estuaries fed by the Gulf of Mexico. Trout roam these locales for a reason: the grass and sand potholes are prime ambush points for tide-driven finfishes and shrimp. Often, when the wind blows or summertime water temps creep into the 80s, strands of grass break free from the bottom and float to the surface. For pluggers, the vegetation presents the problem of fouling the natural movement of lures by catching the trebles. For jiggers, the grass always seems to find the hook. It is frustrating dispensing of the grass after every cast, especially when you know the fish are there but the grass hinders hookups. One remedy is an offset "bass" hook rigged weedless. Originally, this is the way the Bass Assassin 5-inch shad was created to work, then Texans began using the shad bodies with lead heads and the saltwater boon began.

With spinning reels, the soft plastics cast with ease, but the lightweight rig is tough with a bait-caster. To remedy the bait-casting dilemma, D.O.A. offers pinch weights easily applied or removed from the shank of the hook. They provide more weight for longer casts, but the real advantage is the horizontal falling motion the pinch weights add to the action of the bait when jigging. A three-day session of dancing and darting C.A.L. soft plastics in the grass-laden Indian River near Fort Pierce, Florida, convinced me.

SOUND BITE

Fish use sound to locate prey, especially in stained water. This is why popular topwaters are loaded with clanking ball bearings. Not everyone likes to plug from daylight to dark. It is laborious, especially if your rod is limber and longer than 7 feet.

Jiggers use glass and brass rattles that insert into the soft plastic body of their favorite bait. Though the small encapsulated beads do not produce the decibels of a She Dog or Super Spook, they do emulate the clicking sound of a shrimp exiting the mud. Texas Tackle Factory offers the inserts along with special jigheads that rattle (texastacklefactory.com).

Small rattling corks including the Mansfield Mauler, Alameda, and Cajun Thunder are noisemakers that suspend a bait above tangling grass or sharp shell reefs. Jerk- and swim baits attach below the cork according to the depth you are fishing. I have seen a slow bite turn on when the corks come out. D.O.A offers a pre-rigged Cajun Thunder cork and a 3-inch glow shrimp ready to fish out of the package.

Any advantage I can use to coax a bite, I will take. A minute tweak can turn fishing frustration to drag-squealing elation.

Chapter Fifteen

Paying for It

A guide to choosing a guide

My first experience with a "professional" came on the waters of Calcasieu Lake in southwest Louisiana. To say it was an "experience" is putting it mildly. He was a rookie in the greenest sense. Foul language, bad manners, and just being a "goofball" quickly turned the trip into a circus well before he forgot to turn his aerator on to breathe life into our feisty crustaceans. By 8:00 a.m., three quarts of martyrs lay lifeless on the floor of the baitwell. So much for live bait and the $36 it took to kill them.

Honestly, that was the one time I felt cheated by a fishing guide providing a service for my dollar. More often than not, it is the exception and not the rule. Hiring a pro to put you on fish, whether black bass, crappie, stripers, speckled trout, redfish, snapper, king mackerel, or billfish, should be a scrutinizing process so that your entertainment dollar meets the needs of your fishing abilities and desires.

Why hire a guide? Sometimes equipment and inexperience in a

certain local dictate the expertise of someone who knows the water and counts on that knowledge to feed his family. Others have the equipment but are tired of burning fuel day after day and coming home with a light cooler. Some just want the on-the-water classroom lecture and the knowledge gained from fishing with a "teacher." Still, some just want the service and good time expected, like at a fine restaurant.

Here are some tips to help "guide" your expectations so that you can find the right professional to suit your needs:

Most anglers seeking a guide are not concerned with hauling in a "limit." They *are* concerned with the hospitality and cordial treatment that will occupy their eight-hour trip. There are those "fishermen" who think a day without their 10 trout is a wash. A better name for them would be "meat haulers" or "freezer pleasers." Be reasonable, and do not expect to fill your Igloo. Such is the exception, not the rule.

Many things that make a great day of fishing and, unless your guide can walk across the Sea of Galilee, there are going to be days that are tough. Weather and tides are the important variables in the feeding patterns of fish. Wind can turn a clear shoreline into a huge glass of chocolate milk. However, do not assume that you cannot catch quality fish in nasty water. If bait is in the area, the fish will not leave, it will just be harder for the fish to see their prey. Incoming tides will flush new water and bait into vacant estuaries, but days with slack tides do little or nothing to prompt water movement and fish feeding. High pressure associated with weather patterns, usually after a strong front, sometimes causes fish to get "lockjaw," meaning they feel no need to feed. Lunar phases affect tidal movement and fish feeding times. Throw water temperatures into the mix and you see that many variables are out of the hands of the guides. Like it or not, we are at the mercy of the elements.

Guides want to put you onto fish. They know that if there are fish on the stringer, there are usually smiles on faces—and if you leave smiling, chances are you will probably come back and tell someone about your meaningful experience. That is a guide's business. You can spend wads of bills for ads in national magazines and local radio, but word of mouth is priceless. Any guide realizes this, and for that reason every trip is counted as a new opportunity to grow their business. Consequently, this pays off for the consumer by the guide giving you the best trip and service possible. They cannot afford to treat clients badly.

My dad, Danny Grimes of Mont Belvieu (Barbers Hill), is rewarded for an early alarm clock in the Matagorda surf.

When you do narrow your selections for potential guides, get on the phone and call your prospects. Get a feel for who you are dealing with. Ask questions:

- *What kind of fishing do you offer?*
- *Will we use live or artificial bait?*
- *Do you supply the tackle (i.e. rods, reels, lures)?*
- *Will we be wading or drifting?*
- *What kind of boat do you run?*
- *How many anglers will your boat fish comfortably?*

> • *How much for a full or half day trip?*
>
> • *Is fishing cleaning extra?*
>
> • *Are you a Coast Guard licensed captain?*
>
> • *What is the best time to come?*
>
> • *What are your cancellation and deposit procedures?*
>
> • *Can I plot points with my GPS?*
>
> • *How long have you been in business?*
>
> • *Do you provide lunch and refreshments or do we need to bring our own?*
>
> • *Do you have a list of references?*

Costs for full day trips inshore, such as bay or lake charters, range $350-500 depending on the services offered and the number of anglers involved. Normally, a trip includes no more than three clients, with an additional charge for each additional person. Still, some guides will limit the party to three depending on the size of their boat. Offshore trips run $500 and up, with billfishing sometimes running in excess of $2,000. Think it is expensive? Well, maybe. Yet, when you consider what goes into a successful trip, you will find that it is not all profit for the guide service. Your money spent is usually well worth the expense. Remember, guides do this for a living. It is just like a "9 to 5" job, just longer hours. My day starts a full two hours before my clients ever reach the dock, and by the time they leave the dock that afternoon, there is another hour of routine boat maintenance and cleaning. Eight hours on the water makes for a 12-hour day for a guide—a good one that is.

A $400-$800 a month boat payment multiplied by 12 months is a chunk of money. Compare that to the price of a charter and add in the fact that you will be fishing with a professional and most anglers come out ahead, especially if you split the charter with three other buddies.

Put a pencil to it: a ton of trips can be purchased for the price of owning a boat. Say your boat payment is $500 a month: that's $6,000 a year, not including fuel, oil, licenses, insurance, and routine maintenance. If you spend $200 on every charter you take, provided you have friends to split the cost, you can charter 30 trips before you reach the $6,000 boat payment. The best thing about it is you can walk away from the dock when you are done and not have to worry about cleanup or if your boat trailer lights and bearings will hold up for the ride home. Not to mention, you will be fishing with an expert every time, increasing you percentages of catching fish. Most anglers who own boats have not fished 30 times in the last five years. Do the math and decide what is best for you.

If a charter costs $450, the captain does not reap the entire sum. Many pieces of the pie come off before calculating net profit. Factor in accident insurance for clients; collision insurance on the boat; gas; engine oil; live bait; artificial lures; rods and reels for clients; cost of replacing broken tackle; periodic maintenance of tackle and boat; hooks; trailer tires; trailer maintenance; trailer registration; cost of obtaining a Coast Guard Captain's License; advertising in outdoor shows and publications; cost of time and expertise; and long-distance bills that accrue from the nearly two hours of return phone calls waiting on the answering machine after a day of fishing. Indeed, there is much more to it than just gassing up and taking people fishing.

Like any service profession, tips are appreciated but not expected, at least by many guides. If you are treated with courtesy and respect, put a little extra green in the pocket of your guide to show your appreciation.

Do your homework when choosing a guide. Be up front. Express your interests and expectations before confirming the deal so that you end up in a boat that meets your needs or desires. There are all types of guides out there, each with his own specialization. It is up to you to make the right choice.

Most guides require a deposit to hold a date, thus minimizing last minute cancellations. If you stay up too late the night before a trip or just do not feel like going and call the trip off, be prepared to pay. When you book a trip, that date is eliminated from the guide's calendar. When you decide to "no show," you are taking money from the guide. You see, he probably could have booked the trip if you had not already reserved the date. Do not be surprised if your guide is unhappy if you decide to cancel at the last minute. Once that date is gone, the guide cannot get it back. It is like a lost day of work.

If the trip does not go as planned, express your dissatisfaction. Mind you, I am not referring to a lack of catching fish. All a guide can guarantee is the opportunity to fish, not catch fish. All guides have bad days, even the elite. Besides, a bad day is in the eye of the beholder. However, if you feel the guide was not prepared or did not work hard for you, that is a different story. However, do not whine at the dock for a price break if your guide worked hard but you did not catch enough fish for your liking. Doctors still get paid whether they diagnose anything wrong or not. Most businessmen get paid regardless if their day is prosperous or not.

If you are looking for a wade-fishing guide, ask. Some guides never bail off the gunwale, while some advertise wade-fishing as their only option. If a wader hires a drift-fishing guide or vice versa, a long day is in to offing. Do your homework.

The next time you think that fishing guides have the life, consider the other things that go into making their business a profitable one. It is not all full limits and heavy stringers, but full days and heavy workloads.

Chapter Sixteen

Do You See What I See?

Polarized sunglasses—eyes for the fisherman

I always wondered how Aquaman could see fins from above the water surface and call up dolphins to ride them through the depths of the ocean, solving all kinds of malfeasance and crimes. He must have had a pair of polarized sunglasses, or polarized eyeballs. Were he an angler, he would have been an awesome sight-caster with his ultraviolet, glare cutting vision. Redfish, tarpon, snook, and speckled trout swimming the shallows would never go unnoticed.

I feel I have the sub-surface vision like that of the pelagic dwelling superhero. No, I did not have surgery to correct my vision; I can already spot things from afar. My 20/10 vision remains intact. It allowed me to see the laces of hard-biting sliders, paid my way through college, and comes in handy when spotting diving gulls from afar during autumn.

Ordinary sunglasses compared to polarized shades do not compare when trying to locate game- and baitfishes beneath the surface.

Sunny days provide plenty of glare on the water. When light waves strike the water surface, they vibrate together horizontally, producing blinding spots that are uncomfortable and sometimes dangerous to the eyes.

Polarization rearranges the light, relaxes your eyes, and lets you see through the glare while blocking the harmful reflected rays. Polarized sunglasses range from as little as 15 percent protection to as much as 99 percent. The better, but costly shades, offer the highest degree of protection while also blocking the rays before they hit the water. A quality pair will range from $80-$300. When deciding how much to spend, ask yourself what protecting your sight and enhancing your fishing prowess is worth.

Since ditching popular sport glasses for pairs of more sport specific Maui Jim or Costa Del Mar, I have observed a whole new world. I spend countless hours of my world on the bow of a boat or shuffling across the bay floor. "X-ray" vision of what lurks beneath can alleviate a world of hurt in saline circumstances, while enhancing the chances of finding fish. One example is wading and drifting the surf. Although most people do not want to see those big fish with a protruding dorsal fin, the ocean is full of them. Whether the water is green to the beach or sandy, the sharks are there. I spotted sharks in the surf before wearing polarized glasses, but sightings are more common with my new shades. A few summers ago, I saw a couple of 7- to 9-footers roaming the first gut within rod distance of my stringer of trout.

Another surf trip with polarized vision turned a good day into a great day. I was standing on the first bar casting topwaters into the first gut toward dashing, scattering, nervous mullet. Every time I had a hookup with an 18-inch trout, two bigger fish in the 22- to 25-inch class would follow until they saw my shadow and darted away. I looked down and consistently saw fish swimming over the bar into the deeper, sec-

Polarized glasses cut the glare and help waders see below the surface.

ond gut. Like clockwork, the fishing in the first gut slowed. As temperatures were rising and the tides were falling, the trout were heading to the cooler, deeper water. I turned 180 degrees with my back to the beach and began walking the dog in the 5-foot water. Again, my Top Dog was met with a thrashing blow. Sure, I probably would have figured that the fish had moved deeper after another half-hour of futile casts. However, seeing the fish move firsthand prompted me to process the information quicker, logging it into long-term memory for the next excursion.

Popular brands of shades on the coastal scene include Costa Del Mar, Ocean Waves, and Maui Jim. Costa Del Mar is the easiest to find in local sporting goods stores and tackle shops, and offer a variety of models priced from $80 and up. If not for fishing, you can also use them for stylish occasions.

Ocean Waves can be found in specialty shops for the angler. They offer a sleek, contemporary look fit for fashion or fishing. My favorite frame and model is the Stingray in the green mirror finish. Prices start at slightly less than a Benjamin Franklin, depending on frames and prescriptions.

Maui Jim shades originated in Hawaii, but have since hit the mainland with great popularity. They offer traditional frames with some stylishly eye-catching frames of their own. I fish with the Typhoon II model in tortoise frame and grey lenses. I also own pairs of MJ titanium-framed and stainless steel-framed glasses that are too light to describe.

You might think you can catch just as many fish without special polarized lenses; and you are probably right. However, chances are you will have a headache at the end of the day from squinting, and miss the opportunity of enjoying another world just below the sun-glared surface.

Chapter Seventeen

When the Cold Wind Blows

Winter hotspots & strategies

The term "warm winter" is an oxymoron in most places, but on the Texas coast, it is more the norm than the exception.

Winter fishing in the Lone Star state is without a doubt weather driven. Normally, cold fronts that freeze Canadian and upper Midwest waters lose their bite by the time they cross the Red River. It takes a Siberian blast to ruin fishing in Texas' bay estuaries. Texans have dodged the bullet for 14 years now. Not since 1989 has the "Golden Crescent" endured a hard freeze that resulted in a significant spotted seatrout kill, and 2003 marked the twentieth anniversary of the "great freeze of 1983" that depleted Texas bays of their bounty, resulting in poor fishing for several years after. Wind is the one variable that does wreak havoc on coastal anglers during winter. Winds rivaling those of Chicago blow east to northeast with each passing front, leaving less acreage to fish. Anglers must search leeward shorelines that hold fishable waters in sustained gales of 20 knots or more.

So where do Texans fish for speckled trout when Old Man Winter takes a deep breath and exhales? Here are a few sheltered haunts from Sabine Pass to Boca Chica:

SABINE LAKE

The border lake that divides Texas and Louisiana provides protection from gusts in the Neches and Sabine rivers, which flow into the north end of the lake. Captain Chuck Uzzle of Orange said the rivers can be fished year-round: "Barring flood rains that freshen the upper end of the lake, I camp out in the river during the winter. The trout hang close to elevation changes. Depending on the temperature, sometimes they will be in the holes when it is cold, and shallower as the sun shines."

Uzzle likes to jig a pumpkinseed or glow Norton Sand Eel Jr or Bull Minnow when tossing artificials, but said if you want non-stop action, use live shad: "We have a warm water outfall where the shad really congregate in the winter. All it takes is one throw of the cast net and you have enough shad for the whole day."

Uzzle Carolina rigs his shad with enough weight above the swivel to get the presentation down and hold it in the zone with a heavy current. If the trout are there, it does not take long to bend a rod: "They say specks are lethargic in the winter, but they really thump the shad. There is no doubt about it when they decide to eat."

When mercury readings rise, pluggers wade the backside of Sydney, Stewt's, and Rabbit islands—established havens for big trout due to their proximity to the Intracoastal. Uzzle said these spots on the north end of Sabine Lake provide protection from north winds: "The islands are prime in the afternoon when the sun comes out. Trout hang in the area because it is close to deep water. When the tide or temperature drops, it is only a short swim to the deeper Intracoastal. When the

Wading in the afternoon on clear winter days is best as the sun warms the shallows.

water warms, specks come out of the deep and onto the sandy flats of the islands."

GALVESTON BAY

Frozen Point on the banks of the Anahuac National Wildlife Refuge is one of the most popular winter spots to catch a trophy speck. The flats have shell, mud, and marsh—all the amenities that attract baitfishes, thereby attracting yellow mouths. Since its locale is on the north shoreline of East Galveston Bay, it is protected from northerly winds.

She Dogs, Top Dogs, and Super Spooks in black, bone, chrome, or 808 (black/gold/orange) are solid topwater choices. Slow-sinking Corkies, 51M and 52M MirrOlures, and gold spoons often garner attacks.

The North Flats adjacent to the Houston Lighting and Power (HL&P) Spillway in Trinity Bay is a proven winner. The opportune time to fish this area is on a strong incoming tide when currents push shrimp, shad, and mullet to the shoreline. Miles of sandy, grass-laden humps and guts make wading easy. Topwaters, soft plastics, and spoons catch fish. Trout rarely turn down a feisty finger mullet.

The HL&P Spillway has harbored many 10-plus-pound trout. Pluggers stand in the shallows and cast from the rocks into the deeper channel with subsurface plugs and soft plastics. Live-baiters take troll buckets with mullet, piggy perch, or shrimp.

The east shoreline of the Seabrook Flats provides fishable structure parallel to the Houston Ship Channel. Like fishing any flats area, sufficient tides are needed to flood the shallows, especially during the normal low-tide conditions of winter. Its proximity to the Ship Channel makes it a prime winter fishing venue. Fish hold in the deeper, warmer water when the thermometer is low, and head to the flats as the air heats.

PORT O'CONNOR/ROCKPORT

Back bay lakes such as Pringle, Contee, Power, and Twin lakes are refuges from blustering winds. Sandwiched between barrier Matagorda Island and Espiritu Santo Bay, these havens provide drifters a solid trout fishing local, provided you have the gumption and know-how to cross the open bay to get there.

The Welder Ranch shoreline and the Drum Hole near the mouth of San Antonio Bay are two key winter trout spots, according to Capt. Chris Martin of Seadrift: "You can wade these areas, but be careful because they drop to deeper water quickly. The fish hang there because deep water is close and they can escape to the deep when the temperatures drop. When the sun comes out and the water warms, throw a big topwater like a Super Spook or She Dog. However, my go-to bait is a gold spoon."

Martin prefers using a short shank hook and 1/8- to 1/16-ounce jighead when working soft plastics. He said the light heads keep his baits from hanging on oyster reefs: "In the winter, the bite is normally light and subtle. If you feel tightness in your line, lift your rod tip. If you still feel resistance, set the hook."

LAGUNA MADRE

The average depth of Laguna Madre is 3 feet, and with miles of sugar sand flats, stalking trophy trout on foot is a dream compared to other coastal locales, where boggy conditions warrant catching your breath rather than fish. The wind blows down there—often. Diehard fishermen learn to cast in gusty conditions, or stay pinned to the dock the majority of the year. The upside of living in coastal South Texas is warm weather year-round. Lower Laguna Madre in most places is at or near the same latitude as West Palm Beach, Florida. The locals like to refer to it as the "Texas Keys."

Three Islands is the most popular winter trout spot, according to Capt. Danno Wise of Raymondville. Extensive flats adjacent to the Intracoastal produce big fish for sight-casting pluggers. Five to seven-inch red and black "bass" worms, Norton Bull Minnows, and D.O.A.

Shrimp are proven artificials.

Holly Beach, littered with small islands, grass beds, and deep channels, is another traditional sow trout hangout. Wise said to work skinny sand behind the island on sunny days. Holly Beach does not cough up numbers, but be patient—the big fish are there.

Laguna Vista lies four miles north of Port Isabel on the western shore. The area is a classic V-shaped cove with 3-4 feet of water at the entrance and shin-deep water at the back. Mangroves line the shore.

"Fish will work the deeper grass flats, channel edges and sand-bars consistently," Wise said. "Trout will hop on the skinny flats during midday with good sunshine. I will work soft plastic jerkbaits and 51 MirrOlures slow."

Wise said the spoil islands running from the Queen Isabella Causeway north to Port Mansfield are often overlooked: "Just about any stretch can be productive on a given day. Look for water flowing between islands, color changes, and slicks. During midday, try the deep flats between spoils and the ledge of the ICW. D.O.A. TerrorEyz and other heavily weighted soft plastics work well."

Texas offers miles of trout-infested shorelines on the lee of winter blusters. Anglers braving the wind are finding they can catch trout regardless of the weather; you just have to know where to fish.

Starched flags and wind-burned lips are no longer excuses.

Acknowledgement

I did not complete this project overnight. Though it took only six months to write, the experience and know-how written into these pages took years, and there is so much more to learn. When a writer or professional angler thinks he has learned everything there is to know, they are only fooling themselves.

The best fishers out there take every day, every cast, every hook-set, every good day—and especially every bad day—and scrutinize it. They are not happy with just catching a nice mess of fish. They want to realize why it happened, or why it didn't. These are the Chuck Uzzle's, Jimmy West's, Mickey Eastman's, Blaien Friermood's, James Plaag's, Dana Bailey's, Melvin Talasek's, Billy Pustejovsky's, Charlie Paradoski's, Lynn Smith's, and Jay Watkin's of the wade-fishing world.

Consistency is what it is all about. The ability to squeeze out a few fish when all others have failed is what separates the good from the great.

It is a science. The best anglers are professors, ever yearning for more knowledge. Everyone is a hero when winds are light and the bay is loaded with shrimp and mullet, but the true test is catching when the water is stained and a southwest breeze lowers tides and blows your cap off.

It is fun nonetheless, regardless if your drag gets tested. If it is not, well, I really do not know what to tell you. If you cannot enjoy a day on the water, in my estimation, you really cannot be happy. We all love to catch fish, but more often than not, we return to the dock without a limit. If happiness is catching a limit, I am sorrowful 80 percent of the time. Thank the Lord I have matured past full stringers and heavy coolers.

My love for fishing began at age six when my late Paw-Paw, Douglas Farmer, drove down to Barbers Hill from his Navarro County dairy farm to help take care of me while my mother gave birth to my sister. While Dad, Mom, and Mimi were taking care of the new baby, Paw-Paw took me to Gibson's and bought my first rod and reel, a Zebco 202, and tackle box. Little did he know he created a monster, though I think he would be proud today.

His acreage was loaded with ponds and stock tanks and seldom did we travel north without that Zebco packed in the trunk. One of my fondest memories is posing with Paw-Paw and a 36-pound flathead cat. I wish I could have taken him fishing on my boat before he passed away.

I grew up in Mont Belvieu (Barbers Hill), not 10 minutes from Gou Hole Road boat ramp, which leads to the marsh of Trinity Bay. The family fished often together, mostly for blue catfish in the marsh. It is rather comical to think back to our family outings in the boat. I really do not know how Dad remained sane.

My sister, Danyelle, age five or six at the time, always set the hook regardless if a fish struck or not. She just liked to cast. How we managed to dodge those Eagle Claw hooks I will never know. I think Dad might have secretly squeezed the barb to avoid major surgery.

Mom liked to fish, too, and still does, though her unstable inner ear gets her queasy in the bay with a foot or more of chop. It took her a good hour to prepare the sandwiches and snacks for the boat; our family was going to eat, regardless. Mom used to make the best turkey sandwiches, especially after the Thanksgiving holidays when leftovers filled the frig.

Dad was Mr. Caution, and, still is. He worried for our safety and always preached good judgment. His love for us had to be strong to put up with all the flying hooks, running on sandbars, and ribbing he took from Mom and me. He could have said "to heck with the family thing" and called a friend to go. I know his blood pressure would have been lower, and he definitely would have caught more fish. However, he chose *us*, and I thank him for it. We still fish together today. He is not just my dad, but my friend.

My parents gave me everything to succeed in life. I say "gave," but "taught" is more accurate. We were not poor by any means, nor were we wealthy, unless, of course, you count love. They encouraged me to work for what I wanted in life.

My dream was to play professional baseball, so my parents and built a batting cage in the yard with a pitching machine. That may not sound like much now, but back in the 1980s, I had the coolest thing in town. They required me I have a summer job when I was of working age. That taught me responsibility and money management. They stayed on me to make good grades, love God, work hard, and pray without ceasing. They taught me the confidence to succeed in life, and I thank them.

Incidentally, I reached my goal of playing professional baseball. No, I did not make it to the "Big League," but I did get a hit in my first professional at-bat. I also received a college degree, paid for by playing a game I love. Thanks for making it possible Mom and Dad. I have not and will not ever take the things you taught and provided me for granted.

My mother encouraged me to read throughout my adolescent years. She began by reading to me as a child, then subscribed to *Sports Illustrated*, the *Houston Post*, and *Houston Chronicle*. I think I learned writing from her. In fact, she still edits, every column and magazine feature I write (including this book) for grammatical content before I send it to the respective editors, who actually get paid to do it. Good writers are good readers, and I have my mom to thank for instilling the importance of reading.

I still cannot live without my daily sports page. I remain a *Houston Chronicle* subscriber to this day. I owe the *Chronicle* outdoor columnists— Shannon Tompkins, Doug Pike, and Joe Doggett—a debt of gratitude for providing quality reading. Like I said, good writers are good readers, and since I have been reading the sports page since my teens, I have had the good fortune of reading some fabulous outdoor prose. I have mentioned it to all of them before, but I would like to say it again—thanks. I think I took a little from each of the trio's writing styles and formed my own.

Tompkins and I hunt together two or three times a year, and vowed to make our 2002 Panhandle waterfowl trip of an annual gig. He is a "working man's" writer, choosing to do things on his own and write about the process. His Baytown roots are only a few miles from mine, and we have more than once shared tales in the Anahuac marsh. Every time I read his stuff, I learn something. He is a researcher and lover of history, and writes some of the best leads in the business. I try to pat him on the back as often as I can, and tell him how impressive his writing is to me, though in his humbleness, he just shrugs and says, "yeah, yeah, I thought it was garbage." Regardless, thanks.

Doug Pike fishes with me half a dozen times a year, not always for a story, unless he calls and says: "Hey, man, I need something for Thursday. You got anything going?" More so, I think he just likes the comfort of knowing he has no pressure when fishing with me. Much of the time, a writer of his profile is hounded constantly from every captain on the coast wanting on the Thursday outdoor page. Guys like him need the chance to fish without worrying about working on a story or owing someone ink for taking him fishing.

Pike has helped me several times during my writing career, mostly while working as the editor of the Coastal Conservation Associations award-winning Tide magazine. He knows just where to change word structure to make a story flow better for the reader. He has made me "look good" in several issues over the last three years. Sadly, he resigned as editor of Tide last year to pursue other writing interests, including writing a book. His freshwater fishing book should be on store shelves by the time you read this. He and I are working on a few projects together for the future. Thanks, Doug, for the opportunity to be published in a national magazine like *Tide*, and for the things I have learned from your writing and editing. Thanks, also, for the recommendations you made on my behalf to other editors across the country.

When I moved to Bay City, I did not know many people other than my wife's kin. It did not take long to find a few friends at Matagorda Harbor. When you hang out there long enough and say "good morning" to the same people every day, you make a few friends. That is how I met "Pops," or Capt. Melvin Talasek, and others. About seven years ago, he asked me to go fishing with him one morning, then another, then another, until he was hiring me to deck hand for him on charters.

I remember traveling down the Intracoastal en-route to West

Matagorda Bat one morning in June, a good hour before daylight. It was our fourth day in a row to fish, and, quite frankly, we had been slamming the trout for two weeks. Groggy-eyed, still recuperating from previous days wading, I was trying to catch a few winks during the hour-long ride. As we crossed the bay and the sun began to awake, I thought: *I may never leave this place. I can hunt ducks and geese in the winter and catch fish like this in the summer. I think I have found heaven on earth*. Of course, it is not always *that* good, but that summer remains etched in my memory.

Talasek taught me the Matagorda Bay complex, and together we have shared many unbelievable days on the water. I do not believe there is more giving person alive. He would give you his last meal if it meant you could eat tonight. I have seen him at the dock talking to total strangers about fishing, then go to his boat and give them a handful of baits. He is my adopted grandfather, since both of mine passed away several years ago. He always says "that was a good article" after reading my stuff, just as a family member would. Thanks, Pops, for all the rods, reels, lures, and lessons you have taught me over the years. Here's to many more, Lord willing.

Back in June 1999, I scheduled a trip with Chuck Uzzle to do a magazine feature on Sabine Lake. Little did I know the trip would be the best of my life, not only for the number of trophy trout we caught and released, but for the friend I earned. Since that day, we have become best friends, speaking at least twice a week by phone. Our families spent our 2003 summer vacations together in Florida.

When I need a big fish picture, Uzzle always delivers. He put my dad onto a 30-inch Calcasieu hog in 2002. The consummate professional, he is also just a plain old "good guy"—one who still answers his elders with "yes, sir" and "yes, ma'am." He is a true friend, and father to one of the most precious little boys you will ever meet. I nicknamed his boy (Hunter)

"Catfish" because he loves to swim. He is adorable, photogenic, and a pint-sized Chuck. His picture won me a couple of photography awards from the Texas Outdoor Writers Association. He is a breath of fresh air in the disrespectful times in which we live. Believe me, I know. I teach high school English and see it every day. Thanks for the support and friendship, Chuck.

I would also like to thank the folks at Maverick Boat Company in Fort Pierce, Florida. I have run a Pathfinder 2200V since 2000, and feel without a doubt it is the best boat I have ever owned. I have fished from just about every boat on the water, and when it came time to fork over hard lucre, Pathfinder was the clear-cut choice. Thanks to the boss, Scott Deal, for allowing me to run his product. Thanks to Mike Holliday for taking care of my journalistic needs and taking me fishing when I come to Florida. Incidentally, Holliday is a great writer and photographer as well, once working for the *Miami Herald* and *Florida Sportsman* before taking on the marketing and communications director position at Maverick. Thanks also to Art Wright, Gulf Coast sales manager, for his friendship and taking care of my boat needs. Thanks to all at Maverick for making such a wonderful product. If you want to see what quality is all about, tour their factory one day. It is impressive, to say the least. Thanks also to my dealer, Rick and Rhonda Kresta of Kresta's Boats and Motors in Edna and Clute. Thanks also to Michael Chanek and Jason Lawrence, who rig and take care of my boat when I bring it in for maintenance.

Thanks to Eric Bachnik of MirrOlure, for keeping me supplied with Top Dogs, She Dogs, and Catch 2000s.

Thanks to Dean Russell and Mike Haring of Mainstream Marketing, who rep the finest fishing products in the business. Not by coincidence, the people at Mainstream are some of the finest people, too. Names like

Shimano, Stearns, Mad Dog, Bass Assassin, Mustad, Zeiss, Power Pro, Lowrance, and MirrOlure stand for quality. Thanks, guys, for all you have done for me. I appreciate it.

Thanks to Konrad and Bill Wallace at Power Pro. Since Talasek introduced me to this fabulous braided line five years ago, I have not fished monofilament since. This line is the bomb in Florida, and catching on in Texas. I get a chance to fish with Wallace every year in Florida during Mark Nichols' "Outdoor Writer Festival."

Speaking of Nichols, thanks to him for his annual hospitality. Not many people know it, but he is a native Texan, graduated high school in Houston, and attended the University of Texas. Besides that, the man can fish. I thank him for inviting me every summer to his little slice of heaven called the "Indian River and St. Lucie Inlet," where, big snook, trout, and tarpon roam the Atlantic. Nichols always gets me the photos I need. Thanks also to Jerry and Diane, for their hospitality.

Thanks to Tim Locker for being another friend in the outdoors industry. He reps American Rodsmiths and Kent Cartridge Company, to name a couple. He is a classy fellow.

Thanks to friend, Randy Stacy, for taking me on my first trip in Trinity Bay when I was 12. Stacy, now 40, was a former football player for my father at Barbers Hill High School. We grew up going to church together and I worked for him for five years guiding waterfowl hunts. We fish together as often as we can.

Thanks to Keith Rainwater of Texas Tackle Factory and Team NuMark for producing good products and being a solid individual in the outdoor industry.

Thanks to Bruce and Shirley Shuler of Get-A-Way Lodge in Port Mansfield for their annual hospitality. This place is a lot of fun and Bruce and Teddy Springer are great guides and guys with whom to spend a day on the water.

Thanks to Pastor Joel Osteen of Lakewood Church in Houston. Though I am not a member of his congregation, I watch his telecasts regularly, especially when work prohibits me from attending First Baptist Church in Bay City. The words given to him by God speak to me often. Though I have never met the man, I feel like I have known him for years.

Thanks to my most frequent fishing partner, Eddie Sullivan, a good friend who always shows up when he says he will. You have probably seen his mug grace the pages of several Texas and national publications for which I write. In fact, some Florida publications have told me to stop sending photos of him.

Thanks to the most beautiful, understanding wife a guy could have. Through all the overnight hunting and fishing trips I take throughout the year, Shelly still wears a smile when other women would be growling. She is ever supportive, although not particularly interested in reading outdoor stuff. She reads my column every week and always says, "that was good," regardless if it stinks. She always seems to care how I do outdoors, asking: "Did ya'll have a good hunt?" or "Did ya'll catch fish?" She is a wonderful mother to the most precious daughter (please allow her daddy to brag) a family could have. My wife named her "Mallory" after my love for hunting mallards. No joke. I really had nothing to do with it, honest. Get this: if our child had been a boy, she suggested naming him "Gauge" for my love of shotgunning.

Eat your heart out guys. I have what you all dream about. Of course, I knew that when I married her. All joking aside, she is a gift from God and was the catch of East Texas Baptist University. Thanks, Shelly, for being you. I love you.

When all the thank-yous are done and tributes written, above all my relationship with Jesus Christ gets all the glory. I have prayed for the last five years for God to give me the opportunity to write a book. Then one day, out of nowhere, I received an email from *Texas Fish and Game* asking if I was interested in this project. After prayer and consideration, I realized God had provided the opportunity.

One thing is certain in this life: the Lord answers prayers. It may not be "yes" all the time, but rest assured the prayers do not go unheard. A few years before this project, I was offered a similar book deal that fell through. I was disappointed. Still, God was in control. I was not ready to write a book yet, and He knew it. Over the following years, He groomed me for this project.

Every day, I asked Him to bless my family and me, and give me the words to write this book. The words seemed to flow. I hope I have glorified His name. One day, when this life is over, I long to hear Him say: " Well, done, good and faithful servant." To God be the glory.

Index

W

Y

Where the Fish Are

320 pages
only $9.95

- The Top 40 Texas Lakes and the Entire Texas Gulf Coast
- DRAMATICALLY IMPROVED MAPS
- Over 1250 VERIFIED GPS Fishing Hotspots by Species
- Fishing Hotspots Provided by over 75 of Texas' Top Fishing Pros
- Over 2500 total GPS Locations Verified by Lowrance iFINDER ™
- Easy-to-read, Easy-to-use charts
- Best Baits and Seasons

- Road Information
- Boat Ramps
- Fishing Piers
- State Parks
- Boat and Road Access Wadefishing Hotspots
- Bankfishing Hotspots
- Current Water Body Facilities
- Camping and Picnic Areas